BLACK IS THE COLOR OF STRENGTH

AN ANTHOLOGY

BLACK IS THE COLOR OF STRENGTH

AN ANTHOLOGY

FREDERICK WILLIAMS
Editor

Prosperity Publications
San Antonio, Texas

PROSPERITY PUBLICATIONS LLC
510 E. Ramsey
Suite 3
San Antonio, Texas 78216

ISBN: 978-0-9863740-0-5

Cover Art: Dr. Melissa Duvall
Inside Text Design: Terry Sherrell
Printed in the United States of America

DEDICATION

This book of essays is dedicated to the millions
of our ancestors forced into slavery and
to the additional millions forced
to live under the abnormal
conditions of apartheid in
the only country they
knew and loved.

ACKNOWLEDGMENTS

As editor of this unique book of essays, I want to thank each of the authors who contributed their work for publication. Without your perspective on the importance of writing about our heritage, and the beauty of our culture this book would not be possible. A special thank you to Dr. Melissa Duvall who has designed this cover and many other covers for Prosperity Publications. Your creativity adds a necessary dimension to the value of the product. I would like to also thank Dr. Sharon Shelton-CoAngelo for her superior editing of the final draft and Terry Sherrell of One Touch Point Ginny's Printers for the text design. I want to also extend a special thank you to Prosperity Publications' partners, Dr. Loren Alves, Earl Blanche, Tom C. Frost, Theresa Scott and D. L. Grant for establishing a publishing company that is dedicated to producing works that exude the beauty, strength and love of the African American community. Finally, as usual, a special thank you to my wife, Venetta Williams, who allows me the freedom to explore my vision of a company, whose purpose is to produce literary works of a very high quality.

TABLE OF CONTENTS

PROLOGUE

Black Is the Color of Strength is the work of twenty-three African American writers who share one common goal and that is to present this country and the world of cultures with a range of essays and short autobiographies about the grace, beauty, and strength of their culture. As we move through the second decade of the twenty-first century, it is becoming increasingly important that a positive portrayal of the African American culture be recorded for present and future generations. Knowledge of the sacrifices and outstanding contributions that our ancestors made throughout this country's history has often been ignored, with a few exceptions, by traditional history books. This anthology will help to fill that void.

These particular works are very unique in that they consist of contemporary writings by a collection of artists, ranging in age over seven generations. We decided early on in this process that it was important to find writers who shared a common vision. We were careful to ensure that our collective thinking, centered on the need to produce a literary product that delivered a message: Black culture grew out of a deep and abiding love our ancestors had for themselves and each other, despite that constant barrage of negative portrayals of them in the dominant media outlets. They understood the tremendous obstacles facing them on a daily basis during the years of slavery and Jim Crow. It is our contention, as writers, that under the most horrendous conditions any race of people have confronted over such a long period of time, four hundred years, our ancestors remained a very gifted, innovative, and strong people. That belief is expressed throughout the anthology.

In one of his more insightful poems, the great literary icon of the Harlem Renaissance, Langston Hughes, captured the essence of the Black struggle, "Well son, I'll tell you, life for me ain't been no crystal stair...But all the time I'se been climbin' on...And reachin' landings. And turning stairs." In this classic poem, "Mother to Son," Hughes captures the tragedy and triumph of Black life in this country. When our forebears walked into the twentieth century, they confronted a hostile people who ruled over them as tyrants, and were determined to block their road to prosperity, equality and cultural sustainability. The irony of their condition and those people so hostile toward them was that only because of their blood, sweat, and labor did the United States become a major world industrial power.

When we look back at our ancestors' dilemma, we can only be in awe that they survived. Every major institution in this country, from all geographical sections, lined up against them. The national, state and local governments, the courts, the police force, even the military, were of one accord, and that was to keep the Black race subservient. Still, our ancestors survived. They made it up "the rough side of the mountain," and kept fighting back and praying to a just God that conditions would get better for them and their children. They were a spiritually endowed people who never turned to hate, even though they would have been justified to do so. Instead they turned to love, prayer, and an uncanny determination to never give up, never quit, and never succumb to the evil all around them. Langston ends his poem, providing us with the collective willpower of our ancestors to fight the battle. "So boy, don't you turn back 'cause you finds it's kinder hard...For I'se still goin' honey. I's still climbin'...And life for me ain't been no crystal stair."

Our forebears' spirit, strength, and love are the foundation for this anthology. These works are about them and how we must follow in their footsteps to sustain this beautiful culture and also improve upon it.

LETTER TO MY GRANDCHILDREN

AARONETTA HAMILTON PIERCE

April 26. 2014

My Dear Grandchildren:

Granddad Joe and I were honored and grateful to be included in the three-day Civil Rights Summit at the LBJ Library at the University of Texas in Austin on April 10th through the 12th of this year. The Summit commemorated the fiftieth anniversary of the signing of the 1964 Civil Rights Act by President Lyndon Baines Johnson. It was over the top to hear so many icons of the Civil Rights Movement and four American Presidents. President Barack Obama as well as former Presidents William Clinton, Jimmy Carter, and George W. Bush spoke at the summit. The heroes of the movement included United Nations Ambassador Andrew Young, social activist Julian Bond, NBA legend Bill Russell, NFL legend Jim Brown, Founding Director of the Smithsonian's African American Museum, Lonnie Bunch, as well as the daughter of Dr. Martin Luther King, Jr., Reverend Bernice King, former Urban League CEO Vernon Jordan and Congressman John Lewis (Marco, remember that I brought you John Lewis' book last Christmas, *Walking With the Wind*). The authors Doris Kearns Goodwin, Taylor Branch and numerous others added to the scholarly tone of the summit. Mark Updegrove, Director of the LBJ Library, Amy Barbee, Director of the LBJ Foundation, and their staffs and boards, with the support of President Johnson's daughters, Ms. Luci Baines Johnson and Mrs. Lynda Johnson Robb, created a fitting tribute to President Johnson and to this landmark legislation.

After the event, we were fully inspired and wanted to share this remembrance of our cultural legacy with you. More specifically, I

1

wanted to share with you a slice of our family history and our hopes for each of you as you travel into the future. Therefore, Marco, Jasmine and Julian, I am writing this letter to you. I am sharing my thoughts on historical racism in this country and the face that racism wears today. By recognizing and celebrating pivotal moments in our history, and acknowledging the continuing threats to our rights as African Americans, we will hopefully re-fortify ourselves and push to continue our work for a more equal nation.

President Obama's speech has hung heavy on my heart. At the Summit, he issued a call to action: "You're reminded daily that in this great democracy, you are but a relay swimmer in the currents of history, bound by decisions made by those who came before, reliant on the efforts of those who will follow to vindicate your vision." He was, undoubtedly, speaking of President Johnson's legacy and of his own experience as President. But his words, along with the wisdom of the other legendary speakers, spoke to me as an anthem for my life and maybe for yours. The President's words reminded me that our time on earth is really minuscule when compared with the evolution of mankind. Yet, if mankind is to survive and move forward, each of us must use "our time" on earth to advance the principles that define us as a civilized society.

This is a tall order, but as your grandmother I profess to you, my precious jewels, that even as I expect great things from each of you, I pray that you will have joy on your journey and that your path will be strewn with laughter, love and purpose. I hope you will find those things that excite your desire to learn and that you will search for the usefulness and impact of the projects you pursue. Above all, may you choose ways to give back to society, the community and to God who, "Hast brought us thus far on the way," to quote from The Negro National Anthem, "Lift Every Voice and Sing." Dr. King said, "An individual has not started living until he can rise above the narrow confines of his individualistic concerns to the broader concerns of all humanity." Through hard work and sacrifice, your ancestors earned you a place in this country. You arrived here fully accredited with all the rights, privileges and responsibilities of any citizen. More than anything, I want you to own your place in America and in the larger world. Your citizenship is only powerful if you use every facet of its entitlements. The following story will tell you a little more about our family's early journey.

Unlike most Americans whose ancestors came here freely from other countries, I faithfully recall the fact that my forefathers came unwillingly as slaves and that, with all of its injustices, horrors, and brutality, slavery was legal, widely and openly practiced for centuries in this country. My relatives were stripped of their families, language, country, traditions and all forms of autonomy. They arrived in America on slave ships to which they had been chained in the ship's hull for weeks, barely clothed, frightened, angry, and unchained only occasionally in order to be exercised. They traveled the "middle passage" without luggage, tools, instruments, credentials or inheritances. Their value had been predetermined, and it was calculated solely by their usefulness to the owners. Somehow they endured, worshipped, created, procreated, and above all, labored mightily to build this country.

I can hardly imagine such inhumanity to man by other human beings, whose only motivation was to secure free workers for financial gain. Conditions like forty-hour-work-weeks, remuneration, decent housing, decent food, and rules against sexual harassment, legal marriage opportunities, not to mention fairness, compassion, and kindness were not part of the slave-package. Renowned historian John Hope Franklin wrote in his meticulously researched book, *From Slavery to Freedom*, that "for the most part slaves had no time they could call their own, and not infrequently they worked such long hours that periods of free time necessarily had to be used for rest. Even if there was no work and even if an opportunity for diversion presented itself, slaves could never escape the fact that they were slaves and that their movements, as well as their other activities, were almost always under careful surveillance." The fear of being sold at any time to another owner was the slave's constant companion, since the owners did not respect their family units. Amazingly, many slave owners professed to practice Christianity. My ancestors had to be

3

far stronger than I can ever imagine. Somehow our ancestral lineage survived during slavery against almost insurmountable odds.

The Emancipation Proclamation and the Thirteenth Amendment to the United States Constitution freed my ancestors. This all was accomplished through the hard work and dedication of many great Americans like the abolitionists Frederick Douglass and Sojourner Truth. President Abraham Lincoln worked strategically with Congress for the passage of the Thirteenth Amendment (as depicted in the Academy Award winning movie, "Lincoln," and based on the book by Doris Kearnes Goodwin, *Team of Rivals: The Political Genius of Lincoln).* The freed slaves eventually passed the baton to relatives whose relationships were very special to me since they were the first part of our family tree that I would personally know. I am, of course, speaking about my grandparents who were born near the end of the nineteenth century and my parents who were born in the teens of the twentieth century. Their odds were still monumental, but for them and for so many families like them and especially your grandfathers' parents (that is a whole other story), their productivity against those odds was transformational and heroic.

Their backdrop was freedom. But Plessy v. Ferguson, the historic 1896 Supreme Court decision that established the "Separate but Equal Doctrine," kept the races separate but almost never equal, framed it. This doctrine created America's own Apartheid, not quite as severe by law as that in South Africa, but one that permitted a universal brush stroke to paint us as inferior and undeserving of the same quality of life—education, schools, homes, neighborhoods, parks, sport facilities, libraries, as white citizens. Moreover, African Americans could rarely rely on equal protection under the law. My grandparents and even my parents had little recourse but to accept these restrictions; yet they valiantly chose to avail themselves of the best that this restrictive society offered. By doing so, my grandparents were able to pass on tangible and intangible properties and values that set the course for my parents' lives and for all of ours that followed. They chose the path of education.

I wish I had asked my paternal grandmother where she and my grandfather got their motivation to challenge the odds and to push my father to pursue an academic path. They lived in a rural farming community in West Tennessee and had little, if any, formal education and very limited exposure to city life. Such ideas must have been rare and not at all practical in 1920. While they managed to acquire land, they had little else. Their plan took my father on a search for schools near and far. He traveled by foot or by horseback, in rain and sunshine to nearby communities with schools that would admit colored people (the name we were called then). He passed many schools that only admitted white students. Often, he needed to board with willing families in the more distant communities. Ultimately, he finished high school at Saint Mary's Episcopal School near Memphis, and then he earned a bachelor's and master's degrees at Tennessee State University. And in 1959 he was awarded a doctorate degree at Pennsylvania State University.

Happily, my grandmother (your great, great grandmother) lived years beyond her son's final degrees and long enough to see her granddaughters (one of them, your grandmother) graduate from college and become teachers. Later, one (your great Aunt Sylvia) would marry an Air Force Officer and the other would marry a physician, your grandfather. She was still alive when your father was born. She told me that his birth made her great, because now she was a great grandmother. She probably thought that her years of sacrifice, her work alongside my grandfather to produce a good crop in the cotton fields that made the money necessary for my father's education, were worthy labors. My grandparents' "leg" in this relay of our history was certainly productive and measurable. I am so grateful for the commitment and endurance of my parents and grandparents. I wish I had been wise enough to thank them for charting such a course for us.

WOW! It is April 22, 2014 and I finished the previous paragraphs late last night. As I sit at the computer tonight, the media is reporting, "the United States Supreme Court decided 6-2 to uphold the Michigan's affirmative action ban, which prevents the use of race

5

as a factor in college admissions. Today's decision overturned a November 15, 2012 ruling of the Court of Appeals for the Sixth Circuit. The lower court had ruled 8-7 that the affirmative action ban, which Michigan voters overwhelmingly passed in a 2006 referendum, violated the Constitution's equal protection clause. Have you ever talked to your mom about her days as a law clerk in the Third Circuit of the Court of Appeals? As I reflect with horror on today's decision, I cannot help but wonder how the justices can interpret the laws to vote to protect certain inequalities, yet fail to associate the need for affirmative action with the scourge of slavery, a violation of African Americans that this country has never fully acknowledged and from which we still bare scars, not to mention the history of annihilation of millions of Native Americans.

During slavery, it was legally forbidden to teach a slave to read and with few freed slaves having access to schools, many were a long time learning to read. The years of discrimination and deprivation that define the Jim Crow years combined with the poverty that still haunts so many of our neighborhoods, confirm my belief that qualified students should be prioritized for admittance to schools based on their race. Affirmative action is one opportunity for a type of "reconciliation" for thousands of African Americans who have not always had a level playing field where education is concerned. Their enslaved ancestors labored to build many of these colleges. And while these slaves were eventually freed, they had not a dime, nor a home, nor a job, nor an education, nor a reference letter to aid them to "catch up" in their precious freedom.

Today's Supreme Court decision on affirmative action in Michigan reverses past progress. Moving forward, we must commit to getting "stops" in order to counter the erosion of past gains. Two of the most momentous gains for African Americans since the prohibition imposed by Plessy v. Ferguson were the 1954 Brown v. Board of Education Supreme Court Decision and the 1964 Civil Rights Act. Brown v. Board of Education was argued and won before the Court by Attorney Thurgood Marshall, whose case was researched and prepared by Marshall along with the white lawyer, Jack Greenburg; and several black lawyers, like Charles Hamilton Houston and Jim Nabrit, Jr. Historians like Dr. John Hope Franklin (Dr. Franklin was a college schoolmate of your grandfather's mother, Juanita, at Fisk University); and a cadre of researchers all working under the NAACP Legal Defense Fund. In 1964, President Johnson signed the Civil Rights Bill with great celebration and ceremony. Its impact on the quality of life for African Americans was profound. In Executive Order 11246, President Johnson enforced affirmative action for the first time on September 24, 1965. The Executive Order required government contractors to take "affirmative action" toward prospective minority employees in all aspects of hiring and employment. Contractors had to take specific measures to ensure equality in hiring, and had to document their efforts. On October 13, 1967, the order was amended to cover discrimination on the basis of gender.

An additional landmark piece of legislation under the Johnson administration was the Voting Rights Act of 1965. Dr. Martin Luther King, Jr. and Mrs. Rosa Parks were invited to the White House to witness the signing of this vital enfranchisement proclamation. (Did you know that Dr. King was a graduate of Morehouse College? The same school from which your dad's brother, Uncle Michael, graduated; a great source of pride for Uncle Michael.) Prior laws often included burdensome qualifications such as literacy tests and poll taxes that made it very difficult for many poor people and poorly educated people to qualify to vote. These laws denied full citizenship to African Americans and other minority groups. These measures eliminated our voices in choosing our leaders as well as the laws that govern our country, our states, our cities, and our counties.

Over the years brave men and women have fought valiantly to abolish these and other deterrents, but they keep re-appearing. There are several current challenges. One of them concerns the use of specific identification documentation as a prerequisite for voting. The NAACP has long been the leader in the fight to protect voting rights for African Americans and other minorities. I remember hearing that in some southern communities as late as the 1950's, the membership and meetings of the NAACP had to be kept highly secret lest the member lose his/her job or even his/her life. I suspect that many committed people lost both in efforts to gain the right to vote for themselves and other African Americans in their communities. My parents as well as your grandfather and I are Lifetime Members of the NAACP. I was proud to learn from the NAACP web page that as recently as March 11, 2014, a delegation from the NAACP went to Geneva, Switzerland to bring the issue of voting rights in the United States before the United Nations Human Rights Commission. Roslyn Brock, Chair of the NAACP Board of Directors, said, "The United States has always been a beacon of democracy for other nations. When we do not uphold the highest standards, it can have major implications for democracy advocates across the globe."

Additionally, I learned that in 1947, the eminent Dr. W. E. B. Du Bois also took a delegation from the NAACP before the United Nations when he recited his iconic speech, "An Appeal to the World." His appeal addressed "the denial of human rights to minorities in the case of citizens of Negro Descent in the United States of America and an Appeal to the United Nations for Redress." Among the numerous issues he cited, voting rights was one of them. We continue to fight the same voting rights obstacles which deflect and diminish our efforts to improve our lives in other areas.

It is now April 26, 2014. Days are passing as I strive to share this missive with you. Life, cooking, an outing with friends to see a Richard Hunt sculpture exhibit at the Botanical Gardens, the NBA playoff games, and community responsibilities are slowing me down. Add to that, I talk faster than I type. But WOW AGAIN! I believe that the universe is conspiring to compel me with even greater urgency to write to you. Today the media has blown up with the recently- recorded conversations of the voice of Donald Sterling, owner of the Los Angeles Clippers, in which he denigrates Black people as vehemently as a slave owner might have done during the height of slavery. Since your dad is the general counsel for your local NBA team and your grandfather was an investor in the San Antonio Spurs for fourteen years, we care deeply about the standards of the NBA. Furthermore, the league is composed of about 80% African American players, joined by numerous coaches, assistants, other professionals, and one majority owner, all of whom are African Americans. Blatant comments of derision toward African Americans by any owner/employer are too egregious to ignore. If the voice on the recordings is found to be Donald Sterling's, the disgust will be unimaginable. (Later Sterling acknowledged that the voice on the recording was, in fact, his.)

Sterling has made millions of dollars on the backs of African American athletes. Additionally, Dan Wetzel in "Yahoo Sports" reports, "in other dealings…his companies targeted and discriminated against blacks, Hispanics and families with children in renting apartments in the greater Los Angeles area." He further explains that the housing discrimination is completely different from the NBA accusations because as Wetzel continues, "His companies controlled huge swaths of homes and apartments in Southern California and these kinds of actions are what both directly and indirectly force minority families to stay in dangerous, blighted neighborhoods with poor school districts and limited opportunities. It is the kind of acts that run counter to everything America is supposed to be about."

I hope that this story, as astonishing and burdensome as it is, becomes a catalyst that re-opens the dialogue on race in America that is long overdue. Today there are more of our fellow citizens, like Donald Sterling, whose prejudices and bigotry are reflected in their business dealings. They perpetuate the maintenance of barriers to better economic, residential, employment, educational, political, cultural and artistic opportunities for African Americans. These patterns continue even as laws condemn and punish the misguided use of power. Subtleties that allow broad interpretation of the laws and the failure to refine these laws are part of the problem. The eagerness to reverse laws enacted by the opposing political party, which benefit under-served and impoverished communities promote a lack of confidence in the law for all citizens. The unwillingness to recognize that African Americans deserve the same rights as any American citizen and the belief that African Americans are incapable of egalitarian governance, antagonize the problem.

9

Just as dismaying are apathetic citizens whose social, professional, cultural and religious communities have excluded any meaningful relationships with African Americans. This lack of familiarity has made us invisible on their radar as friends, colleagues, and equals. The thought of hiring us or creating diversity in their environments never crosses their minds. I cannot tell you how many meetings, programs, boardrooms, events I attend and find myself the only African American. I am likely the only one who notices my singularity. Friends describe similar situations. It is critical that we add our voice to as many workplaces and boardroom tables as possible, yet it can be challenging and lonely. I hope that one day you will read *Invisible Man* by Ralph Ellison. It is one of the most powerful books that, among many lessons, describes society's role in rendering a person invisible. Dr. Maya Angelou has said, "History, despite its wrenching pain, cannot be unlived, but if faced with courage need not be lived again."

The power to deny equal access to a certain group of citizens limits the overall progress of our great country. Furthermore, it reduces the manpower equipped to solve our many problems, create needed innovations, research cures for diseases, devise strategies to maintain our country's security, conduct our symphonies, paint our masterpieces, and so on. History already documents African American's proven successes in almost every discipline known to mankind. Wider equality of opportunity could multiply these contributions many times over. Lack of opportunities and exposure feeds hopelessness, crushes creativity, reduces ambition, increases lawlessness, and eliminates possibilities.

10 Dr. Du Bois, an 1888 graduate of Fisk University and an 1890 Honors graduate of Harvard University, wrote in *The Soul of Black Folks* (1903) that, "The problem of the Twentieth Century is the color-line." In 2014, even though a lot has changed, it is still the problem. We, as African Americans, have the opportunity and the responsibility to become more aggressive in the solutions to the American racial divide. I wish I knew the answers. I do know that prejudice cannot be eliminated by mere legislation. And while

legislation alone cannot change attitudes, it can make sure that the Constitution and all other governing directives by which we abide today, speak clearly, uniformly, equally, and protectively for all Americans. We can insure the most dynamic progress by voting in every election available to us. Above all, we must use our gifts in our chosen path to "be our best version of ourselves." This is a phrase that I borrowed from Oprah Winfrey who has offered it as an inspiration for all ages.

Once again, what I am trying to say to you, my grandchildren, comes from my heart. You come from a family that has worked very hard to improve their lives and the lives of others. You also are the descendants of a proud, accomplished and enduring race of people. As an excellent example of how a loving family supports its off-spring, Dr. Angelou wrote in *All God's Children Need Traveling Shoes*, about a young protégé, Kojo, who was staying in her home in Ghana. His family visited her to bring gifts, exchange greetings, and express gratitude. They said, "We want you to know that Kojo did not come from the ground like grass. He has risen like the Banyan tree. He has roots and we, his roots, thank you."

You, my grandchildren, are the only ones who can ultimately decide how you prepare yourself to meet all of the opportunities available to you. There is no race of people whose superiority allows them to limit your ascension. No one has the right to deny your place in this country and the world. Know that people who try to do so are lost in a time warp that is no longer applicable. Think seriously about the tools you need for your journey. Be inspired by the positive events that occur daily and which increase your faith in the American spirit. Be warmed and touched by the numerous people in your lives that lift you up—those who are Black, white, and every other ethnicity; and whom you call friends and family.

11

The election of Barack Hussein Obama revealed to the world and, more important, to Americans that we are willing to be led by a qualified African American, and that a beautiful woman whose ancestors were slaves could become the first African American First Lady of the United States; a lady who is both respected and popular.

And that two young African American girls could evolve and flourish under the close scrutiny of the White House microscope. And, of course, we are grateful for the dignity of Mrs. Obama's mother, the "First Grandmother," whose grace has allowed her to shine in every situation.

Hopefully, my ramblings will resonate with you, if not when you first read them, then maybe next week, next year, years from now, someday. As you travel on your journey through life, may you build a strong reservoir. Remember that what you place inside will always be present to sustain and uplift you. Material things can make life interesting, but they come and go. Your integrity, talents, education, compassion, empathy, and faith will form your character and secure your unique place in the world.

Lastly, choose your heroes, mentors and friends wisely. Look no further than your mother and father for the finest models to emulate. Their credentials are impeccable. Ask them questions about problems and situations that inspire, confuse or upset you. Likely, they have had a lot of the same experiences. They may have been the only African American in the classroom, like you sometimes may be when the discussions turn to current events, such as the killing of Trayvon Martin, the struggle around affirmative action, news headlines of bigotry from the likes of Donald Sterling, or lessons on slavery and the Civil War. However, they will share the pressure that you may feel to be honest and faithful in such situations.

I remain proud that your mother, father, like you, have always had numerous dear friends from other races and ethnicities. Your parents have worked so hard to prepare themselves for a competitive world, and they work even harder every day to make sure your lives are happy, safe and prosperous. Your school and extracurricular activities rarely occur without their presence. Their desire to expose you to new places, people and opportunities is endless. Their love for you is boundless.

You are already showing the glow of your parents' loving support by your love of reading, the love of your pets, your joy of sports and physical activity, your hard work in the classrooms, and especially your love for each other, your parents and the extended family. May you grow in your faith in God so that you feel His support and blessings when the challenges you face are beyond your power to control.

Always remember that you have four devoted grandparents and one surviving, extraordinary great-grandmother, Gramby, who loves you unconditionally. Each has lots of experiences, stories, degrees, careers, successes, and failures to share with you. And, as you know, both sets of your grandparents have celebrated fifty years of marriage. Ask us to tell you our stories and the stories of our ancestors. We are all interesting people with a curiosity for life and learning, and you are the center of our worlds. We are so proud of each of you.

Your leg in the "relay and currents of history" is before you. Swim On!

With everlasting love,
Grandmommy Aaronetta

COMING OF AGE TO MANHOOD

DR. LOREN ALVES

The final weekend in January 1963 will burn deeply and be etched in my memory for the remainder of my life. Events out of my control had a profound effect on me. At age twelve, I wasn't sure if I would ever recover from the sorrow and trauma I experienced that weekend. I did, and that is why I am sharing that short period of my life with you. I want to reveal what happened to me as living proof that we can overcome most obstacles placed in our pathway to a successful and happy life.

Levi Cobb was my closest friend. He had moved into a house right down the street from the DeSoto Bass Courts, the projects where I lived with my mother, two sisters, and three brothers. Every year we walked to Miami Chapel Elementary School together. We would be punching, shoving, heckling each other, as all young friends do at that age. We went from the third grade to the seventh together, and had just begun our second semester when everything fell apart.

In the seventh grade, our favorite teacher was Mrs. Mesmer. Although she was a white teacher from the other side of town, she instilled discipline, respect, and friendship in her teaching methods. She had also been my older brother and sister's teacher when they were in seventh grade. They had told me I would have fun learning from her, and I did.

Our last class that Friday in January 1963 was Home Economics. Our other close friend Harvey was in that class with us. We all joked about how poorly we had stitched our aprons and then argued whether Jim Brown, the star running back for the Cleveland Browns and our hero, would rush for over one hundred yards that Sunday.

We also agreed to meet after school and play a couple games of "scrambled eggs," at the field near my apartment in the projects.

I had also become one of the school's patrolmen. Now, instead of waiting around for Levi in the morning and walking home with him in the evening as I had done for years I needed to get to my post two blocks from the school.

That final Friday in January leading into the fatal weekend, right at 3:25, five minutes before school dismissal, I hurried out of the classroom, picked up my pace as I rushed down the hallway and finally out of the building. As soon as I stepped outside the cold wind slapped me right in the face and my nose turned red instantly. I could see my breath every time I breathed out. Cold chills shot through my body as the wind penetrated through my coat and other clothes I was wearing. But it didn't deter me from my safety patrol post a couple blocks from the school. I took my job as a patrolman seriously. It made me feel real important, wearing my bright orange safety patrol strap. There was a silver badge attached to it in a spot right over my heart. I proudly held a stop flag attached to a six-foot pole always in my right hand.

Exactly at 3:30, I heard the bell ring and like a herd of cattle the students ran out of the building and headed to the corner where I stood in control. They rushed up to me, but I stood firm, with arms extended, stopping them from running out into the street.

"Look at Mr. Important," a young skinny kid in my class said.

"Yeah, we should all rush him at the same time and then see how he can stop us," another young boy who liked to act tough scowled.

Every day was a repeat performance. They threatened to overtake me, but never did. They just loved to tease me. Ignoring their taunts, when traffic cleared I raised the stop flag pole in the air and shouted.

"All clear traffic, you can now cross the street."

The kids ran into the street with Levi and Harvey in the last wave of students to cross over. As they shot by me, Levi got in one last taunt.

"Hey, Mr. Policeman, I guess you going to grow up and put us all in jail," he shouted.

"Yeah, he ain't going to be able to hang with us anymore, cause he's going to be trying to arrest us," Harvey shrieked in his high-pitched voice. "Probably won't even show up for our game of scrambled eggs today." He reached out and tried to knock my stick out of my hand. He missed and kept on running.

"We'll see you at the field in an hour," Levi shouted from the other side of the street and headed up the block.

I stayed at my post until 4:00 and then ran all the way to our apartment. I rushed through the front door and tossed my bags on the couch.

"Why you in such a hurry and running around all crazy?" my older brother, Donald, shouted at me. He sat on the couch with my other brother, Ronald, watching television. Barbara, my sister hadn't gotten home yet. Delores, the oldest of us all was never home. She was the only one who had a different father. Mama had been married prior to marrying my dad, Big Raymond. Even though some would say we were only half sister and brother, we all looked at her as one of us.

"Got to get out to the field and kick some butt," I answered and went into the bedroom I shared with my brothers. Clothes were scattered everywhere and the beds were half made up. I quickly got out of my school clothes and changed into jeans. I grabbed my heavy Cleveland Brown's Jersey, slid it over my head pulling it down tight. Then I slipped into my old gym shoes and shot out of the bedroom. Without saying anything to my brothers, who both gave me a hard stare, I ran out the door and headed towards the park.

When I arrived, the other boys were already there, with the exception of Levi. I found that strange because he never missed the opportunity to show off his speed and agility.

"Where's Levi?" I asked, rubbing my freezing hands together to keep warm.

"Don't know," Harvey replied. "He'll probably show up. Let's get this game going. It's cold and we need to move around to keep warm."

"We're not going to wait on him?" I asked still concerned that Levi wasn't there.

17

"No, we going to get started before it gets too dark," Larry said. He was a friend of ours but a year older than the rest of us. He loved to show off his physical superiority.

"You right, he's probably baby sitting his little sister or his mamma got him doing chores. She always got him doing something," I chimed in.

Being the smallest in the group I don't know why I even played the game of scrambled eggs, which simply was a game where one of the players would catch the ball and run like crazy from everybody else. It was a test of brute strength and endurance. My disadvantage was quite apparent, but in my neighborhood you never backed down or showed any signs of being afraid. Knowing those were the rules of the projects, I lined up in a circle with the other five boys and Harvey tossed the ball in the air.

Larry caught it before it hit the ground. He then took off running towards the line barely legible in the frozen turf. Gregory tried tackling him around his shoulders but with no luck. John and Bernard both grabbed a leg and I tried to get my arms around his waist. Larry was so much stronger and he just dragged us along with him to the goal line. Once he crossed the line, he shook us loose and I voluntarily released my grip on him. Harvey threw the ball in the air four times and each time Larry would grab it punishing the rest of us. I wasn't about to go for the ball and get pummeled by all those boys bigger than me. I figured my punishment was minimal if I limited my involvement to reaching out and grabbing at Larry. After four games we decided to call it quits. In the heat of the battle we forgot about Levi.

Exhausted from our game, we found an icy park bench and sat on it. Larry stood in front of us tossing the ball up in the air. The temperature had dropped, but we were so heated we paid no attention to the cold. Instead, the conversation turned to Sunday's football game. The Browns would be playing the New York Giants for first place in the Eastern Division of the National Football League. It was the last game of the season and the winner would go on to play the Los Angeles Rams for the championship.

"We going to beat their butts, you know." Harvey said. "Ain't no way the Giants can beat Cleveland at home, not with Jim Brown running the ball."

"I'll bet he goes for 125 yards." Bernard said. "He's going to run over that sorry linebacker Sam Huff for the Giants."

"Yeah, just like I ran all over you all." Larry bragged with his chest stuck out.

"Where is Levi?" I asked again. It was really bothering me that he hadn't showed up. I didn't quite accept the earlier explanation. I had a weird feeling about him not being there.

"Who knows," Larry said with a little attitude in his voice. Evidently he didn't like me changing the subject about his defeat over us. "If you're concerned why don't you go over to his house and find out."

"No, I'll call him later." I said. "Let's bet on how many yards Jim Brown's going to get. I bet my Pay Day candy bar he goes for 130."

"You got a bet!" Gregory chimed in for the first time. He was always quiet until it came time for betting. He always thought he might beat someone out of something. "I'll bet my Baby Ruth against your Pay Day."

"You're on," I said.

After placing a couple more bets on the game, we finally broke up and headed home.

The next morning it felt good to sleep in late. The temperature had dropped and it was snowing. It was Saturday and I didn't have to go out in the freezing cold. But I had a strong urge to run over to Levi's house and make sure he was okay. Instead, I picked up the phone and dialed his number. I had to get his bets for tomorrow's big game.

"Hello, Mrs. Cobb," I said when his mother answered the phone. "Is Levi home? We missed him yesterday and we all made our bets for tomorrow's game. I wanted to find out if he was going to take the Browns?"

There was a long silence and I could hear heavy breathing. It frightened me. For the first time I considered the possibility that something had happened to my best friend.

19

"Mrs. Cobb, is Levi all right?" I asked with a lot of anxiety in my voice.

"Loren, Levi was in an accident last night and he's in the hospital." she shouted into the phone.

"Is he all right?" I asked.

Again a long hesitation and finally she said, "yes," in a very faint voice.

We hung up and I nervously called Harvey and the other guys and repeated what Mrs. Cobb had just told me. We decided to stay in touch in case one of us heard anything about Levi's condition.

On Sunday morning I got the answer, as did the entire neighborhood. I sat at the breakfast table, while my brothers and sisters sat in the living room watching television when the station cut it to bring a special announcement. I couldn't believe what I heard.

"Friday evening a twelve-year-old Negro boy, Levi Cobb, was accidentally shot and killed by his uncle while trying to break up a fight between his father and his uncle. Police are still investigating the incident. No one has been arrested as of yet."

I dropped my fork, jumped from the table and ran to my bedroom, slamming the door behind me. I didn't want to talk to anyone. The television reporter was lying. My best friend was not dead. I had just seen him Friday and he was alive, laughing, and enjoying his youth. This couldn't happen to us. It couldn't happen to my best friend because those kinds of things didn't happen to a twelve-year-old. I was ready to go right back out there and confront that reporter on the television and insist that she admit to everyone she was lying and that nothing as vicious and ugly as the murder of my best friend had actually occurred. But I was afraid because in all reality nothing would change. The reporter wasn't lying and I was trying to stop time and go back to Friday. I wanted to say good-bye to my best friend and tell him I'd see him in the park in a couple hours to play scrambled eggs. But Levi hadn't shown up, and his mother told me he had been hurt. Finally, the lady on the television told me he was dead. My best friend was dead at twelve years old. I was forced to confront a reality of inner city life. Death seemed to be a constant companion to being poor, Black, and trapped in deplorable conditions that no person, young or old, should have to confront.

The next few days at school were the saddest of our lives. We didn't talk about Jim Brown running for 135 yards and the Cleveland Browns beating the New York Giants. In fact, no one remembered the bets. Suddenly none of that mattered. We all viewed life from a different lens. Being quite young we thought life was forever; we were invincible and nothing could happen to us. We talked about football, girls, and sometimes school but never about death. But sitting in Ms. Messmer's class waiting for her we were silent for the first time. I believe all our thoughts were similar: Levi wasn't there. Where was he? Was he in Heaven or could there be a place that young kids went because they were still too young to die? We just didn't know and because we didn't we sat silently waiting for our teacher to help make sense out of it all. Finally, she strolled into the classroom with a sense of authority as if she knew what had to be done.

"I know you all are feeling a lot of pain today," she started. "We all are. It is so difficult when we lose someone so young but it happens and we must learn how to go on. You all must learn how to go on for Levi. That's exactly how he would want it and it's exactly what you all must do."

Ms. Messmer's words were soothing and made me feel better. They didn't quite take away my pain and depression but helped considerably.

"Now we do have some work that must be done so let's try to concentrate on that for right now," she continued.

We all tried to concentrate, at least I did, but my mind kept wandering back to Friday. I could picture Levi running across the street and disappearing around the corner. He had waved with his back to me. If I had any idea what would happen later that evening I would have shouted out to him to turn around so that my last memory would have been of his face. I couldn't hold the tears. I tried my best to hide them from the other boys. They probably were all crying as well.

That week seemed to drag on forever. We went through our usual routine. I manned my post at the corner. However, there was

21

very little teasing from the other boys. They didn't even run up to the corner. No one yelled and laughter was totally subdued. By Friday I was exhausted, but knew on Saturday I would have to conjure up enough strength to attend Levi's funeral.

I was up and about early the next morning. All night I'd tossed and turned knowing I would have to look at my closest friend lying in a casket. With the sun shining through the bedroom window I jumped up, tossed on my pants and a shirt, and hurried into the kitchen, being careful not to wake my brothers. I sat alone at the kitchen table staring out the window. It was a clear day and the sky was a radiant blue. Because there were no clouds, I knew it would be awfully cold. The sun helped to lift my spirits. Mama began to move around in her bedroom and I knew real soon she would come out dressed and would be ready to go to McLin's Funeral Home. A nervous energy invaded my body and I could hardly put the spoon of cereal up to my mouth. My mind began to wander. I could visualize Levi as an angel singing and praising God. At least that's what they taught us in Sunday School classes. I would look around the church and think that everyone with gray hair, slumped over bodies, or walking with canes had to worry about those things. Death didn't come visit young boys; we were immune to its invasion.

But death knew no age, race, or gender and when it was ready for you, it just came and took you out of here the way it did Levi. As Mama came out of her room dressed and ready to go, I knew attending the funeral would age me more that what I was ready for. Mama and I walked out of the apartment and got into her old Oldsmobile that we called the "Beast" and headed for my first experience at growing up.

McLin's Funeral Parlor was one block from Levi's house and I stared at his front porch as we drove by. I tried to will Levi to walk out that door and run down the front steps as I had watched him do so many times. But I knew the house was empty and a dark ambiance surrounded it. I wondered as we drove by how people can make happy sounds in such a sad time? How can they express joy when there is so much pain? Why did God have to create death? At that moment it made more sense to me that we should live forever. All of us boys were happy going to school, playing scrambled eggs, and betting whether or not Jim Brown would run for over one hundred yards. We were content with this life; why did we need the other one?

Mama pulled into the parking lot at the funeral home. She turned off the car and opened her door. I did not move. I felt paralyzed like some terrible disease had taken over my body, and I could only sit there. I would have preferred that much more than going inside that place.

Mama sensed my hesitancy. "Kind of hard to do, isn't it?" she asked in a very mellow tone.

I didn't answer. Instead I stared out the window.

"Come on, Loren, you'll be all right," she said. "Just remember that Levi is with Jesus and he is happy."

Mama's voice was reassuring and her words gave me strength. Most importantly, I knew she would be with me. I opened my door, got out, and we hurried inside.

I practically came to a stop when I looked to the front of the church and saw Levi in the silver casket. He was so quiet and still with his hands crossed in front of him. We found seats in the same row with Larry, Gregory, Bernard, and Harvey, all sitting with their parents. No one spoke; we were all fixated on Levi's still body. It was an awful feeling seeing someone whom you had known as a friend, always energetic, admirably funny, spastic at times, yes, even bothersome, but now, lifeless, motionless, eerie, and lying there in what could only be described as his last resting place on this side of the universe. We sat there in disbelief, each of us trying not to express emotions, shed tears, or make eye contact, showing our fear of the moment.

Throughout the entire service my mind was oblivious to the funeral proceedings taking place right in front of me. I disappeared into my own world. My mind drifted from place to place and also to nothing with real relevance or significance. I tried desperately to look away from the casket. But, I still knew Levi was lying there, not moving. I looked up into the ceiling lights. I stared at the windows and read different scripture passages above the pulpit. However, my eyes would wander back to that silver casket and tears flowed freely

23

from them. I didn't want to cry but every once in a while it all got the best of me, and I would give in to the emotions.

Mama decided that we would not go to the burial site. When the funeral was over we expressed our condolences to Levi's family, climbed into the Beast and headed home. I tried to make my mind wander to anyplace far from the funeral home and my friend's body. As we drove by Levi's house, I didn't look over at it. After seeing him lying in the casket, I knew for sure there was no chance he would come bouncing out the front door ever again. I vowed to never go to another funeral; they were just too depressing. Even at that age I knew there was something wrong with how we buried our loved ones. Everyone was so sad. It seemed like we were cheating Levi of his right to leave here on a happy note. I wished they had sung "Oh Happy Day" in celebration. The songs they sang sounded real good, but they left me feeling depressed and wanting to cry more when the choir finished.

I glanced over at Mama; she hadn't uttered a word since leaving the funeral parlor. Maybe she was grieving in her own way or maybe she was just giving me some space to deal with loosing my best friend. Suddenly, she gripped the steering wheel tightly with both hands and the car began swerving and pulling to the right. I heard a loud flapping noise coming from outside. Taking my lead from Mama I gripped the armrest on the door.

"What happened?" I asked as calmly as possible.

"We just had a blow out." Mama shrieked.

She managed to steer the car over to the curb bringing the "Beast" to a stop.

"I need to find a phone booth so I can call your brother to come and change it," she said.

A couple times while riding my bicycle I had stopped and watched two men change flat tires on their cars. I was a quick learner and from observing them I figured I could change our flat. I had to act like a man in this situation.

"I think I can change it Mama," I said. "You don't have to call Raymond. I can handle it." I opened the door and headed to the back of the car.

"Boy, you can't change that tire. Now get back in the car and I'll find a phone booth and call your brother," she scowled at me.

"Mama I can do this!" I said with more determination than before. "I watched a whole lot of people change flat tires." I exaggerated but figured it was necessary in order to convince Mama I could do this.

"You trying to show Mama that you're grown," she said smiling. "Go ahead but be real careful, that stuff is heavy." She put the emergency brake on and got out of the car.

Mama stood off to the side as I opened the trunk. I didn't know if what we needed to change a tire was all in the trunk, but as I began my search I found the jack, the jack stand, the handle and the lug wrench. They were all so heavy, and I struggled to get them out and put them on the side of the car. After lining all the tools up in an orderly fashion, I grabbed the spare tire. With one strong effort I lifted it out of the trunk and placed it next to the tools. I was beginning to gain confidence that I could actually change a tire.

I removed the hubcap and loosened the lug nuts on the wheel. Then, I placed the jack setup on the rear bumper and hoisted the car up. I was proud of myself and shot a quick glance over at Mama. She was beautiful with a slight smile and a look of amazement that enveloped her face.

"Look at my man. You're doing just fine, Loren, just fine."

Finally, I got the rear end jacked up just enough to get the tire off the ground. I finished removing the lug nuts from the wheel then I removed the flat tire, grabbed the spare, and then struggled to get the tire onto the frame, but it wouldn't work.

"Loren you have to jack the car up a little more. Remember, the tire you just removed was flat and you have to lift the car a little higher to get the other one on." Mama said reassuringly.

I dropped the tire on the ground and hurried back to the jack. "Oh yeah, I knew that," I proudly proclaimed.

I lifted the car a little higher, got the spare tire on, tightened the nuts and put the hubcap back. After loading everything into the trunk I jumped in the front seat with my chest sticking out a mile. For a few minutes I had forgotten that I was depressed because of the funeral. Proving to my mother that I was man enough to change a flat tire had given me sufficient joy to temporarily replace my sadness. But what happened next deflated my positive feelings and shocked me to no end.

"How old are you Sonny Boy?" Mama asked.

What a strange question I thought. "I'm almost a teenager," I said.

"Precisely." she said without hesitation. "That's why I think I can tell you about who your father really is."

Stunned by what Mama said made my eyes widen. My mouth tightened and I looked straight ahead. At that moment I wished I was driving the car so I could just slam on the brakes and shout, "What did you just say?" Instead, all I could do was stare at the front windshield as if I were a deer fixated on the headlights of the Beast.

"Loren, I was truly astonished today. I watched your coming of age to manhood," Mama continued. She reached over and touched my leg as reassurance. "You boys showed a great deal of courage today at the funeral. I am not sure I could have been as strong as you all were if it had been someone as close to me as Levi was to you all. And the way you handled changing the tire for your Mama. You are growing up on me."

I heard Mama's words but they really didn't register. I wanted her to get back to the subject of my Father.

"Mama what do you mean, my real Father?" I asked, with my voice cracking. "Isn't Big Raymond my real Father? You mean I'm just like Dolores? I have a different Father from everyone else?" I began to feel lost and out of place.

We pulled back into the parking lot at the DeSoto Bass Courts. She began looking for a parking space and gestured with her finger for me to stop asking questions. I turned my body away from her in protest. When she parked I jumped out of the car and not waiting for her rushed into the apartment. She followed closely behind me.

Mama closed the door and motioned for me to have a seat at the kitchen table. We were the only two in the apartment. She sat right across from me and folded her hands on the kitchen table. She had a look on her face that I had never seen before and it made me nervous. What exactly did she have to tell me that caused such concern on her face?

"Before watching you today, Loren, I still looked upon you as my little baby boy," she started in. "I asked you how old you were because your behavior today seemed much beyond your age and I figured that it was time." She hesitated and stared at me. I assumed she was allowing me time to take it all in. "I knew someday I would have to tell you the truth, but I didn't know it would come so quickly. The funeral also made me aware of my life. If something were to happen to me then you would never have known the real truth about your father and that wouldn't be fair to you."

"What real truth, Mama? What are you talking about?" I was getting anxious and wanted her to cut through all this other talk and get right to the facts.

"After the divorce from Big Raymond times were hard," she said. Her words were hard and tough. "I had to do domestic work just to try and make ends meet. I wasn't getting any help from Dolores' father or from Big Raymond. Taking care of your brothers and sisters fell on my shoulders. I met a real good man who helped us out. He put food on our table and paid some of my bills." Again she paused, looked up at the ceiling and then back at me. "I felt obligated to give him what would make him happy since he was helping me and my kids. In the process I got pregnant with you."

"Where is he now?" I asked not really wanting to hear the rest.

"Let me finish telling you the whole truth." Mama got up and poured herself a glass of water. She sat back down and continued. "I figured the people I worked for would fire me if they knew I was pregnant and not married. So, I didn't eat well to try and stay thin and hide my condition. I never ate the foods I should have for your nourishment. You were born in the middle of one of the worst blizzards in Dayton history. Because of your father's insistence I was able to have you at Miami Valley Hospital. But you were extremely underweight and terribly undernourished. At eighteen months old you suffered from a terrible vitamin D deficiency (Rickets) that caused you to have knocked knees and missing teeth. With the help of welfare, I was able to get you braces to straighten your legs and special care.

"Where is he now?" I insisted.

"Loren, your Father is dead. He was killed in a car accident."

"So I never saw my Father and now I never will?"

"Yes you did meet him. You remember the man who used to come by here and would give you a dollar every time he left."

"Yeah." I said vaguely recalling a man who would come by and sometimes bring groceries and would always give me some money.

"That was your Daddy," she said. "When he died, they notified me that he had left you part of his insurance money but I refused it. You are an Alves and that money was not going to set you apart from the other children, so I turned it down."

It made me feel good knowing that my real Father had left me part of his inheritance. Big Raymond did nothing for any of us. It didn't make me feel good knowing that Mama had turned the money down but I understood why.

Mama stood up from the table. "Loren, you are man enough now to handle the truth. Don't let it stop you from believing that you can accomplish anything you put your mind to. Just like you made it through Levi's funeral and you changed that flat tire for your Mama, you can do anything. You can handle what I just told you and not allow it to stop you from becoming the man I know you will be." She turned and walked away.

I followed her every move until she finally disappeared up the stairs and out of sight. Her final words resonated with me. At twelve years old I was mature enough to handle the death of my father who once in a while stopped by our apartment and dropped off some money for Mama and was now dead. That was my unofficial welcome to the projects and to poverty.

As time passed, Mama had been right all along. I handled all those issues well. I accepted the challenge to overcome the obstacles placed in my way. The ill health, death of Levi, and never knowing my real father would not stop me. In the eighth grade I advanced to the A-classroom. In fact, I did so well I was qualified to apply for admission to Patterson Cooperative Vocational High School, comparable to a magnet school today. I finished the ninth grade at Paul Laurence Dunbar High School and then entered Patterson in the tenth grade. I pursued three years of auto mechanics and was fortunate to land a job at Delco Moraine, a division of General Motors during my junior year of high school. The cooperative partnership the school district had with Delco allowed us to work for two weeks and then attend school the other two weeks. This was a year-round program.

Having graduated Top Senior Mechanic, I was offered a full time job with the Vehicle Test Laboratory Department at Delco Moraine in the summer of 1969. At eighteen I was convinced I had found the career and job for the rest of my life. But when Delco began to lay off workers, I knew that would be the end for me since I was the employee with the least amount of seniority. Although I didn't get laid off, that incident made me understand and realize the importance of an education. What looked tempting at eighteen may not be as inviting and might not be available at age forty. I needed more security and began to look around for other opportunities.

God has a mysterious way of living up to his promises to us. All I could think of then was what Mama would say to me all the time, "and this too shall come to pass." I was in the right place at the right time when my neighbor, Phyllis Dillon, heard from my brother, Donald, that I was interested in dentistry. She looked me straight in the eyes and said, "You can pursue the answer to your missing teeth if you want to know it bad enough get busy and serious.

I was nineteen and afraid to give up a great job with General Motors but certainly was influenced by her challenge. Mrs. Dillon invited me out to her job at Wright-Patterson Air Force Base Oral Maxillofacial Prosthodontics' Dental Department to get a taste of the workplace. I was totally awe struck and needless to say blown away with what I learned about the science of missing teeth and the opportunity for a career in dentistry.

Feeling the need to get busy and serious about my future, I enrolled in Sinclair Community College in Dayton, Ohio. On a tip from my brother Donald I enrolled at Bowling Green State University in the fall of 1970. During the two years I spent there I became a dormitory resident advisor. After that, I then transferred to Central State University in Wilberforce, Ohio. That summer I also married my high school sweetheart, Phyllis Arnold. In 1975 I graduated from Central State with honors. I was now married, a college graduate, but definitely wanted to continue my education.

Because of my missing teeth, my dream had always been to become a dentist. So when I received the opportunity to enroll in an eight-week summer program at Meharry Medical School in Nashville, Tenn. I didn't hesitate. This was an opportunity of a lifetime! I would be assured a seat in their fall dental school class if I finished among the top five in the summer program. When I was into my sixth week of the program, Phyllis called me from our home in Dayton and told me that Washington University in St. Louis, Mo., assured me a place in their fall dental school class as well. I jumped at the opportunity. Meharry still hadn't offered me a place in their class. As a firm believer in the saying, "A bird in the hand is worth two in the bush," I dropped out of the eight-week program at Meharry. I hurried back to Dayton to pack up my belongings. Phyllis and I headed straight to St. Louis where we spent the next four years. I finally graduated and passed the dental examination. Following dental school I was commissioned as a Captain in the United States Dental Corps and served my country for twenty-one-and-a-half years. I retired as a full Colonel with a specialty in pediatric dentistry and now serve my eastside minority community, currently as the first and only Board Certified Black Pediatric Dentist in San Antonio, Texas.

There were many obstacles I confronted growing up in the projects in Dayton, Ohio. I lost my best friend at twelve years old and struggled throughout childhood without my biological father, but I made it. It wasn't easy, but no one is promised an easy life. Some are born with privilege and others, like me and many of my fellow young Black men in the real world, are not. I refused to allow my circumstances to stop me. To all you young men out there, do not let anything prevent you from fighting for your dreams. As the old song goes, "You can make it if you try." I did and so can you.

Even now, many years later, I am eternally grateful for that time in life that afforded me the opportunity to mature right before my mother's eyes. I am especially grateful to my brother, Donald, for referring me to his Vietnam War friend at Bowling Green University in 1970, where I learned how qualified and ambitious, but poor young men and women could get into college. I will always remember my neighbor, Mrs. Phyllis Dillon, who challenged me to "get busy and serious" about my goal to become a dentist.

And finally, I am unequivocally thankful to my wife Phyllis for taking the call from Washington University School of Dental Medicine at a time when I was away from home, and getting the message to me, which ultimately led to my career as a dentist.

I HAVE OVERCOME

A L E X I S   W I L L I A M S

All I can remember of my childhood is pain and suffering. I don't have memories filled with love from my family. Instead, I only envision the pain inflicted on me at a very early age, which led me down a path of destruction. I grew up in a single parent home. My mother had her first child when she was fourteen years old growing up in Detroit, Mich. By the time she was twenty-one she had four girls and one boy, all living in the inner city with no father in our lives. We moved from Detroit to San Antonio, Tx. when I was four. And my nightmare began when I was nine years old. It was a nightmare no young child should have to endure.

That Friday in the spring of 2001 began like any other day, but would end in a nightmare. After school my two cousins and I hurried over to Aunt Marie's house. I ran through the front door, threw my backpack off, and headed for the backyard. My cousins and I played so much that time flew past like ice cream melting on a hot day. Just as it began to get dark we went back into the house, settled on the couch and began to watch cartoons on television. My Uncle Edward was stretched out on the other couch on the far side of the room. We could hear him snoring. It was early evening and we knew he was already drunk.

After about an hour of watching television, Aunt Marie came out of her bedroom and stood at the entrance to the living room.

"All right, kids, time for bed," she said and pointed her finger toward the bedroom.

My cousins bounced off the couch and hurried into the bedroom. For some reason I decided not to go to bed but instead remained sitting there. Once my cousins got up and headed towards their room, I stretched out, propped my head up on the armrest and continued watching cartoons. I could still hear Uncle Edward snoring. Aunt Marie disappeared back into her bedroom so there were only the two of us in the living room.

About a half hour later my eyes got heavy and I drifted off to sleep. I don't know how long I had been sleeping but I was awakened as I felt and smelled smoke in my face. I opened my eyes and was startled to see Uncle Edward standing above me with a stare on his face that frightened me. He put his fingers up to his mouth like my teacher would do when we were being too loud in the library. Not knowing what to do, I sat up, and he plopped down next to me.

I tried to move away but he grabbed my arm with one hand and began to stroke it with his free hand. His hands felt heavy and rough, and every time his palms cuffed my shoulders he squeezed them.

Filled with fear, I began to cry. I wanted him to stop. He finally got up and I prayed that he would go away. I closed my eyes tightly trying to wipe this all away by not looking at him. But I could hear his belt buckle hit the floor. I opened my eyes and he began to undress.

"Oh, God," I gasped. It wasn't over.

He came closer and stood over me with parts of his body exposed.

"Don't! Please leave me alone," I cried out. I pulled the covers tightly against my body. I even pulled them up over my head.

I felt the covers being pulled away from me and then my spandex shorts were lifted from the front. I began to shake all over. My fear was so strong I thought I would faint. He began to stroke my exposed body and it felt terrible. A man had never touched me before. I was so scared I felt chills throughout my body. He hovered over me and finally dropped his body down on top of mine practically smothering me. I could hardly breath. I felt like a mat under the weight of his body pressed against mine. I didn't know how to defend myself. I just lay there, unable to move or to cry. I held both arms, with balled fists, in front of my body. He grabbed both my arms and forced my hands open. He tried to force me to rub him in certain places, but I refused. Fear had totally engulfed me and I knew I would die. The pain was excruciating, and his sweaty face against mine with his alcoholic breath made me sick. I wanted to vomit. But I couldn't do a thing because my body was paralyzed.

After he finished I felt numb all over. He slid off me, grabbed his clothes and headed for his bedroom. But before he left, he again placed his fingers to his lips as an indication that I should keep this quiet. I could not contain the tears as they flowed freely down my face. I feared what would happen next. Would he decide to come back and do the same thing all over again? Or would he come back out there and hurt me to make sure I didn't tell anyone what happened? I felt cold and began to shiver. The darkness seemed darker than usual. I didn't dare move and I couldn't sleep. I tossed from one side to the other always looking at that door for fear he would walk back out. With every little sound I jumped straight up. I imagined he was back on the couch across from me, and any minute would get up and attack me again. I needed my mother, but I was afraid to get up and dial her number to come get me. The night took forever to end, and I felt some relief when the sunrays crept through the cracks in the blinds.

The house was quiet as everybody still slept in their rooms. I had to get out of there before he got up and I would have to face him. I finally mustered up enough strength and courage to get off the couch. I rushed over to the phone sitting on the end table across the room. I looked back at his door fearful that it would swing open any minute and he would attack me again. I dialed my mother's number. Every number I pressed sounded like a car's horn as it echoed throughout the phone.

Suddenly, my aunt's door slowly opened. My eyes widened in fear. They were riveted on that door waiting to see who opened it. I put the phone down and frantically ran back to the couch. My heartbeat sped up as I watched my aunt's cat run out of her room and into the kitchen. I took a deep breath and headed back to the telephone.

35

I dialed mother's number a second time and listened as it rang. She had to pick up. This is one time I didn't want to hear the answering machine. She had to come and get me before this animal of a man could attack me for a second time.

Again, my heartbeat quickened as my mother's voice began to flow on the answering machine.

"I'm sorry I can't come to the phone right now. Please leave a message."

Fear and disbelief shot through my body. She hadn't answered and I needed her. "Mama come and get me," I said in a whisper. I managed not to cry. "I wanna go home." I placed the phone back down, crept back over to the couch and sat there with my legs crossed tightly staring at the wall.

It seemed like I sat there for an eternity with all kinds of frightening thoughts rushing through my head. Was I a terrible person because my own uncle had violated me? Was it my fault since I didn't go to bed when Aunt Marie told me to? Did God hate me? Would boys never want to talk to me?

Finally Mama came through the front door and she immediately knew something was wrong with me.

"What's the matter?" she asked

I started crying. "Nothing, Mama, I just wanna' go home."

"Where's your Aunt Marie?" She looked around in confusion.

"They're all still sleep." I answered meekly.

"Let me wake her up and let her know we're gone." She headed towards my aunt's bedroom door.

"No!" I shouted.

"What's wrong with you, girl?" She stopped dead in her tracks.

"Nothing, Mama. Can we just go home? Don't wake anybody."

A frown crossed Mama's forehead. She stood there for a couple seconds staring at me. She then turned and started for the door.

"Okay, then let's go," she scowled. "But I'm sure going to call your Aunt Marie later this morning and find out what happened. Why were you the only one up and nobody else was? Something strange is going on." She finished and we walked outside.

36

We both got in the car and she drove off. I wanted to hurry up and get home so I could hide in my bedroom. On the drive home the usual scenery that would have normally excited me, like the sky, trees, and flowers looked different. Nature's beauty that once used to catch my eye now looked dull and unattractive.

We pulled in the driveway at our house and I jumped out of the car and ran straight to my bedroom, slamming the door closed behind me. Feelings of an intense sense of guilt overtook me. I crawled into my bed and pulled the covers over my head. I mourned for what happened to me. I knew that the assault would change my life forever. Suddenly, I became angry with myself. Why hadn't I told my mother right away what happened to me? And how could I possibly tell anyone that my uncle had raped me?

Since the age of seven I always loved to write. I had pages and pages of writings about my feelings. When I was depressed, when I hated the world, and when I felt unhappy, I wrote. It was my therapy. Writing made everything all right. With that in mind, I jumped out of the bed, grabbed some paper along with my pencil and began to write what happened. I wrote two identical accounts of the rape and addressed one to my favorite teacher, Ms. Marie, and the other to my physical education teacher, Mr. Welch. Convinced this was the right approach to handle my crisis, I climbed back in bed and would stay there until Monday morning when it was time to go to school.

The rest of the weekend, Mama never asked what happened and left me alone in my room. I only came out to eat and use the bathroom. Sunday flew by fast and then Monday morning came and it was time for school. I climbed out of bed dressing in pants and a shirt. I pledged to never wear a dress again. I would never let anyone see my legs or my developing body. It was the reason I was abused and to prevent it from ever happening again I wouldn't expose any of my body ever again. I was dragging that morning as I thought about the day ahead of me. I clung tightly to my two letters.

I arrived at school just before the tardy bell rang. As I walked into my first class all the kids looked at me like they knew I had something to hide. I lowered my head and sat at my desk. The bell sounded signaling the beginning of class. Ms. Marie strolled into the room and took her place behind the desk in front of the class.

"Get into your groups," Ms. Marie said.

I raised my hand.

"Yes Alexis, come up front," she said.

Trying to keep my balance and not fall over from nervousness, I hurried up to her desk, placed the letter in front of her, and walked back to my seat. It wasn't unusual that I gave her a note to start her day. I did it all the time, but this was different and I am sure she noticed my unusual demeanor. I watched from my desk as she read my letter. She smiled as she opened it, probably assuming that it would be another positive and sweet message from me to her. But her smile disappeared as she read the contents. A solemn expression came over her face. I began to cry. I could tell she wanted to as well because her nose had turned red.

The bell ending class sounded off like a fire truck siren. I let everyone get up and leave class. I didn't want them to see me crying. Finally, I got up and walked slowly out of the classroom.

"Alexis, wait a minute," Ms. Marie said.

I turned around and slowly walked toward her. My emotions were now out of control. I didn't know how to feel. I started crying again.

"Don't cry, honey," she said softly and reassuringly. Her warmth toward me made the tears continue to flow. "I will handle this for you. You just go on to your next class and it will be all right."

The warmth in her voice gave me the courage I needed to make it to my next class.

That class was physical education, and it was the fun class for the day. When I walked into the gym I handed Mr. Welch the other letter and hurried to my assigned seat. He stared at the paper and then stuffed it into his pocket. Before he could say anything to the class, the intercom came on.

"Coach, can you have Alexis Williams please come down to the nurse's office?" the female voice carried throughout the gym.

Mr. Welch looked at me, and before he said anything I got up and walked out of the gym. As I hurried down the hallway I felt relieved and afraid. I was relieved because I knew the only reason I would be called to the nurse's station was because Ms. Marie shared my letter with the principal. I was afraid because everyone now knew that I was involved in something bad, and I figured they might blame me. Often times Mama would blame me for things I didn't do. They would probably do the same.

As I walked into the nurse's office, Mama and her boyfriend were the first two I saw. The nurse took me by the hand and led me into a private room. She asked me to tell what had happened. I didn't understand why I had to do that? It was all in the letter I wrote to Ms. Marie. But I managed to recall for her, every detail of what my uncle did to me.

"Get this poor child to Methodist Hospital quick," the nurse said. She handed my mother some papers. "Doctors and nurses will be waiting for you there."

We rushed out of the school building and into Mama's boyfriend's car. He took off speeding out of the parking lot and onto the main street. I curled up in the corner of the car with my body resting against the door. My head was bowed and I felt drained.

"Is there anyplace you want to go that would make you feel better?" Mama asked looking back at me against the door.

"McDonald's," I answered in a timid and low voice.

Mama smiled and James made a quick left turn and headed to the McDonald's only three blocks away. He pulled into the driveway and headed to the drive-up window.

"What do you want baby?" Mama asked.

"Big Mac and a coke."

She ordered my food and James pulled up to the window. They grabbed the hamburger and coke and handed them back to me.

I took one bite and felt sick. I wanted to throw-up. I laid the Big Mac, still wrapped, on the seat and held the drink in my hand. I drifted off to sleep but did not spill the drink. I must have dozed off for a good fifteen minutes and was jolted back awake when the car came to an abrupt stop.

"Where are we?" I asked still clinging to the coke. I stared up at the giant building in front of me and again fear took over. I didn't want to go in there.

"The hospital, baby," Mama said. "We have to see if anything is wrong with your body." She sounded convincing and I felt relieved.

We walked through the double doors and two policemen, two doctors, and a nurse greeted us.

"You must be Alexis?" one of the doctors asked as we approached them.

I nodded and the nurse took my hand. She guided me into a small room with white walls, a thin bed, and a table with shiny metal objects on it. There were a number of chairs and my mother took one. James was not allowed to go back with us.

The nurse lifted me on to the bed with my legs hanging over.

"Are you comfortable enough to put a gown on for us?" the doctor asked.

"No!" I blurted out. The thought of my bare body being exposed and examined frightened me. I clinched my clothes tight against my body.

My mother got up and walked over to the bed. She took my hand.

"If you put the gown on we can get out of the hospital faster." She knew how to persuade me to do things I did not want to do.

Mama took my clinched fists, released them and loosened my clothes. I changed into the gown.

"I need you to lay on your side facing me," the doctor said.

I shifted my body to the left side. The bed was cold and I just wanted to get up and run out of there.

"I'm going to examine your lower body," the doctor said as she separated my legs. She began to press and pull my inner thighs.

I clamped my legs together. "That really hurts." My voice was weary and tired.

The doctor pulled out a small device and again pried my legs open. "What is that?" I asked.

"It's a tiny camera, the size of an ant," she said as she hooked it

40

onto a long tube-like stick. "What I'm going to do is examine the inside of your body. The camera can see places where there might be damage that my eye cannot see."

As she inserted the instrument into my private area, my face tightened and I began to cry. "It's hurting me," I shouted.

"It's okay, honey," the doctor whispered. "It'll all be over in a couple minutes."

She finally pulled the small device out of my body. I put my clothes back on and ran over to Mama.

We walked back out into the waiting area. The doctor rushed over to the two policemen and said something to them. I couldn't hear them talking but whatever she told them, they hurried out of the hospital. She walked back over to us.

"She has internal tearing along the walls of her private area," she said. "I can tell something happened to her, but to make sure I will contact you when the results are in."

"Thank you, doctor," Mama said. She took my hand and we walked back into the foyer and out of the hospital.

Later that day we received word that Uncle Edward had been arrested and was in jail. The court also notified Mama that his trial for molestation of a juvenile would begin that following Monday. This ordeal was tearing our family apart. My brother wanted to get a gun and kill Uncle Edward. Mama and Aunt Marie had a verbal fight over the incident. Aunt Marie claimed it never happened. Mama told her that she would make sure he went to prison. And the fight continued for the entire week before the trial.

Mama was able to convince the principal at my school that it would be best that I not return until after the trial. She arranged to get all my homework for the next week and helped me with it at home. The rest of the week dragged on forever. I stayed in my room most of the time. I was depressed because I began to feel I was to blame for our family falling apart. If I had just kept my mouth shut and said nothing then none of this would be happening. I wished it would all go away. But I knew it couldn't. We had to see this through. No matter how difficult it might be for me in court, I had

41

to make sure my uncle didn't get away with his vicious act. He stole my innocence and he had to pay. By Sunday night I was a nervous wreck. I wondered what would happen in court and would I have to see my uncle, a person I really didn't ever want to see again in life?

"Get up, Lexi Pooh, it's time to go to court," Mama said as she walked into my room.

I wasn't ready for the day to start. I really wanted to pull the covers up over my head and just go back to sleep. In fact, at that point in my life, I wanted to sleep forever. But Mama went over to my closet and chose the clothes for me to wear.

"A dress!" I shrieked. I threw it under my bed along with the sparkly shoes she had laid out for me. I couldn't believe she picked that hideous dress. My feeling about girly clothes was changed forever. I rummaged through my closet and found my favorite pair of jeans and my football jersey.

"You're not going to wear that, are you?" Mama asked.

"Yes, Mama, all I want is pants and a shirt." I was still upset that she would suggest I wear a dress.

Mama didn't argue with me or force me to wear a dress. She understood that my rejection with anything female had to do with the incident. She shook her head and walked out of the room.

This time it was just Mama and I. James did not go with us. I sat in the front seat staring out the window as she drove toward the court building.

"Now remember, Alexis, it is important that you tell the truth. Just let the judge know what happened and everything will work out just fine," she preached.

"Yes, Mama," I kept repeating to her. She told me everything would be just fine, but I was not convinced. Everything wasn't fine. Our family had fallen apart and now I was about to send my aunt's husband to prison. That would cause an even greater rift within our family.

We pulled into the parking lot at the courthouse, quickly found a space, and then hurried through the huge wooden doors into the building.

"Right this way, ma'am," the officer said as he guided us through the metal detector.

We then headed into the courtroom filled with many people, some I knew and others were just faces. A very tall man, whom I didn't know, guided me through a small swinging door and to a table.

"Alexis, I am the District Attorney," he said to me in a mellow tone so as not to frighten me.

My tiny body sat at that large table in a big chair and looked up at this woman sitting high above us and dressed all in black. An overwhelming feeling of helplessness took over and I felt intimidated by it all. My body began to shake when they brought my uncle into the room and sat him at a table to the left of me. It was the first time I'd seen him since that frightful night and I just wanted to get out of there. At that point I needed someone but as I looked around I couldn't trust anyone, not even Mama. I was alone. Where was my father who should have been there to protect me? He was only not in court, but where was he when I was attacked? Where was that male figure with the strength to make me feel secure?

"This court is now in session?" a man in a police uniform called out.

The first few witnesses were the nurse from school and the doctor who had examined me. One of the police officers that arrested my uncle also got in the witness chair and talked about the arrest. By that time I was so light headed I didn't hear anything being said.

Finally I heard the district attorney call my name.

"Alexis Williams," he said, "I need you to come up here so we can ask you some questions."

The walk up to the witness chair took forever. I saw Uncle Edward out of the corner of my eye. He frightened me, but Mama and the district attorney told me not to be afraid because he could no longer bother me. With their words echoing in my ear I sat in the chair. The judge turned to look at me.

"You comfortable?" she asked.

"Yes," I said in a low whisper. My head was bowed. I refused to look up because if I did I would see Uncle Edward.

43

With my head bowed I could still see the District Attorney and Uncle Edward's attorney talking with a lady who I recognized from Child Protective Services. They huddled for about three minutes and then the lady opened the railings and approached me. She had a doll in her hand.

"Are you okay?" she asked

"Yes," again I whispered. Why were all these people asking me if I was comfortable and was I okay? I thought. No, I wasn't comfortable or okay.

The lady held the doll out toward me. "Alexis, I want you to take this doll and point to where on your body you were touched?"

I didn't want to do it. I held my fist tightly clenched next to my body. I could feel my emotions building up and knew any minute I would cry. I kept my head bowed.

"Alexis, honey, you have to do this," the lady coaxed me. "If you don't, we can't continue. Don't you want the man to pay for what he did to you?"

When she said "man" I shot a quick glimpse over at Uncle Edward. He looked so ugly and ominous to me. I just knew he was going to come out of that chair and attack. But Mama and the District Attorney assured me it would be all right. Without raising my head and with my hands shaking, I reached out and took the doll. I placed my finger on the doll's lower parts. It sickened me and I wanted to vomit.

I tried to relax back in the chair. Now that I had done it, I felt it was over. But it wasn't.

"Can you point to the man who did those things?" the lady asked.

I couldn't hold it any longer. The tears flowed freely down my cheeks as I remembered Uncle Edward's fingers in front of his mouth as a warning that I shouldn't holler out. I felt traumatized. Why was this happening and why would they ask me to point him out? Why wasn't he the one that was being questioned, after all I was only nine years old? They placed the responsibility to prove him guilty on my shoulders, and that didn't seem fair to me. I started hyperventilating and momentarily felt paralyzed. I couldn't raise my arm to point him out. I was overwhelmed as my body began to shut down.

I could feel all their eyes were on me as I now cried hysterically. I looked at Mama and she was also crying.

"Please take her down," the judge said. "We will take an hour recess and then see if she is able to continue."

The lady took my hand and helped me down from the witness chair. I ran to the railing. My mother jumped out her seat and met me at the railing, taking my hand. We followed the lady to a small room right outside the courtroom. They called it a children's playroom. Mama sat me in a chair carved into a giraffe's head.

The lady gave me some blocks to play with, and I built a house while she watched. I calmed down as I stacked the blocks on top of one another.

"Do I have to go back in there?" I asked the lady.

"No you don't," she answered.

I took my fist and crashed the house I had built with the blocks. I then laid my head on the table and closed my eyes wishing everything, the incident, and the people would all go away. I must have lain there for a good hour and then another lady woke me, picked me up and carried me out of the room. Mama was waiting right outside. The lady handed me over to Mama and said.

"Time to go home, young lady, all your worries will be gone now."

Holding my hand tightly, Mama and I walked out of the courtroom. I thought it was all over. I thought I would be able to put it all behind me and forget what happened. But it wasn't going to be that easy. I had lost all respect for everyone. Why hadn't Mama done something to this man and where was my father? In fact where was any man that would protect and take care of me? I began to believe that, at nine years old, the burden of my existence rested on my shoulders. I had become a statistic, just a number. I was nothing more than a young girl who had the terrible unfortunate luck to be raped. My first experience with a part of life that should have come much later, came much too early and what should be a beautiful experience was an ugly ordeal. I turned against the world and for the next five years became labeled as a juvenile delinquent.

I did nothing but sleep for the next two days after the trial. We got word back from the court that Uncle Edward was found guilty and given a three-year prison sentence. My Uncle Edward's violation of my innocence and the short sentence of only three years for such a dastardly act set my brother off. I was awakened on Wednesday morning to the sound of loud voices in the kitchen. I heard the rattling of silverware and the slamming of a drawer closed.

"Put down that knife, Jeremy," Mama shouted.

"No, I'm going to kill him," Jeremy said. "They only gave him three years and Alexis is going to have to live with this for the rest of her life. Someone got to act like a man around here."

"Jeremy, if you do something stupid, then this family will have suffered twice. First Alexis being abused, then Edward going to prison, and your cousins losing their father. If you do something to him, then you'll be gone also.

"I don't care, Mama," Jeremy said. "He shouldn't have hurt my sister. I'm the only man around here and someone's got to protect her."

"She'll be all right," Mama said. "She'll recover and get on with growing up."

I ran back and got in my bed. I pulled the covers over my head. How could Mama excuse it so easily? I was hurting badly. But I was so tired I felt like never getting up again. It didn't take me long to drift off to sleep only to be awakened by two loud voices.

"Your husband is a sick man, and he needs to stay locked up for a long time. Only consolation we have is that he'll be labeled as a child abuser for the rest of his life," Mama said.

"You don't really believe Edward raped Alexis do you?" It was my Aunt Marie's voice. "She lied and you know she did. She ain't nothing but a problem child anyway." There was a moment of silence. "Edward told me he was just looking for his lighter he'd left on that couch earlier in the evening."

"A lighter in my daughter's pants," Mama shot back. "Give me a break."

"Well you need to know that Alexis just broke up my family

when she sent my husband and my children's father to prison," Aunt Marie said.

"That's where the sick bastard belongs," Mama shouted.

"I'm out of here," Aunt Marie now shouted. "Your daughter is tearing this family apart. She is the one who needs help."

I heard the door slam and then silence. My aunt and mother had fallen out and I felt guilty for that happening. But I hadn't lied. Uncle Edward had raped me and the damage to my body proved I was telling the truth. Why didn't my Aunt Marie believe me? Did she love that man so much she would question something so obvious it was beyond doubt?

Days went by and my aunt, who usually came by our house all the time, didn't call or come over. My cousins didn't come over either and I had no contact with them. Our family had now fallen apart and I blamed myself.

Carrying the burden of responsibility for the break-up of our family weighed heavily on me. I felt fear all the time. I withdrew and didn't want communication with anyone, not even Mama. Returning to school was difficult because I told myself, "If you let your guard down, bad things will happen." My body was developing into that of a teenager and I wanted to hide it from sight. I felt comfortable with my clothes hanging off my body. I walked around with my head down unable to look others in the face because I knew deep inside I couldn't trust anyone. I was unable to let the hurt go, but as long as I kept it in my heart and on my mind, I was only hurting myself.

Trouble arose like a match striking the ground. My outlook on life became increasingly negative and belligerent with each passing day. Small things that happened sent me into a rage. I fought everyone who got in my way or I thought had crossed me, including Mama. Our home was dysfunctional with Mama's drinking and the number of men in and out of her life, all of them looking at me with that Uncle Edward gaze. By age thirteen, my battles with Mama were so vicious that we actually exchanged blows. Fights eventually landed me in a juvenile detention center.

My run-in with the authorities started in 2005 when I entered Roosevelt High School. One of the girls in my class made what I considered a derogatory comment about me and I attacked her. That fight earned me a trip to alternative school. I was fourteen years old at the time. Once in alternative school my problems escalated.

One morning while walking to school with a friend, who also attended alternative school, the boy slipped some prescription drugs into my backpack. During first period, the authorities did a random search and they found the drugs. I didn't tell them my friend put them in my backpack. A cardinal rule among teenagers was that you never told the authorities on each other. I had to take the hit for the drugs alone.

Once again I was in court, but not as a witness or victim. I was the defendant. The judge sentenced me to six months in a Juvenile Justice Academy, which essentially is a prison for young people. Being locked up like a prisoner was an excruciating experience. The girls in that place were tough and in order to survive I had to become a much tougher person than I was before going inside.

After six months I was finally released and put on twelve months probation. The authorities did give me a choice of going back to alternative school or I could attend a charter school if I could find one that would accept me. I did not want to go back to alternative school because they are merely breeding grounds for more trouble. I wanted a new start away from all the negative influences that had invaded my life. I had a couple weeks to get accepted so I put all my energy into researching the possible schools that were available to me. I chose a charter school on the east side of San Antonio, close to my neighborhood. I had found a new kind of joy knowing I would now go to a good school with excellent teachers who I believed would have my best interest at heart. Little did I know but would soon discover, that this school did not think much of kids like me. I went to the school and did everything they asked of me. I filled out all the necessary paperwork and went home to wait for their answer.

A week later I got it. A big fat NO! They did not want young people who had drug convictions. They didn't give me the opportunity to discuss that conviction with them. If they had I could have explained what happened. But they judged me by the conviction. The school's administration didn't even take the time to call and interview me in order to determine if I was deserving of an opportunity for a better life. It was obvious that they wanted only what they considered to be good kids. I did not fit into that category so I got that big fat NO and went back to alternative school.

I was now fifteen and convinced I had dug a hole that I would never be able to get out of. Life for me might as well have ended because I had no future. The charter school had told me I had no place in their world. Since the "good" world did not want me, the only option was the world of "trouble."

Mama and I had grown increasingly confrontational with each other. We argued all the time and often it came close to blows. When she was inebriated, which was all the time, her boyfriends would look at me in ways that made me uncomfortable. Mama fought with them all the time, but not because they were seductively looking at me. One day she was in a real battle with her boyfriend. He had blackened her eye and left heavy red marks around her neck. I watched in horror as he grabbed her and threw her across the coffee table. She crashed to the floor. He turned and ran out the door. I'd had enough. I ran to my room and packed a few things I owned into an old duffle bag. I hurried back out of my room and raced for the front door.

Mama stepped in my way and started shouting at me.

"Where do you think you're going?"

"I don't want to be here anymore. I'm leaving," I shouted back at her.

"You're not going anywhere. Get back to your room."

"Move Mama. I'm leaving." I tried to get around her but she kept blocking my way. I ran to the patio door, but she beat me there and blocked my exit.

While standing there she opened her cell phone and called the police. "Emergency," she shouted into the phone, "please help me, my daughter has attacked me and I need help." She hesitated for a moment and then continued. "My address is 1630 Copper Road, hurry I need your help."

My efforts to leave were now in vain. I fell back on the couch and waited for the police to arrive.

Within fifteen minutes they knocked at the front door. Mama told them that my probation required that I not leave the house without her permission and I had jumped her and given her the black eye and bruises on her body in an attempt to leave. They believed her lies and the next day I found myself back in Juvenile Detention Center. The charge against me was assault and attempt to violate probation. Once again the courts were not interested in listening to my version of the incident. I did not inflict those bruises or the black eye on my mother, but they believed her.

I stayed in Juvenile Detention for three months and was released, but I received eight more months' probation. This time I did not go back and live with Mama, but moved in with my older sister. Mama didn't object because I really don't think she wanted me back in her home. Somehow she had gotten this crazy idea that all her problems were caused by me. I began to doubt that she really believed I had been raped. She also knew that her sick boyfriend had actually tried to molest me also, but she turned a blind eye to that reality. She had gotten to the point that she preferred to believe I was not telling the truth than accept the truth that her boyfriends were sick perverts.

Again, I was given the choice of going back to alternative school or seeking out a charter school just like before. This time I didn't even bother applying at the first charter school, but did apply and was accepted at Southwest Preparatory School. Living with a sister only two years older than me and her boyfriend only three years older, was not the perfect arrangement, but it was better than Juvenile and living with Mama. I had to try and make the best of a less than perfect situation. It had been six years since the rape, and I felt like I was adjusting well to being back in school and then trouble reared its ugly head again. I wasn't looking for it, but it found me.

On January 18, 2008, I had made plans to attend the King Holiday march with some friends. I was going to take my younger sister with me. The march started at ten that morning, so she was supposed to meet us at our apartment at nine. She was two hours late and the two of us got into an argument. That argument turned into a fight. During our struggle, I damaged the outside mirror on the passenger's side of a friend's car. She became irate and insisted that I pay her immediately for the damage. I had no money so there was no way I could pay for the damage. The entire day turned out to be a disaster.

That evening, I stopped by Mama's house to explain to her why I had tried to whip my baby sister and how she had fought me. Mama wasn't about to listen to anything I had to say. She went into a tantrum, and started hitting me. About that time, the friend whose car mirror I had damaged showed up at Mama's house and insisted on me paying for the damage. Before I knew what was happening, everything seemed to fall apart and again I found myself in the backseat of a police car.

The charges this time were assault and damage to another person's property. Again, no one cared to hear my side of the story. And again I found myself in Juvenile Detention Center. My sentence was for three months and I served two. I was given six months probation. During those two months in Detention, I was under the supervision of a guard named Noel. She was in her early thirties and took a strong interest in me. She noticed that I loved to write. Throughout all of my ordeals I would always write. When I was raped I wrote about it, when sent to Juvenile the other two times, I wrote about it, and when refused admission to the charter school, I wrote about it. This time, while in Juvenile I began to write nonstop. I let Noel read some of my writings and she was surprised at the depth and clarity of my thoughts. One day I told her of the tragic events that I had suffered over the years and she encouraged me to always fight back and never give up. She was the first person to ever appreciate me as a person. I no longer felt like some kind of object to be abused by anyone who felt compelled to do so. Because of Noel, I finally believed that I could be somebody. More than anything in the world, that somebody I wanted to become was a writer. Noel was the first positive female, someone who could serve as a role model for me, that I ever had in my life. She started me on my journey to turn my life around. It only took one additional person to make the change complete. That happened once I got out of Juvenile Detention, finished the semester at Southwest Preparatory, and was finally admitted back into public schools.

First Sergeant Donald Halford, who is in charge of the ROTC program at Sam Houston High School, was the first positive male role model in my life. I was sixteen and every man whom I had dealt with over the years left me practically hating all men. I didn't know my father at all since we left Detroit when I was very young. I believe he was in jail when we left. Mama's male friends, who were all Black, had either made lewd gestures or tried to molest me. So when I first walked into First Sergeant Halford's ROTC class I knew I would confront the same kind of Black man once again. It fills my heart with joy to admit I was wrong.

My second semester at Sam Houston High School, I was assigned to ROTC. I had very little interest in the military, but if it made the counselors at the school happy I agreed to it. First Sergeant Halford was a no-nonsense man who conducted his classes just like we all were in the military. I quickly ascertained that this was a man that could be instrumental in helping me change my life. I became very active and volunteered to carry out specific assignments whenever possible. Sergeant Halford noticed my enthusiasm and began to nurture my growth and development. He instinctively knew I carried a lot of troubled baggage and began to spend time talking with me and giving me encouragement. I needed a great deal of help because I still suffered from low self-esteem. But with Sergeant Halford and Noel I began to gain confidence in myself.

During the spring of 2009, I was chosen to participate in a cross-country bus ride sponsored by an organization called God Parents Youth Organization. Even though it was an all-expense paid trip, I still needed additional clothes and money for myself. Sergeant Halford provided me with the funds that I needed. I went on the trip that started in Los Angeles and visited over thirty cities in thirty days, taking us across the country. We visited a number of Historical Black Colleges and Ivy-League institutions also. We visited Washington, D.C. and went up to New York and Boston, finally making our way back to Los Angeles thirty days later.

As of the writing of this essay, I am planning to graduate from Sam Houston High School within the next month. I had once thought I would join the United States Air Force, but since I was given the opportunity to participate in this anthology, I have decided to attend college. I want to pursue a writing career. I am not sure in what genre, but I do know I want to write. I believe the many encounters, mostly bad but a few good, have prepared me for my mission in life, and that is to continue my writing in order to share with other young people. I want to share with others who have also been abused to let them know that there is hope for them. I want to encourage them to never give up. During those dark days, I never dreamt or could even imagine that I might be given the opportunity to participate in an anthology with such outstanding writers. I know I am blessed and look forward to a future filled with rewarding opportunities that will help eradicate all the negatives that dominated me for the first sixteen years of my life.

BEATING THE ODDS AND WINNING THE BATTLE

DAVID FLOYD

According to statistics I should be either strung out on drugs, in prison, or dead. The so-called experts on human behavior categorize Black men based on their sociological/economical criteria. I was a young Black boy who his entire life battled the pathologies that are destroying the Black communities all over this country. I grew up in the middle of a vice-ridden Black neighborhood. It was the east end of Freeport, Texas, sitting right at the banks of the river where the shrimp boats docked for the summer. After being out to sea for up to three weeks, the shrimpers got off those boats ready to party and party they did, right in my neighborhood. Heavy drinking, prostitution, gambling, and every once in a while, a murder took place all around my brothers, my childhood friends, and me.

My family was not immune from the effects of those vices. For most Black families, survival was their goal and they were determined to do that by any means necessary. Mama understood that struggle and all the games associated with it. We survived because Mama knew how to manipulate around the many pitfalls waiting to swallow up those too weak to fight back. I guess I got my no-quit attitude from Mama. The more obstacles that were placed in my way, the more determined I was to defeat them.

My battles began from the first grade on when it became quite apparent that I could not read. At six-years-old I couldn't understand why I was unable to do what all the other students had no trouble doing, and that was to read passages from a beginner's book. I began to believe something was wrong with me, and my teacher, Mrs. McWilliams, did nothing to dispel my fears. I dreaded eleven o'clock because that was the time we had to read out loud while the rest of the class listened. I sat there hoping that somehow the words would come to me. As the rest of the class took turns, I tried to figure out exactly what I would be called upon to read. Sometimes I asked the little girl sitting next to me to tell me the words with the hope of memorizing and simply reciting them when my turn came around. That always led to a paddling from Mrs. McWilliams because she claimed I badgered the other students. She called me to the front of the room, paddled me, and sent me back to my seat, hurt and embarrassed.

I could associate certain words with objects such as the word dog placed below or next to the picture of a dog. Same for cat, cow, house, and tree. I did just fine with those words, but others that had no association with objects baffled me. It made me angry and frightened at the same time. To add to my consternation, Mrs. McWilliams would actually taunt me.

"Come on, David, we don't have all day," she would scowl. "David, these words are easy. A kindergartener could read this. I believe you are just being lazy."

Her attacks made it much more difficult. I could feel all the other children staring and just waiting for me to mess up so they could laugh. That was the most difficult part of all, the others staring and laughing. If I stuttered or failed to pronounce a word correctly, they laughed and it reverberated like an echo chamber over and over again. The laughter increased the longer I stood there with that book in my hand. Readings, stories, and words seemed deliberately designed to humiliate me. They gave others a reason to look down on me, and that gave me a reason to fight them. After a while, I no longer cared about reading and I only wanted revenge. I wanted to hit and hurt the ones who laughed, and through the power of my fists let them know it was no fun not being able to read.

The real tragedy is that Mrs. McWilliams simply gave up on me. She conveniently placed the blame for my failure on Mama. Many times she would shout, "If your mother or someone in your family would only come to one of the parent meetings, they'd know you can't read." If she had taken the time to contact Mama and tell her of my problem, then that would have been enough to let her know

I needed help. But no one did a thing and with each week I became angrier and much more violent, because the other students could read, and I couldn't.

Whippings by the principal of the school and Mrs. McWilliams became practically an everyday occurrence for me throughout that entire year, and I was only six years old. After a while, I don't believe Mrs. McWilliams needed a reason to whip me, she just assumed I did something wrong. I was the target of her wrath. My teacher and I had a confrontational relationship. I no longer cared about my behavior in the classroom. I talked all the time, laughed at the other students, played tricks on Mrs. McWilliams, and sometimes threw a punch or two. The whippings would continue throughout elementary school because my defiance grew with each year that I fell further behind the other students in reading.

By third grade I had really come to hate school because I was such a failure. My teacher, Mrs. Brown, was no different than Mrs. McWilliams in that she was relentless in her demands that I read.

"David, take your time and concentrate on each word," she said.

I would tightly grip the book, stare at the words, but nothing registered.

Her patience was short. "Don't you want to pass third grade?" she scowled.

"Yes ma'am."

"Well read for me."

"Jjjjohhhnnn lllliked tttto." As I stuttered the others laughed. "Leave me alone," I shouted. "Leave me alone." I threw the book on the floor and ran out with tears flowing down my face.

Mrs. Brown caught me in the hall, grabbed my arms, and jerked me all the way to the principal's office.

"Why did you throw your book down and run out of the class?" Mr. Waniack, the principal, asked, even though he knew why. I did it so many times over the years it seemed rather ridiculous for him to ask. Before I would cry and tell him that no matter how hard I tried, the words just wouldn't come out. And when the others laughed I couldn't stand there and let that happen. But he never heard me.

57

Mr. Waniack did not feel my pain and embarrassment. He didn't understand that I wanted to read the words in that book more than anything else. Or maybe he just didn't care. His response never changed. He'd simply grab his paddle and say.

"Bend over."

I must hold the record for bending over and getting paddled at O. A. Fleming Elementary School. After a while I became immune to the whippings since they happened practically everyday. Mr. Waniack never considered the possibility that something was wrong with their teaching methods. Or possibly, they really didn't try to understand. The teachers at that school humiliated me every day for five years, but still passed me on to the next grade, knowing that I could not read. How could they possibly not know that I wanted to desperately overcome my handicap?

Mama never knew I couldn't read. She assumed, that since I was passed from one grade to the next, all my learning skills were developing as expected. I was too ashamed to tell her and the other kids knew they had better not. So Mama was in the dark. I compensated for my failure with an extremely competitive spirit in other subjects. While in the third grade, we had a math contest. The student who knew their multiplication tables best would win a Baby Ruth candy bar. Mrs. Brown actually tried to convince me not to compete. With reading she badgered me to do something I couldn't; with math she discouraged me from doing something I could do. I won that contest and it was the proudest moment in all my elementary years. I really enjoyed that Baby Ruth.

My three years at Freeport Intermediate School were just as traumatic for me as were the previous years. My reading worsened, my behavior worsened, and the paddling continued. Not only did I get paddled regularly, I also received in-school suspensions. They bused the students at our school to another intermediate school to serve out the suspension. We were housed in a separate room away from all the other students and marched like prisoners to the cafeteria for lunch where we ate at separate tables. We stayed at that school the entire day in a room without windows, and then were bused back to our school. Students at both schools stared at us like we were prisoners. They might as well have put a big X across our foreheads. Our schoolmates viewed us as being different. Just as students scorned me because I couldn't read, here was a second time I faced the same kind of embarrassment.

The teachers at Freeport Intermediate knew I could not read; however, just like at O. A. Fleming, they passed me on to the next grade. It made no sense, but I didn't complain. I sure didn't want to spend any more time there than necessary. My teachers did not want me for another year and the feeling was mutual. It worked best for all of us. What I didn't realize was that, in the long run, I would be the only one to suffer.

David Floyd, the boy who could not comprehend a kindergarten reader, was now in high school. They assigned me to developmental classes, including developmental English. I would be called on in that class to read orally from different books, but I no longer feared my failure because all the other students in the class could not read much better than me and had no right to laugh. The school system had categorized us for the entire student body to recognize as slow learners or non-learners.

I had no illusions about learning to read at all in my life. But somehow I would make it just as I did in the past. It became clear that the school officials did not care if a Black child couldn't read, do math, or any of the subjects you were asked to pass in order to graduate. Many young Blacks in my condition had graduated with no chance of success, and many of them were stuck in prison with no future. That's how I felt at that time in my life. Eventually I would come to realize that my attitude was self-destructive and sometimes used as an excuse not to learn. I was doing exactly what they wanted and that was failing.

Basketball saved me during my three years at Brazosport High. I eventually became one of the star players and the teachers passed me because of that reason. My friends and I also concocted an ironclad scheme for cheating. When we had exams, they would find a way to get me the answers to the test. It worked quite well in all my classes and now as I look back on it, the teachers probably knew all along what was happening. They didn't care; they just wanted to get me out of their class.

At that time I didn't think anything was wrong with cheating. It was survival for me, and without cheating I never would have graduated. Ultimately, it served me well. If I had failed to graduate from high school, my will power to achieve may have been broken and I never would have learned to read. I inevitably would have become one of those statistics assigned to me by society.

When I graduated from Brazosport High School I was literally reading at the second grade level. With hopes of winning a basketball scholarship to San Angelo State University, I took the ACT examination as part of the requirements for admission to the school. I scored a nine on the exam and five points were given to you for just signing your name on the exam. There was no way I could read and comprehend the questions on the exam. This time there was no one to help me. My reading disability had finally caught up with me. All my life I had depended on my basketball skills to compensate for my inadequacies. I knew someday I would be in the National Basketball Association and reading would be inconsequential. But when I received that nine I then realized the consequence of not reading.

I still refused to give up. I recognized and accepted the fact that I would never make it to the NBA. That's when I decided I would never lean on any other crutch for a balance. I would confront the problem and win the battle. I had no idea how I would do that, I just knew I would. It was two wonderful men and one beautiful lady who showed me the way.

I will always be grateful to the late Mr. Maceo Smedley, one of the few Black administrators at Brazosport High School. He helped me identify the college that would be willing to help a young Black man who lacked the ability to compete at the college level, but had all the determination to succeed. I will never forget my meeting with him in his office.

He sat and listened as I explained my intentions to him.

Every once in a while he smiled, especially when I expressed my determination not to be stopped by anything or anyone.

"So you want to get a Ph.D. in accounting?" he asked.

"Yes, sir, no doubt I will get a Ph.D., not I want to."

"You can't read, David." He gave me a hard stare. "How you going to go from an eighteen-year-old boy who probably shouldn't have graduated from high school to a Ph.D.?" he continued, not being mean but realistic.

"With great will power and your help," I said. "Please help me pick the right school."

Mr. Smedley presented me with three choices. The first was Texas College in Tyler, Texas, the second Paul Quinn in Dallas, and the third was Huston-Tillotson in Austin Texas, all historical Black Colleges.

I choose Huston-Tillotson and it turned out to be the very best choice I could have made. It was there that I met the other two people responsible for my overcoming my reading disability.

With the exception of fighting and playing basketball my skills were limited. I had very little knowledge of the world outside of Freeport, but as I walked onto the Huston-Tillotson campus in January 1987, failure was not on my mind. I was entering a new world I know very little about; however, I did know I must not fail or my life would, as Langston Hughes poetically put it, "fester like a sore and dry up."

It didn't take long for me to find out just how little I knew about the world beyond Freeport or for that matter how little I knew about something as simple as getting admitted into college. The depths of my naiveté became quite visible as I stood in front of the registrar's desk with my application all filled out.

"Your name," he asked without looking up. A notebook of green bar computer paper loaded with names sat on the table in front of him.

"David Floyd," I said almost in a whisper.

I watched as he leafed through the pages looking for my name. He turned a page and then the next, doing that a couple of times.

61

"That's interesting," he mumbled. He spent another half-minute studying those pages. "Did you attend Huston-Tillotson last semester?"

"No sir, I didn't."

"So you're a second-semester transfer?"

"What's that mean?"

The registrar stared up at me with a slight frown. "It means you're entering college in the spring semester and not the fall when most students enter."

"Yes sir, I guess so. Is something wrong with that?"

The man continued staring at me now with a frown on his face. "Most students start in the fall, but no, there is nothing wrong with it," he answered. "But there is a problem because I don't have you listed as a registered student." He looked back down at the names on the computer sheet. "When did you send in your application for admission and when did you receive your acceptance letter?"

"I have my application with me and it's all filled out," I said.

"You didn't submit your application for admission earlier?"

"No I didn't. I thought I could do that when I came up here. I do have my approval for financial aid."

"That's only half the procedure, young man. Financial aid means nothing without first being admitted to an institution."

"So what does that mean?" I asked.

"It means you are not admitted to the college and you'll have to wait until the fall semester to be admitted."

My knees weakened under me and I almost fell to the ground. This man had just told me I couldn't attend Huston-Tillotson when classes began in a couple days. I had to get into college right then because there were no other options open to me. I didn't even have enough money to get back to Freeport. I knew no one in Austin and had no place to stay. There was no way I could go back to Freeport. There was nothing there for me but trouble.

"Sir, you have to let me register," I pleaded. "You see I can't go back home. In fact, I don't even have enough money to get back home and no place to stay here."

"There is nothing I can do," he said. "I have no record of you and as far as the school is concerned, you just don't exist. I'm sorry." He sounded sincere. "The only person with the authority to admit you now is the president."

"Where is he?" I asked.

The man pointed to a large white building across the grassy mall. "In that building. When you get inside turn left and you can't miss his office."

What happened next is a wonderful testimony to our Black colleges and the kind of care most teachers and administrators show toward their students. Dr. Joseph T. McMillan Jr. did not have to help me when I showed up in his office. After all, I should have known that my application had to be submitted to the university before the semester began, and most importantly I had to be accepted as a student. Dr. McMillan could have easily taken the attitude that anyone who didn't know the basic procedures for admission had no business going to college. He could have turned his back on me and forced me to give up my dream at that moment to go to college. He didn't do any of those things; instead he took a chance on me. I wasn't the smartest applicant, but he sensed my determination. He invited me to come into his office and in doing so, opened the door to my successful pursuit of a dream.

"How can I help you, young man?" he asked as he removed his glasses and stared across his big oak desk at me.

"I need your permission to register for classes." I felt nervous energy burning through me. I was actually talking with the president of a college. "The man outside at the registrar's desk told me the only way I can get into college is if I see you. He said something about I didn't apply ahead of time and that only you could let me in." I was beginning to feel foolish having to reveal me naiveté again.

"Why didn't you apply?" he asked in a very somber tone.

"Honest, sir, I didn't know I had to. I applied for my financial aid and got approved. That's all I thought I needed." I showed him the financial aid papers. "See, sir, I got them right here."

He took the papers, glanced at them and handed them back to me. We stared at each other and that's when I broke down. Tears

63

flowed freely down my face. Again, my legs buckled and I placed my hand on the edge of the chair in front of the desk to keep from falling.

"Sir, you got to let me in. I can't go back home because there is nothing good for me there." I paused to wipe the tears. "I don't want to end up as just another statistic, either in jail like a lot of my friends or dead."

Dr. McMillan just kept staring at me and I knew he was not touched by my story. Why should he be, and did I think he would care for a boy who didn't have enough sense to get admitted to the school before showing up to register? He must have thought I was some kind of ghetto fool.

Assuming I had failed, I prepared to leave.

"I'm going to admit you on a special provision," Dr. McMillan said. He pulled some papers from inside his desk drawer.

Stunned, I stood there while he filled them out and handed them to me.

"Take these to the registration desk. They'll have to schedule you to take some tests in order to determine what classes you should take. We need to test your skills in reading, writing, and math." He stood up and glared at me. "You said you wanted a new life and a new start. This is your chance. Huston-Tillotson is giving you that opportunity. Don't let the university or me down."

"Thank you, sir," I said in a choked voice. "I'll never let you or the university down. I promise you that." I turned and hurried out of his office.

I meant exactly what I said. There was no way I would disappoint him or the university, for in doing so, I would disappoint myself. I knew the real battle was just beginning, after all, I still couldn't read, and that would surely be reflected in my test scores. It did and I was assigned to remedial reading and writing classes. It was in the remedial reading class that the other individual to whom I owe so much of my success came into my life.

The second week of classes Mrs. Roder, the remedial reading instructor, called on me to read a paragraph from a fourth grade reader.

"Tttttthhhhe bbbbbboy wwwwwho…,"

"That's okay, David," Mrs. Roder stopped me. "We'll come back to you. Relax and realize we are all friends."

But we weren't all friends. My reading level was the very lowest and when I tried to read, just as it happened in elementary and intermediate school, college students laughed. The irony was that they were also in remedial reading class.

After a few weeks of the laughing and teasing, I decided to sit down with Mrs. Roder and discuss the problem. Unlike most of my teachers throughout elementary, intermediate, and high school, Mrs. Roder really cared. She was Black and I believe that was the difference.

"What is it, David?" she asked as I took a seat in her office. "What's bothering you?"

"It's the reading exercises in class," I said.

"I know. It's the laughing and snickering isn't it? I try to control it as best I can, but they're so immature."

"Mrs. Roder, there was a time in my life when I would've fought every one of them laughing. I would've come out swinging, but I've matured beyond that point."

"That's good, David. That makes you a better person." She walked from behind her desk and took a seat next to me. "How do you want to handle this? I don't want you to be uncomfortable in class. You'll never learn to read that way."

"What if you don't call on me in class?"

"David, you have to do the reading exercises. That's the only way you'll learn to read."

"Could I do it privately with you?"

Mrs. Roder sat there silently for a moment, obviously thinking about the situation. I prayed that she would allow me to meet after class and read to her privately. I almost got what I prayed for.

"I tell you what we'll do," she finally said. "Instead of meeting with me after class, you'll meet with Ms. Phillips, my assistant, and read to her. You still must come to class and please do not miss any of your scheduled meetings with her."

I choked up and again tears welled up in my eyes. The faculty at Huston-Tillotson was becoming my best friend.

"Mrs. Roder, that is something you'll never have to worry about," I said. "I will be here on time and ready to learn."

"Good, David. I know you will." She smiled at me as I turned and walked out of her office.

Over the next four years, I never missed a scheduled meeting with Ms. Phillips who became a very special person to me. She was that third person I mentioned earlier responsible for my success.

We began our sessions with a kindergarten reader, *Buttermilk Bill and the Train*. It was the same book my teachers at O.A. Fleming tried to force me to read and I was never successful. But this time the circumstances were different. I felt like I was with a friend and for that reason I knew I would win this battle. I asked Ms. Phillips if we could start all over whenever I stumbled over a word. She agreed and we started over many times. But I finally mastered it, and we moved on to other books at a higher-grade level. Because of Ms. Phillips' incredible patience and her outstanding teaching techniques, my reading skills increased quite rapidly. With each threshold I met my pride grew. Despite a full load of classes, I always found additional time to practice reading. After a while, I would catch the bus and go over to the library at the University of Texas. There, I spent endless hours reading all kinds of books and especially ones dealing with history.

Due to just sheer determination, I graduated with a Bachelors Degree from Huston-Tillotson in three years. Also, because of sheer determination, I was accepted into the Masters of Science program with a major in Accounting at Bentley University in Boston, Mass. Bentley is recognized as one of the top business colleges in the country. David Floyd, who grew up in a dysfunctional community, dysfunctional family, and dysfunctional school system, competed in a graduate program with students from Harvard, Massachusetts Institute of Technology, and many other elite Ivy League universities and succeeded in getting a Masters Degree.

I am now a full time professor of Accounting at Austin Community College and will receive my Doctorate Degree in the next two years. I have authored an autobiography that chronicles my struggles and determination. There are a million other young Black boys who have experienced the same hardships as me, and hopefully my story will serve as the inspiration they need to never give up. My determination never wavered, and my hope never died. No one could destroy the burning flame that lit my spirit and drove me to succeed. For all the young brothers and sisters who read this and then my autobiography, please remember that in many ways you are the captain of your soul and the master of your fate. Always be encouraged by the words in a song by Sly and the Family Stone and that is, "You can make it if you try."

ON BEING A PRINCIPAL

Dr. Mateen Diop

I was vacationing with friends when I received a call from the deputy superintendent for the San Antonio Independent School District. "Congratulations you have been named principal of Hirsch Elementary," the voice on the other end of the phone extolled. I must admit all the challenges I faced in my life came to mind as I drove to our district offices to meet with the superintendent. I had my daily talk with God, wondering why the road I travelled was wrought with so many hills and valleys. I wondered how I would lead a group of teachers and students to success. Every fear imaginable crept into my mind, but I knew I was prepared for the challenge.

After receiving congratulations from district level supervisors, I drove over to my new school. As I steered into the school's parking lot, I immediately recognized the first problem to be resolved was the dilapidated marquee. I made a note that I must put that as an initial "to do" on my list. The marquee may seem like a small thing, but first impressions are extremely important. I surmised that whenever someone visited our campus, the first attribute they would notice would be the condition of our grounds, grass cut, area free of clutter and the marquee. Since our sign needed obvious repair, I knew that had to be the first hurdle I crossed before school opened.

I walked into the school's main office and there sat my new secretary. She didn't recognize me as the new principal, but before she could say anything, I cheerfully told her who I was. She gave a slight smile and directed me into the retiring principal's office. The person whom I would replace was actually my Sunday school teacher from many years ago, and he couldn't be happier that I was taking his place. As I sat in his office, I noticed that he wasn't close to packing. I guess he also noticed my expression of concern.

"Don't worry man, I'm moving out of here, just give me a week," he said.

We sat and talked for several hours as he counseled me on what to expect, who to look out for and the challenges I might face. I didn't care; I just wanted to get busy being successful.

After a week passed, I went back to the school, and as promised, he was packed and ready to move out. He handed me the keys to the school, gave me a tutorial on the alarm system, and I was now on my own.

My secretary was trying to figure out how we would work together. I wish I could have told her then that I'm probably the easiest and hardest person to work with. My only goal was to achieve student success. After meeting with her, I asked if she would summon our campus leadership team for a meeting. Since this was still summer, I had to coax the team to meet with me by providing lunch. I believe they would have come anyway because they wanted to meet the new principal.

The campus leadership team consisted not only of teachers, but also parents and instructional assistants. When we gathered for that first meeting, the first thing I did was to have them look outside my office window as plastic debris fell from the shabby school marquee. We agreed to hold a fundraiser to purchase a new sign within the first few months of the school year. "Great," I said, "but now on to the reason we all are here—student achievement," I continued. I had already thoroughly analyzed our school's data. I knew our strengths and weaknesses, but I wondered if they really knew what our students were capable of achieving. Initially, I articulated my vision for the school and then we spent the rest of the time discussing our data and what our initial staff development would look like. Hopefully, they did not notice that I was more nervous that day than I would be the actual first day of classes. After the meeting I went back to my office to recount the discussion we had. "Okay, I can do this," I whispered to myself.

The next issue for consideration was the budget. The majority of our student population was considered "at-risk," which meant they were vulnerable to dropping out of school. The federal government provides additional funds to schools servicing at-risk students; however, those funds were carefully distributed and also carefully spent. As principals we had to plan for and spend every dollar of those funds every year. We had to identify our strengths and weaknesses, and then develop a plan to meet the needs of our students.

While visiting classrooms before school started in the fall, I noticed that there were very few working computers in the building. I asked the secretary about technology on the campus to which she responded, "We have very little." I immediately amended the budget crafted by the former principal, to include the purchase of new computers for every classroom. I am a strong advocate for integrating technology into the classroom, so every year while at Hirsch I allocated funds to purchase new technology. By the time I left Hirsch we had more new technology in our classrooms than any elementary school in our district.

Now that I had met with the campus leadership team, planned the staff development and worked up a budget of our funds for the school year, the only detail left was to ensure that the building was ready. No job was more important than ensuring the building was clean and safe for the students. Our custodians polished the floors, as well as cleaned all the classrooms and offices. They made sure the grass was cut and perhaps most important, our cafeteria was spotless. The cafeteria was where we held most of our staff development sessions. It was the place I called the battlefield. Data was strategically placed on the walls, tables decorated and themes for the year and all the technology at our disposal was setup and ready to go.

71

August 14 arrived and, of course, I couldn't sleep the night before. I kept replaying in my mind all that was needed for a successful staff development session. I woke up early and arrived at the school before daylight. At this point, I had yet to meet all of the teachers, so I was anxious and as I am sure they were as well. The clock ticked away as 7:30 got closer I knew the teachers would begin finding their way into the battlefield for our first of many sessions together. Finally teachers began to arrive and one by one I greeted them as they entered the battlefield.

"Greetings, welcome back," I said to everyone. "Please help yourself to refreshments before we get started."

My suit jacket was drenched with sweat and I prayed that no one would notice. As the clock reached 8:00 and the room filled up with my entire staff, I took the microphone.

"Good morning," I began. "As you all know I am your new principal, Dr. Mateen Diop." I then shook hands with the entire staff, told them about my background and called on each person to stand and tell us something about themselves. With the introduction complete, nerves began to settle and we all began to relax, and ready to get down to business.

Our first topic for discussion was centered on the misperceptions about the public schools. The critics lament that such schools are "failing." I often wonder what measuring stick they are using to determine if a school is successful or not? Most pundits point to test scores or some other measure such as graduation rates to determine a school's effectiveness. However, as a leader in the public schools, I can tell you that a principal has several measures by which to gauge effectiveness; test scores being only one of them. Data drives every decision we make as school leaders. If reading scores are down, we must allocate financial and human resources to fix the problem. But how do you fix problems not noticeable through testing. My staff and I concluded that it all depended on planning for success and that is exactly what we would do as the school year began.

Planning for Success

As I began to visit classrooms, I realized that we needed more than ninety minutes of instruction in certain subjects. Along with extending the school day with after-school tutoring, we hired several tutors to address our struggles in reading and math during the school day. I also instituted single-gender classes for the fourth grade. The all-boys class, although challenging, showed marked improvement in every campus and district based assessment the entire school year. The all-girls class outperformed every class in every subject.

The data for my all-boys class improved with every campus assessment. When word go out that we were experimenting with single-gender classes and implementing technology, I began to receive visitors from everywhere. District and community leaders wanted to visit our classrooms to see what we were doing. I should have known this would happen; midway through the school year, the teacher for the all-boys class was promoted to a district level position, which left us with a serious void in the fourth grade. How could I find an effective teacher midway through the school year? I am not one to use excuses for my failure in any endeavor, so I found what seemed to be a great fit for my boys. Although the teacher had energy and enthusiasm, she didn't have the experience at the time to handle twenty-two young boys. Needless to say, instruction in the class suffered just as we were preparing for the upcoming state exams.

The day of the state test arrived. Our instructional coordinator ensured everyone was in place logistically and the day went off without a hitch. At the end of the day, teachers showed their anxiety when I asked the question, "how do you think they did?" Many teachers would remark, "I hope they did well." Not a good indicator to me.

Toward the end of the year our results arrived. We were actually at an end-of-year social event when the email arrived. I am sure teachers did not notice when I excused myself for several minutes to peruse the results and just as I thought, my fears were confirmed: Reading: 75% passing, Math: 67% passing, Writing: 65%. I knew the teachers would be disappointed, so I let them enjoy the rest of the evening before I divulged our results.

The next day I called in my instructional coordinator and we discussed the results at length. We decided to conduct meetings with teachers during their conference to inform them of the results. Although there were some bright spots, as a campus we were not where we wanted to be. My area superintendent called me to discuss the results and inquired as to my plan of action. At our final staff development of the school year we celebrated our successes, but I made sure teachers understood what would be required the next school year.

The 2010-2011 school year would be much different. At the very outset, I reminded teachers of our challenges, of what our community expected from us and what we should expect from ourselves. I reiterated our mission and goals for the year. "We will effectively integrate technology into every facet of our lessons." I am sure teachers grew weary of my musings, but I was being redundant on purpose. The message of success had to sink in.

This staff development was probably the deepest we had ever disaggregated our data. We used every identifier we could find to pinpoint our strengths and weaknesses. I even went as far as providing a picture of each and every student, with their demographic data next to the picture and previous assessment results. My goal in that exercise was to remind teachers that we were dealing with the lives of real students and not just numbers on a page. It was a very empowering activity since you could hear teacher's conversations: "I remember John, I had him in Kindergarten," or my favorite, "She was a very smart girl in first grade, what happened to her?"

Those types of questions and conversations about students reminded me of my sister. I wondered if Mavis' first grade teacher would have talked to her fifth-grade teacher, maybe they would have noticed her sinking grades and how she went from a model student in class to a disruptive force a few years later. Since we knew exactly what student we were talking about, we could use data to tell us why there were huge gaps in certain student's learning. We knew we couldn't control every aspect of our students' lives, but we could control every aspect of our teaching and learning. I used many analogies from my days of playing sports. I stressed to my teachers, "We would leave everything on the court."

One of the challenges when leading an inner city public school is the perception that we are failing our students, and they are somehow inferior to their peers in the suburbs. My school was no exception.

Today, there are at least four different charter schools located in my school's attendance zone. Whenever I run into one of my students at a local supermarket and I hadn't seen them for awhile, I would ask where they were attending school and the answer would likely be that they are attending a local charter school. When I asked their parents why they left my school, the answer would always be, "I like this or that school better." I wondered what they "liked" better about their chosen school, but my resolve would be strengthened to make sure my school was even better. I know my parents were forced to attend my school due to income, but if they had the opportunity to live in the suburbs, I am almost sure they would attend their community public school over a charter school—but back to our success story.

As the school year progressed, I could feel the energy of success around the campus. Since we disaggregated data so thoroughly, teachers knew exactly what was needed for each student. Behavior improved to the point that our suspension rate was next to zero. I even noticed that some of our students who withdrew earlier in the year to attend charter schools were now enrolling. That was probably one of my biggest joys as a principal; to have parents re-enroll their children based on the success and improvements we made from year to year was affirming to me that we were moving in a positive direction.

As the day of state testing grew closer, another phenomenon began to take place—although we were prepared for it this time. In Texas we have what is called the snapshot date. This date (normally in October) is when the state takes an axiomatic "snapshot" of a school's enrollment. Whoever is enrolled in your school on the day will count toward your final accountability rating—provided, however they are enrolled at your school on testing day. For example, let's say the snapshot date is October 31, Johnny is a fifth grade student on your campus and therefore counts toward your membership of students. On November 1, Johnny withdraws from your campus and enrolls at an elementary charter school (or any other campus). Johnny attends the Charter Elementary for the entire year and is not making adequate progress so Charter Elementary withdraws Johnny and he enrolls at my school on the day of the state test. Since

Johnny was enrolled on my campus on the snapshot date AND he was enrolled on the day of the test, his scores (pass or fail) will count towards the accountability rating for my school. That is probably the most disheartening part for his teachers because we never had an opportunity to teach Johnny. Yet if Johnny fails the state assessment, that teacher and my school will shoulder the blame.

This was a common practice with the charter schools in my area. As principals we would always wait for the day just before testing when our enrollment would increase and immediately following the testing season, those same students would be recruited to return to their charter schools and our enrollment would decrease. I would tell my teachers, to their frustration, that was one of those details we had no control over, so we must do what we can with whoever walks through the doors—this is true of public education.

We strategized often about how to achieve student success. Schools were opened on Saturday and several of my teachers spent many evenings tutoring our students. Once all the data was analyzed, we had to devise a plan to ensure our students would be successful on the upcoming state assessment. One point I knew for sure was that we had to make our classes smaller. The first detail was to summon my campus leadership team. However, this meeting would be a little different from the earlier ones. Since time was of the essence, it was imperative that our strategy begin immediately. I listened to some input, but I had already developed our game plan. Based on data collected the entire year, I decided that our strongest teachers would be used to tutor during the school day. It did not matter what grade they taught, or what they felt "comfortable" teaching, if we were going to make this work, it would mean everyone had to buy in!

I gave each teacher copies of recent data, filtered down by subject and student expectations in those subjects. I explained to the teachers that they would be tutoring students based not only on the subject they struggled with, but the skills necessary for success in each strand or learning objective in those subjects. For example, it was not enough to tutor Johnny in mathematics; we had to identify which area Johnny struggled with the most. Did Johnny struggle with problem solving? If so, what exactly about problem solving was giving Johnny the greatest amount of difficulty? It was amazing to see how many of our students were struggling with the same skills, which actually made it easier for teachers to prepare.

Perhaps the most rewarding part of that particular testing season was Julio (pseudonym). Julio was a fifth grader who had never passed a state assessment. Each year he fell further behind. Julio's parents considered holding him back. Every day at roughly the same time I would see Julio walking to the nurse's office. I would ask him where he was going during the reading hour and he would always utter, "I forgot my backpack at home, so I called my mom." This was Julio's way of dealing with the fact that he was struggling in class and too embarrassed to sit through instruction. On any given day there were twenty-eight students in Julio's class. For a student like him to struggle was not uncommon. Part of my plan to address Julio's needs was to carve out time during the school day when he would receive a very small group instruction. I reasoned that since Julio did not want to be in class during the day, I am almost certain he would not want to remain after school.

There were several students like Julio who also needed more personalized instruction during the school day. After identifying those students, I changed the master schedule to accommodate their needs. Every day for at least two hours per day, these students received personalized instruction. I knew teachers would not immediately accept the changes, but in my mind this was the only way we were going to be successful on the exams and ensure our students would be ready for the next grade level.

Another problem we faced was students being tardy. It seemed many students, in particular our fifth graders, arrived to school at the end of the reading block. However, when they were given small group instruction at eight in the morning, they seemed to arrive on time. Another strange phenomenon occurred; Julio stopped "forgetting" his backpack. I would visit his classroom and Julio would be focused and actually asking questions. Even though Julio was in the fifth grade, he received his math instruction from a very strong third grade teacher and his reading from a very strong fourth grade teacher. Teachers were actually enjoying what they were doing because students were attentive and actually learning.

As I visited classes, I noticed Marlena (pseudonym), a painfully shy girl who always wore her hair covering her entire face. She arrived to school late practically every day. One day as I was visiting her class, I checked the teacher's roster and her name was not there. This was the first day of our new schedule, so I asked the teacher where was Marlena? Since this was not her regular teacher, she did not know where or who she was. Almost the second I began to radio to our data clerk instructing her to call Marlena's home, she walked through the door. I spoke to her privately to remind her of the importance of getting to school on time and I also reminded her that she missed the reading lesson for the morning. I then introduced Marlena to her substitute teacher and continued my daily "learning" walk.

A few weeks passed and I was reminded to check on Marlena. I went to her class and was surprised to see her actively engaged in the lesson. I almost did not recognize her because I could actually see her face. She was asking questions and having conversations with other students and the teacher. At the end of the day I asked the teacher about Marlena's progress and she praised her effort and said she was doing well. This sort of behavior continued daily among many students much like Marlena, and I knew we were ready for the test. When I asked teachers to tell me what they thought about certain students, they spoke with ease about how well the students would do.

On the day of the state test, Julio was one of the first students in the class. He seemed eager. I had implored parents to ensure their child received a good night's sleep the night before the test. Walking from room to room, I noticed that students were focused and seemed sharp. No one was distracted by my presence and from what I could tell they were using every strategy they had been taught. At the end of the day, I asked my usual questions; "How do you think they did?" "Did everything go okay?" Students seemed confident but I did not want to get too excited because I knew how hard my teachers worked and they would be highly disappointed if our students did not succeed.

Weeks went by and finally I received the email notification that our test scores were ready. When we received our results, the first name I looked for was Julio. His results read: Reading-Pass; Math-Pass. He did not just barely pass. Julio scored high enough for us to send him to middle school comfortable, knowing that he fulfilled his mission. Marlena was the next student I looked for and I am proud to say that Marlena passed every subject as well. My instructional coordinator also served as a math tutor during this time. She looked for the scores for every student she taught and I could hear the excitement when she exclaimed in her sweet Caribbean accent "hallelujah." All the students she had tutored were successful.

We went down the list and with utter jubilation, noticed that our math scores were the highest they had ever been, increasing by nearly 20% from the previous year. Perhaps most notable was that our writing scores increased by over 23% and 94% of our African American students were successful. Although we achieved our goals, I was still more excited for Julio. I still think about him and wonder how he is doing in school, but if anyone is proof positive that inner city public schools still work, you only need to look at Julio.

THE FORTY-YARD DASH IN 4.2 SECONDS

Anthony Prior

In the pursuit of a dream there are people who defy the odds and push through life's obstacles. My dream was to play professional football, and I refused to allow all the pitfalls, problems, and disappointments that are a part of life's journey, prevent me from accomplishing my goal. When fans watch the athlete perform, they are often mesmerized by the effortless talent, but fail to realize the long hours and years of development it took to get to that point. And that is exactly what it took for me, beginning at the age of eight to achieve my goal.

Ask any football player in the world what question his peers ask him most often and he will tell you, "How fast can you run the forty?" Most of the time athletes will exaggerate their speed. If any player says speed doesn't matter, usually they never possessed any. Over half my life has been based on forty yards, the most important length in considering any athlete's potential in sports. I have one of the fastest times recorded in history for the forty-yard dash, having run it in 4.2 seconds on a consistent basis. The forty yards sprint has motivated and inspired me much of my life. I dedicated my time and all my efforts to achieving and maintaining that speed. I recall training four hours a day, six days a week for five solid months to reach that plateau. Those 4.2 seconds would take me away from family and friends, but that is how we elevate towards greatness. We must be willing to sacrifice for those things we believe are important to our success. Let me assure you that I didn't always have that kind of speed. It took time to develop it once I found out I did have the potential to be a standout runner and football player. I was ready for the long journey to the NFL.

As a teenager in high school all I heard my father and brothers talk about when it came to playing football was their speed in the forty-yard dash. My brothers were pretty fast, often racing against each other in the streets of our neighborhood. Since I was the youngest, it was my job to line them up and holler, "Go" when they raced against each other. It usually took several tries to get them off to a fair race because one of them would always jump the gun and take off early. I stood at the finish line, waving my arms frantically as they argued over who won the race. They never took my word for it because the finish was always very close.

I stood in awe of my brothers and never thought I would ever become a fast runner. I struggled with my speed when I first entered high school. I had no technique, but had a strong desire to win. My first year in track was a learning experience. I finished last in the one hundred yard dash. I never wanted my parents to come to any of my track meets. I was finishing last, sometimes third place or fourth, but never first. But I would come home and tell them that I took first place.

After my first track season, the following fall I tried out for the football team. I became so frustrated, I was ready to quit, but for some reason decided to stay the course. That decision changed my entire life because the next day the coach put the team through some speed drills. He explained and demonstrated to us the art of running with higher knees. As I began to implement what he showed us, I immediately experienced a difference in my running ability. My speed and my confidence kicked in like a cowboy riding a hungry bull. After practice I began to have visions of doing great things with my speed, from playing college football to going to the National Football League.

This new speed revelation was somewhat of a phenomenon for me. I was so fast and was able to cover so much ground with every stride just from the lifting of my knees, all I wanted to do was test my speed over and over again. Each time I would sprint it was like discovering something new within myself. This gift and talent was an unstoppable force of inspiration. I had ballistic speed. At that point

I really didn't care about playing football; I had my sights on track. I wanted revenge for all those times I had been beaten badly by others on the track team.

When the football season ended, I refused to take time off and began preparing for the upcoming track season. There was a hundred-yard dirt trail on the side of my parent's house. I cleared out all the rocks and debris to make sure there was nothing in my way that could slow me down or cause an injury. My brother Stanley used to watch me and was amazed as he noticed my speed increasing with practically every practice. I ran the forty as a training exercise for football and the one hundred for track. I concentrated on all aspects of the art including the start, acceleration, duration, form, breathing, footing, posture, and confidence. Every day after school I would run up and down that trail until I was too tired to run anymore. I would always run full speed and walk back. I was at the point that I believed I could beat my brother. He was still faster than me, but I was closing in fast like a cheetah on its prey.

One day I hit a gear like none I ever felt. The weather was perfect for running. It was about 102 degrees outside and my brother Stanley and I started off jogging at first. After we reached the starting point we thrust into full speed simultaneously. I felt myself reaching with my knees, and it was effortless. My brother was even amazed. At first I thought he let me win, so I tested his manhood and told him the next time we sprint together I would give him a two-yard head start. The next day when we lined up to race, with him two yards in front, his facial expression said I was a little too ambitious to be challenging him. We began to jog and for some reason his jogging was faster than usual. Before I could say, "hold up," there were two explosions one after another. I saw my brother's feet and elbows take off in front of me. But his progress seemed to come to a halt as I began to accelerate. With controlled but relaxed anger I saw my knees reaching beyond him, and before I could blink twice I was running alone on a trail leading to something greater than myself.

When track season finally arrived I was running varsity. That same spring, my brother stopped running with me. He proudly admitted that I was faster than him and he wanted me to go all the way to the NFL. "If you have to rely on your speed, ride it all the way to the top," he said. "Anthony, run so fast the coaches will have to make a spot for you." My brother and I never owned a stopwatch. We ran strictly on instinct, technique, and feelings. The first time I was clocked running the forty-yard dash was my junior year during spring football drills. I ran a 4.3 and everyone was saying, "Wow, did you see that?" They asked me to run it again for verification and I proved my speed was legitimate. They loved my form because when I run I loved to look good.

I had gotten so fast and good at football I received a scholarship to Washington State University. The coaches there told me I had a lot of potential, but what they were really telling me was that I was so fast they would take their time with me and see if I could develop into a good player. My problem was, even with my speed, they didn't know where to put me. I didn't catch well enough to play as a receiver and didn't cover well enough to be a corner back. They let me know that without my speed I wouldn't have a scholarship. I began to take the attitude that I would see just how far my speed could take me. At that point in my life, all things revolved around my speed, whether I was studying for a test, on the track, or in bed asleep. I meditated on those forty yards day and night because I knew if I wanted to be great at anything, then I had to master it and get rid of all distractions. I had what I call, "Positive Tunnel Vision."

My speed was the result of what many fail to do and that is prepare themselves as best they can. My purpose was to distinguish myself from everybody else. My determination kept me out of the box of mediocrity. To elevate I understood there must be less talk and more action leading to my objective. My brothers and friends watched me practice and perfect my craft in many different ways, whether lifting weights or running in the rain. I became isolated and alone, as they were not willing to make the same kind of sacrifices I made. When they were going to parties, drinking, staying up all night, I was by myself.

Three weeks before the National Football League scouts were coming to Washington State University to test players in the forty-yard dash and other drills, my roommate decided to throw a party. About ten o'clock that evening, many of the guys on the team were partying and they asked me to relax and just party with them.

"Are you crazy?" I said. "The scouts will be here in a few weeks. I need to train."

"What are you going to do, run the hill outside?" my roommate asked.

"Exactly," I replied.

I took my roommate's truck, and turned on the bright lights so they could illuminate the hill. I walked up to the top and ran down so fast I fell and scarred my knees and elbows. While stretched out on the ground that voice of distraction spoke to me, telling me to quit this nonsense, go into the party, and allow life's alleged pleasures to get in the way of my destiny. I ignored that temptation, got back up, and ran with a passion between anger and inspiration. I could see people going into my apartment, drunk, talking, and laughing essentially about nothing. I enjoyed listening to the music coming from the building while I ran. My brother's words filled my mind, "Let your speed take you where you want to go."

The following few weeks flew by and on March 13, 1991, the NFL scouts witnessed a record-setting time in the forty-yard dash ever recorded at Washington State University. I ran it in 4.21 seconds. The men who were partying that night made their own choices; we all do. However, at that young age I had a vision and my joy at setting the record far exceeded any pleasure I may have experienced at that party.

I did not become a starter on the football team until my senior year when I played free safety. I could not cover that well, but the coaches saw in me, a kid who was not afraid to hit and could run like a deer. I am thankful for my coach, Mike Zimmer, who recognized my ability and gave me a chance to shine. During one game we were playing against the University of Southern California, always a powerhouse in the Pac 12, he put me on kickoff returns. Because of his confidence in me, I was determined to prove that he had made the right decision. I caught the kickoff three yards deep in the end zone and took off. I saw an opening to the left and shifted to high gear. To this date, I cannot recall my feet ever touching the ground I was moving so fast. Before I knew what was happening I had an open field in front of me. I knew at that point I would record the longest kick-off return in Washington State history because no one could catch me. I was also aware that this feat would create an interest in my potential among the NFL scouts. That is all the inspiration I needed to look beyond the present challenges and consciously focus on greatness.

After my senior year, I was invited to the NFL combine in Indianapolis, Ind. It was a dream come true. All I had to do was run the fastest forty and I knew I would have a chance to go to the big show, the NFL. At the combine I did not run the fastest; I ran very average. I felt like a pigeon in the pack with the others. I thought, when it came to the forty, I would be an eagle. Usually I soar alone—there is me and then there is everyone else. But for some odd reason I don't know what happened to me that day. The forty is all I had going for me. I wasn't one of those players who had four great seasons all through college to fall back on. My only stronghold was my speed, and it disappeared that afternoon.

That evening in the hotel lobby I sat with a professional scout named Sutherland. He bought me a coke. At first he asked me if I wanted a beer, and I initially said, "yeah," to a professional scout. I quickly caught my error and said I would take a coke.

He said, "You ran pretty well out there."

Average is what he really meant.

I said, "I'm way faster than that."

"I know," he replied. "I'm coming out to Washington State in a couple weeks to check out your time again."

His words were like magic to my ears. When I returned to school that Monday, I broke up with my girlfriend and started living with friends. I began a relentless regimen of training and couldn't afford any distractions. One fact that most young athletes fail to recognize is that involvement, especially sexual, is one of the greatest distractions they can face, and one of the greatest temptations. I loved and cared dearly for my girlfriend, but quite honestly it was a love I couldn't afford at that time. My concentration was totally on working out the problems I faced in Indianapolis with my speed. The great Nelson Mandela's words were my inspiration; "The glory in living does not lie in never failing, but in rising every time we fail." I had to rise to this perceived failure and nothing would stand in my way.

One morning, about 5:00 am, my roommate heard me getting cleaned up in the bathroom and shouted.

"Man, don't you ever sleep?"

I replied, "I have to train because the NFL scouts will be here next week. Sleeping is a distraction just like sex and drinking. I have to find my 4.2 speed again and I have to do it fast.

He got up, walked, and stood at the entrance to my bedroom. "What will you do if football doesn't work out for you?"

I turned and glared at him with sheer determination in my voice. "It will work out. Greatness is always around the corner, and it depends on whether or not you have enough of what it takes to go and look for it." I paused for a moment to gather my thoughts. "We can always look for the negative things in life. But I have looked for great things and, with that attitude, I will do great things." With those words I hurried out of the apartment and up the hill to work on regaining my speed.

The scouts did return to Washington State University and I did redeem myself by running a 4.26 in the forty. Even though it was a cloudy day, I knew that somewhere behind all those clouds was sunshine. That is how I lived my life. I felt really good about what I did that day; the scouts and Sutherland seemed to be impressed. I was fortunate to have the New York Giants draft me because I ran such a great forty-yard dash that day.

The night I was drafted, I cried and laughed out loud at the same time. Turning my head from side to side my thoughts took me back to the days when it all started, running with my brother on the side of my parent's home. I thought of Stanley who inspired and encouraged me every step of the way. I didn't get a million dollar contract. I wasn't even on ESPN, and there were no major endorsements coming my way, but the reality of setting a goal, putting a dream in motion, and actually watching it come true right in front of me was beyond expression. Along the road of inspiration, there are always those who want to bring you down to mediocrity. There were people who were full of doubt in the beginning and envious of my accomplishments, because I was living my dream. The great long distance runner Roger Bannister said, "The man who can drive himself further, once the effort gets painful, is the man who will win."

I left Washington State and went home to California for a month before leaving for New York. I trained with my brother Stanley for the entire time, running on the side of my parent's house. It was such a special time because it took me back to where the dream started. When I left for New York, I was ready for the new challenge in my life, playing football at the highest level.

On my arrival in New York, all the other rookies talked about their college stats and accolades. While they bragged on past accomplishments, my thoughts were firmly on the next day when we all had to run the forty. That next morning, the rookies had a big workout, doing drills and running the forty. I had tunnel vision. I didn't care how well I did in the other workouts; my specialty was running. Everywhere I have traveled I have always been the fastest. My drills were okay, but I was the very best in the forty and I was not going to give that up. And yes, I wore the crown once again, this time on the east coast.

However, after a long, tough, grueling training camp I was cut. I was devastated. I figured I was playing pretty darn good, making good plays, hitting hard, but in the end I came up short. I called my parents and then my agent and gave them the bad news. I then started my long drive back to Washington. As I drove across country, I would do a little stretching every time I stopped for gas because my agent told me that I could get called anytime and needed to keep in shape. I stopped at a rest area in North Dakota to do some drills and sprints in the grass. People were looking at me like I was crazy. I didn't care because I was on this journey they call chasing a dream. When you are truly motivated by something, you often look like a fool to other people. I guess that is the cost of greatness. Sometimes you have to look silly, but strangers can't see the passion that takes over when you are in between chasing a dream. Because failure is not an option.

I finally arrived back in Washington and stayed with some friends. I was so excited that night I couldn't sleep. It was snowing and I didn't care. I got up, went outside and marked off forty yards in the snowy night. I started running back and forth. I felt like I was cheating myself because I couldn't go full speed in the snow. Next morning, I went to the gym and spent the entire day running the forty yards. While running I thought of another quote to keep me motivated. It kept going around in my mind. Winston Churchill once said, "Success is going from failure to failure without losing enthusiasm." Even though I had experienced a major setback, I was still motivated and enthused about my prospects for success. When I got back to the apartment, my agent called to tell me that the New York Jets wanted to work me out as soon as possible. I knew this time something good was going to happen, and once again, it would be determined by my performance in the forty-yard dash. I was ready to fly to New York the following morning.

That next morning, I woke up late and the airport was all the way to Spokane, about seventy miles east, an hour and a half drive. My plane was leaving at a quarter to nine and I woke up twenty minutes before eight. I jumped out of bed like a wild animal frightened by the night.

"Oh, my God," I shouted. "I'm going to miss my plane."

I ran to the car with my bag, jumped in my Porsche, and was speeding the entire way. I didn't care; I had to be on that plane. This was my opportunity to show the Jets what I could do. But I missed the plane. I called the Jets coaches and told them there had been a mix-up at the airport. I wasn't about to tell them I overslept. They accepted my explanation and put me on a later flight leaving at ten that morning. When I arrived in New York, the man who picked me up told me what was expected that next morning, eight o'clock wake up and nine o'clock workout.

That night I left the hotel and asked a taxi driver to take me to the Jet's facility. He dropped me off and I jumped the fence about ten o'clock at night. I walked along the turf where I knew I would probably be running the forty-yard dash. I walked every inch of that stretch of turf, closed my eyes, and thought about that dirt trail along the side of mom and dad's house. The Jets facility was close to the hotel so I walked back. I slept that night knowing in my heart this time that I wasn't going home.

The next morning, with the scouts watching on in awe, I ran the forty so fast they didn't bother telling me my time, nor did they ask me to run a second time. One of the scouts excitedly said.

"I'll be right back."

He hustled up a few of the coaches and brought them back over to where I had just run the fastest forty they had ever seen. They put me through a few drills and I signed my first professional contract with the New York Jets that afternoon. At that time in my life, I was leaning on one thing, my speed. There comes a time in life when, for a moment, the things you do make sense, and I was having one of those moments. I thought about forty yards and realized this was a relationship that had no end in sight.

Being a New York Jet was a lifetime fulfillment. It felt great. I was a professional football player, something millions dream about, thousands sacrifice for, and only a few accomplish. It gave me the opportunity to play with one of the men I most admired as a football player. Before I arrived at Washington State University, James Hasty held all of the running and lifting records. I had never met him until I became a Jet. He would eventually help further my career and make me a better football player.

My joy was short lived, because half way through the season I was cut. They told me it was because of a numbers game. I prepared to fly back to Washington and when I arrived my car, which had been parked there for months, had two flat tires. I just laughed it off because sometimes you laugh to keep from crying. When I got home that evening, I started running and after my work out, my agent called and said that the Canadian Football League (CFL) was interested in me. I agreed to fly up there and the next morning I was on a plane to Calgary, Canada. I wasn't very excited about going to Canada because it was not the NFL, just CFL.

I flew into Calgary and was supposed to work out the next day. I had convinced myself that I didn't like the place at all. I didn't like the guys around me and I didn't like the food or the hotel. I had decided that my forty was in a class all by itself, and all I wanted to do was embarrass the other players. I didn't want their times to be even close to mine. Just as I did in New York, that night I went to the stadium and walked every inch of the field where I would be running the next morning. I walked every corner and meditated, reaching back to the dirt trails where it all began, and embraced the moment.

The next morning I ran the fastest forty in the team history and they asked me to sign a contract right then. I said no thanks. The general manager asked why I refused to sign with them and I told him because it was not the NFL. He laughed and said they didn't want me, but I responded that I'd take my chances.

The next day I went back to Washington. I spent the next month complaining as I watched the NFL season come to an end. I told myself over and over that I should be on an NFL team because nobody could run as fast as me. I was still young and had to make darn sure that my aspirations to play in the NFL didn't fade away. I wanted to keep that dream strong and fresh in my mind. I immediately started training for the next year. That same year I watched as the Calgary Stampeders won the Grey Cup Championship, and said, darn, maybe I should have signed that contract.

A few weeks later during the cold winter, I decided to run in a track meet in Cheney, Washington. It was a 50-meter dash and I won it easily. I called the New York Jets and told them. Several weeks later I was back in New York preparing for mini-camp with the team. This time I was determined to regain the respect of the players by running the forty so fast there would be no way they could ignore me. All I concentrated on was that forty-yard dash. The team's strength and conditioning coach asked if I wanted to do some cornerback drills and I told him no. All my energy was focused on the four seconds that would bring me fame, not those football drills. Besides, no one ever got recognition for their skills by doing drills. On the other hand, you get noticed for your speed.

The night before I was to run the forty I had a sore ankle, but that was not going to slow me down. As usual I took my ten o'clock walk and meditated. The next day, I ran a 4.2 forty and that got everyone's attention. I made the team for the second time and this go round I would be there for four years.

As the years went by I began to develop into a pretty good football player. The Jets had a few coaching changes within those four years, bringing in different personalities, with new philosophies. I managed to weather the storm with each change. However, there are some storms in life, no matter how well you are prepared, those rare slips can eventually turn into a fall. In life there are some things we have no control over and so one spring morning after four years with the Jets, I got a call telling me I had been cut again. I grabbed my running shoes and started sprinting that night with a rage..

A week after returning home, I received a call from the Cincinnati Bengals. They told me they would honor my contract I had with the Jets. I was excited. They sent me a schedule of their mini camps. My excitement grew stronger when I found out at mini camp everyone would be required to run the forty at least two times. I called my brother Stanley and told him.

"Man, I'm going to show that organization who is the king when it comes to running the forty."

I didn't care about football drills; all I could think about were those four seconds that had been so good to me. I began to view the forty as my specialty to sustainability.

I arrived in Cincinnati pumped and ready to go. When I got to the hotel I waited until about ten at night, called a cab and went to the training facilities. As I had done in the past, I walked along the turf reminiscing about where my journey began, the dirt trail on the side of my parent's home. I got in the cab and headed back to the hotel.

Perhaps, the driver thought I was a little weird, but when you are on a mission, you do what needs to be done.

Back in the hotel, I smiled confidently at myself in the mirror. I slept well knowing in the morning I again would catch the attention of not only the coaching staff, but also all the media there covering the practice as well. The following morning, I thought if anyone in Cincinnati didn't know who I was, they were going to get to know me in about three and a half hours. And they did. I ran the fastest time in Bengal history. I made the six o'clock news that night and once again those forty yards brought me back to the place I wanted to be. I couldn't wait to get home and tell my friends and family about my success. My enthusiasm was destroyed two days before training was to begin. I received a call from the Bengals' management informing me that I had been cut because of salary cap problems. I was stunned because teams already had their rosters together for training camps. Once again, I found myself left out.

Days passed and I finally got a call from the San Francisco 49ers. The following day I flew to their training camp in Sacramento, Calif. I was a late addition and knew I faced an uphill battle. When I arrived they told me I would be working out the following morning and that the workout would be on grass. That evening I walked along the grass with my eyes closed and thought only of my beginnings and that dirt trail.

The next morning I warmed up and was ready to run. However, they surprised me and told me they were going to put me through some drills and that would be all.

"Don't you want me to run the forty?" I asked.

"No, just drills," the coach said.

Even though they signed me that morning, I was disappointed. I wanted the chance to wear the crown as the fastest man on the team. I wanted to run that forty. In the football world, word spreads fast, and we often make a name for ourselves if we are able to do something outstanding. The 49ers already knew of my speed so they were concerned with my agility and football skills.

I played my rear end off and had a great camp. I made big plays, hit hard, but despite all of that, I came up short and was cut before the regular season began. I drove back home to Riverside, Calif., about a seven-hour drive. I got there about nine in the morning and by noon was at the local high school training again for another shot at running the forty. I trained alone for the next two months.

There were no calls from teams or from my agent; then one day out of the blue, the Denver Broncos called. I was thrilled because at the time they were the hottest team in the NFL. When I arrived in Denver, it was extremely cold, but that didn't matter. Once again I would have the opportunity to wear the crown of the fastest man on another team. I ran that morning on wet grass and I was so fast they had me wait for four hours at their practice facility while they tried to work out a deal. But I came up short once again. They told me that they were not going to release anyone or make any changes at that time. I was crushed. My reliance on my speed had failed me this time. I spent the next day in a state of confusion. But like a warrior, I returned home to California and began believing in those forty yards once again.

The following week the Minnesota Vikings called and asked if I was in shape. Was I ever in shape! They flew me to Minnesota the very next day. When I arrived I was a little tired, but still had enough gas in the tank to feel good about everything. When I arrived at the Viking facility, I was told by a coach, "Head coach Dennis Green doesn't like to wait so be ready to run as soon as he opens those double doors." He pointed to a set of doors in the facility. "You'll have about one minute to get to the starting line and run."

I stared anxiously at those doors and when he opened them, I threw my hands up in the air and said, "Let's do this right now."

I had nothing to fear. "I'm not only good at the forty, I'm great," I declared to everyone within range of my words, "I am speed." At that moment, I transcended into something greater than myself. I ran a sensational forty. They originally wanted me to run two times, but after the first time all they could say was, "Wow, let's do some drills."

I did some drills and that afternoon I signed with the Vikings. That year I played in my first career playoff game. Forty yards had delivered for me once again.

I spent two seasons with the Vikings, and again I was a free agent. That spring I went to the Carolina Panthers for a free agent work out. I blazed in the forty, but they did not sign me. I wasn't disappointed because it was early in the year and I had plenty of time to sign with a team. A week later my agent called and said the Kansas City Chiefs wanted to work me out. I was excited because James Hasty was now playing for them. I called him and told him that I would be working out with the team. He wished me the best and told me he would love to have me as a teammate once again.

I arrived in Kansas City with an old teammate from the Vikings who was also trying out. The personnel director and coach said they wanted to offer me a contract. I called my agent while they were working out a deal. I waited in the hotel thinking about forty yards, not the contract. This time I wanted to get a substantial signing bonus. I believed if I ran an awesome forty the next morning I would get that bonus. I didn't sleep that night and all I could think about were those forty yards. Once again I was placing all my trust in four seconds.

The following morning I ran those forty yards so fast the Kansas City Chiefs gave me a signing bonus that was better than I had imagined. While riding back to the hotel, all I could think about was that I could have run a little faster. There are gifts we all carry around. Some discover their craft and master it, and some die with it, never knowing what ability they possessed. That day I figured I was actually living and mastering my gift. Forty yards once again came up big for me, and before I knew it, I was in training camp.

I was actually having a great training camp, and then I hurt my lower abdominal muscle. I was forced to miss a week of practice. I played average in the last pre-season game and was cut the following morning. I flew home to California and that evening once again was at the local high school training for the forty.

After a month and a half of inactivity, a few of my friends called pretending to be NFL scouts. I got all excited only to find out it was a joke. Shortly after that, the Oakland Raiders called. I thought my friends were again playing a trick on me, but came to find out it was the real thing. Later that evening I was on a plane to Oakland again ready to showcase my speed. However, this time I was somewhat intimidated. The Raiders were known for always having the fastest players in the NFL. We all knew of Davis Love's speed, but then it hit me they hadn't seen speed like mine. When I landed in Oakland, the words of the famous tennis player, Arthur Ashe, struck me. "One important key to success is self-confidence. An important key to self-confidence is preparation." If his words were applicable to any athlete, it was me.

I packed a lot of clothes because I knew I would be staying. I reminded myself that I train for moments like this; it was my time to shine. The following morning when I warmed up, a good sized crowd and a number of players stood there in anticipation of my performance. It was a cold day and the grass was wet, but it didn't slow me down. They timed me and were shocked at my speed. I was put in the category with all the other world-class forty-yard dash sprinters.

The Raiders signed me and by the following Sunday afternoon, I was playing on the field. I played that 1998 season with the Raiders, but was not signed the following year.

The next call of interest was the San Diego Chargers. They brought me in for a workout in early 1999. I knew my speed would again get me through the initial workout. When I arrived on the field, I noticed that the finish line was very close to a brick wall. I pointed this out to General Manager Bobby Bethard. I asked if we could back up a little because there was not enough room for me to slow down. He smiled and said, "Okay."

As I had done time and time again, I shot out like a canon and ran, some say, the fastest or one of the fastest times in Charger history. Because of my speed, they offered to sign me, but I turned it down. I didn't feel the signing bonus was as large as it should have been. Often when we get good at something, we expect the same commitment from others as we have committed to ourselves. But life does not work that way. I failed to realize I was not being paid to run a forty, but to play football. I ended up not playing for any team that year.

That spring, I hurt my hamstring one morning and had to turn down a work out with the Carolina Panthers after the San Diego

Chargers in 1999. I ended up sitting out the whole season of 2000. No phone calls, no opportunity to show my talent. No thrills. Even though I didn't play football that season, I trained as if I was going to get a call at a moment's notice. I had decided to always be prepared so that when the call came I would be ready. I was in shape to run the forty, but no one was calling. I reluctantly concluded that I had run the last leg and put my gear away.

That night I sat outside staring at the millions of twinkling stars and a full bright moon. I was sending my thoughts to God. I was not praying, but listening for the voice of reason and I began to look back over my career and counted the many times I had been rejected. When I reached the number seven, I couldn't believe I was still motivated. I had so much confidence in my speed I overlooked my weaknesses. I stared up at the moon one more time and then went back into the house. I sat on the couch feeling desperate for answers. In desperation I picked up my Bible and randomly searched for a passage that would give me some relief. Would you believe I opened it up and I looked down immediately and found in Proverbs Chapter 24, verse 16. "A righteous person may fall seven times, but he gets up again. However, in a disaster wicked people fall." For some reason those words from the Bible inspired me. I changed my clothes, put on my running shoes and took off outside to do sprints at 10:30 that night. I ran past midnight.

The next week I found out that the pro scouts would be at UCLA so I drove to the campus because they were having timing events. I showed up like a thief in the night with only my running shoes in hand. At first, they weren't going to let me run. Then I found the athletic director of football operations. He must have seen the desperation and hunger in my eyes when I explained to him that I needed to do this. He spoke with the scouts to make sure it was all right for me to run. They agreed and I blew everyone away in the forty and in the overall workout. But still there was no call.

That next week the scouts were at San Diego State. Again, I blazed in the forty. My problem, however, was that I needed to run in front of a general manager of an NFL franchise, and not scouts.

My greatest concern that I might not ever be able to play in the NFL again was growing but I wasn't concerned about my ability to run the forty. I knew that covenant was secure because I owned it, and established it long ago. There are certain things we all possess and the forty was my secret weapon, my angel, my expertise, my mastery, and my life.

Several weeks later, the Calgary Stampeders from the Canadian Football Leaague called. Remember them from earlier? They were holding a big workout in Los Angeles, right in my backyard, and no one could outdo me on my own turf. During the warm-up, I glared at the other guys trying out. They didn't stand a chance. I thought about every individual there, and how they all had a dream like I did. We were going to run the forty and they had no chance at all. However, I had now come to a new realization that the forty couldn't knock down doors. It couldn't be used as a sledgehammer to get what I wanted. Yes, I wanted to be back in the NFL but sometimes a person has to let the past go so they can make room in their heart for new adventures and new memories. I was ready for this moment and this time running the forty became a new starting point for my life.

As I ran the forty a strange silence came over me, it was an unexplainable peace that can only come when a person embraces their destiny. After I ran, I spoke with the head coach, Wally Buono. He was blown away because the coach standing at the finish line said he didn't hear my feet hit the ground. A few days later, I signed a contract to play in the Canadian Football League. I rationalized at that point it shouldn't matter where you do your best, and a bird in the hand beats two in the bush. I packed my bags and headed North to play in the Canadian Football League.

TESTING POSITIVE:
WHAT I DID TO HAVE SEX WITH HER

CHRIS CANNON

Friday night at about eight-thirty in downtown Detroit was when it always happened. The sounds of the hottest music, the sight of the finest women, and the confidence of knowing twenty-two other young men had my back if anything jumped off that night was reassuring. Although we had each other's back, we also were in a competitive battle that could have caused anyone of us to abandon the friendships if necessary in order to win.

As we prepared that night for our weekly ritual of excitement and testing our ability to win, each boy bragged that he would get the most telephone numbers or end up leaving with the best looking girl. For me, I always went for the very finest girl because it proved that I had the most confidence in my ability to score and, of course, I held that title. Later that night, I knew, even if I didn't get the finest one, somebody was going to get lucky enough to have sex with me. It was scary how confident I felt, knowing I could have sex with someone who I hadn't even met. I used young ladies to build my confidence, enhance street credibility among the brothers, and most important, to prove my manhood.

That one particular night as I began to work my magic, my life changed because I recognized something then that I wasn't aware of before. All of the young ladies I met on the streets of Detroit who were willing to grant me access to their most prized possession had one thing in common: none of them had a relationship with their father. I didn't care about their personal lives, but it came out in general conversation and I viewed it as a great opening to score. When I made this connection with young girls and their fatherless lives, it took my game to a whole new level. I began to seek out girls without active fathers in their lives because they were easier to manipulate than those who did have fathers living with them or taking time to be involved with them. In the process I also recognized something about me and the other brothers hanging out in down town Detroit every weekend: we were all trying to fill some kind of void in our lives to compensate for our fathers not being around.

It soon became clear that every girl willing so easily to have sex with me was only looking to find in me what she never received from her father. And conversely, what I was receiving from them was validation of my manhood. The reality is that we all were trying to establish our identities, find someone to appreciate us, make us feel good, love us, and care for us in a way that made us feel special, even if it was temporary.

The greatest fear young men must confront is the fear of failure and their greatest need is for respect. That is why young men use young girls for competition. We are programmed to believe conquest of the female will gain us that respect because we have conquered the coveted prize that most young women don't realize is their greatest asset. On the other hand, a young girl's greatest need is security and their greatest fear is abandonment. The primary reason why she might have sex is not because the guy is the man like I thought I was, but in most cases her fear of being alone. When I finally understood this, it crushed my ego because I believed I was special, not ever realizing what they were offering me was probably offered to others also.

The reality is girls use sex to get love, and guys use love to get sex. Think about it, a guy might tell a girl anything he thinks she wants to hear just to have sex with her, and she might have sex with him just to get that security she never received from her father. The fear of abandonment in young ladies and the fear of failure in young men cause them to reject truth and rationalize having unhealthy relationships. My action toward females was strictly driven by fear. It wasn't love, respect, or commitment. The fact that my friends were watching what I did is what influenced my behavior because my identity as a man was based on what they thought of me. Honestly, I was so insecure I had to use girls to build my confidence and make me feel good about myself. It wasn't only me, but all those young men standing on the street corner every Friday night in downtown Detroit.

However, what I never took into consideration were the consequences for my actions. What I have since learned about life is that you can do anything you want to get short-term pleasure and fulfillment, but what you can't do is chose the long-term consequences that come with the lifestyle you may chose. When dealing with the consequences, people act like they don't know how it happened. All things have a process that leads up to the outcome. Out of all the crazy things my eyes have witnessed, I have never seen two naked people skipping down the street and the man accidentally slips and falls on top of the woman and gets her pregnant. Besides that, there are some diseases out there that will cause your testicles to swell to the size of grapefruits. I know some people would probably like that, looking down on their stuff saying, "Now that's what I'm talking about; I'm the man, I'm the man, BIG BOYYY." They may be thinking that the fairy God penis delivered them the big one, not realizing they have a sexually transmitted disease.

All right, seriously, I know I don't have to lecture you about disease or pregnancy; you already know about those things. And, no, I am not going to tell you to just use a condom either, because a condom cannot protect you from a female who has gone flip crazy because her emotions were played with and now she's looking to hurt someone for REAL! Condoms also will not solve the issues young men have that make them depend on sex to feel good about themselves and to help cover up their insecurities because their fathers never taught them about being a man. Besides, condoms only cover 1% of your body. Yeah only 1%. A real man relies on self control, not birth control and treats a lady with honor and respect, two words that are foreign when it comes to how we should treat females, but they can become common, starting with you.

I fully understand the beauty and pleasure derived from sex, but without knowing you, I do know that you have dreams and goals that you want to accomplish in life. Never trade what you want most out of life for what you want at the moment. I promise you, it is never worth it. So many young people have future goals and dreams just like you. But they never accomplish them because they rationalize that they'll just have fun for now and come back to their goals later. Right at that moment they are just going to do their thing, never realizing the price they must pay later on in life. It is necessary therefore, to make your expectations greater than your temptations, because your behavior is the true measure of the success you claim you want.

Your desire to become sexually active is natural. However, sex is just like a fire. Let me explain what I mean. In my home, my wife and I have a fireplace. At times we might just sit and talk or have a nice romantic dinner in front of a crackling fire. We even use fire to cook the food we like. If we took that same fire and put it on the carpet in front of the fireplace what do you think would happen? Quite naturally, the carpet would burn. Not only the carpet, but the furniture and possibly the entire house would burn down. Tell me this: Did the fire change? No, the fire did not change. The only thing that changed was where the fire was placed. When the fire was kept in its proper place, it was warm, romantic, and helped to cook our food. But when it was taken out of its boundaries, it was very destructive and could have possibly killed someone. Always remember, boundaries keep good things in and bad things out. Sex is just like that fire. When it is kept in its proper place, it is a great thing, but when it is not, it can be destructive and possibly take someone's life just like that fire. If you have already let the lion out of the cage, no worries. My job is not to judge or look down on you. I want to encourage you to choose and live the best life you can.

I now wish that I could have told my wife that I was man enough to wait to have sex until I married her, but I couldn't because I was weak and tried to live my life for others. I understand now that a wish changes nothing, but a decision changes everything. Make every decision as if a generation is depending on it, because everything you do in life will have a positive or negative impact on someone else's life. Think for a minute about someone who did something that impacted your life and how it affected you. If it was good, I am sure you feel good about that person. If it was bad, I am also sure that both persons regret it, especially if they are aware of how it made you feel. Never put yourself in a situation where you cause someone else pain that you will grow later to regret. If you don't remember anything else, always remember there are two major pains in life, the pain of reward or the pain of regret. With every choice you make, always ask yourself is the risk worth the reward? If you have to think about it for more than a few seconds, the answer is NO.

You may be the kind of young person who claims that this isn't really relevant to your life because you never plan to marry. I totally understand because I felt the same way. During the earlier years of my life I was against marriage and thought it stupid because of what I saw from the people around me. The one married couple I saw on a daily basis didn't even like each other. Usually when I saw them, she was upstairs, he was downstairs. When she was in the kitchen, he was in the garage, and when she was in the living room, he was in the basement. They did everything in their power to stay away from each other. As I watched them evade each other, I surmised that if this is what marriage is like, I don't ever want to get married. I also pledged to always be faithful—to three different girls. Sounds crazy, I know, but when I was in high school I had three girlfriends and I constantly stressed that I wasn't going to be with anyone else outside of the three. Keep in mind they didn't know each other. This was all Chris Cannon trying to make himself feel more like a man in order to hide his insecurities.

As I mentioned earlier, I always went after the best looking girl in the school or neighborhood. My senior year I decided to jet on the three. I had to go after the prettiest young lady in my senior class. She looked so good I would brush my teeth before calling her on the phone. When we got home after being with each other all day at school we would call each other ten minutes after we parted company. Sometimes we wouldn't say anything, just listen to each other breathe into the phone. We used to go out to eat, go to the movies, have sex, and we even went out of town a few times together. She and I dated for two years before she went off to college. I thought I was in love and wanted to spend the rest of my life with her. About three months before she graduated, I didn't eat lunch for two of those months and saved up all my lunch money and bought her an engagement ring just before her graduation night. I remember going to the mall with a few twenties, a whole lot of dollar bills, quarters, nickels, dimes, and, yes, pennies.

The night she graduated, I got down on my knees, grabbed her hand, and asked her to marry me. The question I have for you is did I really love her? Before you answer, keep in mind we spent all of our time together, and we had a lot of sex. Now, I'll ask the question again, do you think I loved her? You would think the answer to that question is obvious because not many people would sacrifice lunch to buy an engagement ring. Right? If you think I loved her, I have to disagree with you. The reason is because I knew she wanted to graduate from college and be a psychologist. Every time we had sex my actions proved that I was more concerned about my sex interest than her best interest, and that is not love. When true love is not understood, people use sex to prove their love for another. The act of sex only lasts as long as it takes to perform, but love lasts a lifetime. Sex is what many people build their relationships on and when it is removed they have absolutely nothing left, which was the mistake I made. Sex should never be used to define a relationship; it should only be used to celebrate the commitment of it. Think about if my girlfriend had gotten pregnant, it would have made it that much more difficult to finish college.

After only three weeks of dating, I told my girlfriend that I loved her almost every day. That experience taught me that communication without demonstration is manipulation. If you are not demonstrating what you are communicating then you are manipulating someone. That is exactly what I did because when I told her that I loved her, what I was really saying is I love me, and I love you for what you can do for me. When you love someone you want what is best for them and you put their needs before your desires. A real man understands that you have to control your desires, not satisfy them, especially at the expense of jeopardizing your own future or the future of someone else's. Just like oil and water do not mix, sex and manhood do not mix either unless marriage is in the center of it. The primary role of manhood is to protect and to provide, and having sex before marriage will only jeopardize your future and go against EVERYTHING that manhood represents.

As young men you must acknowledge that marriage itself is not the problem; it is always the people within it. Let's look at college basketball as an example. The team that won more championship titles than any other in the history of the game is UCLA. There was a time when they were winning championships back to back and other teams didn't want to play them for fear of getting embarrassed. Why were they so successful? Did they always have the best players? The answer is no. What made them successful were the principles they lived by, their discipline, sacrifice, and work ethic. But recently, they had their worse season ever. They lost 19 out of 29 games. That meant every time they won a game, they lost two. What happened that this team once considered the king of the court went from winning almost every game to losing so many? Was it the college? Was it the team? No, it was the players and the coaches that made up the team. Those players and coaches moved away from the morals, values, discipline, and work ethic that built their success. They tried doing things their way instead of following what had worked years before they arrived. Marriage and sex is just like the players on the team both the winners and losers, based on their decision to stay disciplined and follow the proven plan or try to go against what has always worked.

I have experienced the adventure of having sex with multiple females, especially in college, and can tell you from experience that it never brings fulfillment. After sex, I felt empty, lost, scared, depressed, insecure, and even contemplated suicide. That kind of sex never solved my problems or filled the void that was in my life. The insecurity I felt always led me to seek out more sexual partners. With each conquest I would brag to my friends trying to impress them and find manhood, the further it took me into depression, insecurity and confusion. I did not trust or respect the females who were willing

105

participants in my sexual escapades because I knew my confusion and thought they were stupid for being involved with someone like me. I never considered them marriage material. I didn't trust them with money, my secrets, and definitely not my heart. Let me make it quite clear: The problem was not them it was me. I didn't trust myself, and my insecurities caused me to accuse them of being as promiscuous as I was. Without trust, all relationships are worthless, especially when they are built on sex only. When a young man has sex with a young lady, it brings out his insecurities in most cases because he starts to think about her having sex with somebody else. Why? It's because in the back of his mind, he knows that having sex with her is only to satisfy his insecurities and lack of self-control.

A real man understands it is better to have one woman one thousand different ways than one thousand different women. When I graduated from being a grown boy to a grown man, I stopped trying to convince myself that I did not want to get married. There was nothing wrong with marriage; there was something wrong with my thinking. By not getting married, I could reconcile having sex with as many ladies as possible. However, the concentration on sex interfered with concentrating on those things that could provide me with a more productive life. I remember while in college studying for an exam I had to take the very next day. In the middle of my studies, a young lady called me and asked, "Are you busy?" I said no, what's up? To this day, I do not remember her name, but I can tell you she was not worth the time and money it cost me having to repeat that course because I failed that exam. Distraction and lack of focus will always be the case when sex is taken out of its proper context and the desire for it exceeds the importance of priorities and purpose for one's life. As young people, I want you to make the best possible decisions when you set priorities for your life. I know that you have goals, dreams, and immense gifts to offer future generations that can positively impact them. Believe in yourself! You can do it. I can assure you that people who do not expect anything out of life will jeopardize your future also if given the chance because they don't feel they have anything to lose or anything to offer outside sex. You are different, though, because your talents, skills, and abilities are the solutions to someone's problem and the answer to somebody's question. Believe it or not, you are the model for others to follow. Children younger than you are looking to you right now for direction, and your choices will have a positive or negative influence on their lives.

More than anything I want to advise you to wait and have sex with your wife, because she is going to be the best thing that ever happens in your life, besides the birth of your children. You will be able to accomplish things with her that were never possible without her. We all need someone in our lives to show us how to be better than we know how to be and this is what a wife will do for you. This is why I appreciate my wife so much, because she's brought freshness to my life that was never there before, so that I cannot imagine living without her. She knows my thoughts before I think them, my words before I say them, and my needs before I need them; it's a beautiful thing! I get emotional just thinking about my wife at times, because what we have together cannot be explained; it can only be experienced.

Marriage is the greatest gift ever given two people to express their love for one another. Before I ever had sex with my wife, I knew it would be different because she was different and I had to be different also. When it came to sex with my wife I knew that foreplay for us involved a wedding ring. The man that I needed to be and the man that she desired was what I was practicing to be, long before we connected. Just like you, I was told that practice makes perfect, but that is not true. Do you think all the practice I had with the different females in high school and college prepared me to have a perfect relationship later in life? Of course not. The truth is practice makes permanent. Whatever lifestyle you practice will permanently be your experience.

I knew I wanted better and different so I began to change my lifestyle to meet the desire of my heart, which was for someone to love, honor, and respect me as a man. The reality is most people marry someone who is of equal quality, which is why you want to start now on being the best that you can be for that special young lady later. There is a famous saying, "Give and it shall be given back to you." So you definitely want to give the best to your future wife so you can receive the best in return. With all the mistakes I made I can tell you I was an exception and feel very fortunate to have married my wife. There is no doubt in my mind that if I hadn't changed my lifestyle early to a better model of true manhood, I never would have married my wife. Avoid the same mistakes most men make by thinking they will start making better choices later in life, when the time is NOW. Anyone who disrespects young ladies and risks their future for three minutes of pleasure, or uses women to cover up their insecurities can always continue that lifestyle, but they also have to do one thing, drop the title because they are not men!

Remember this, future generations of young people are depending on you. Here is my last question, I promise. When others from your generation or generations to come are looking for direction and examples on how to respect themselves and how to treat a young lady, or how they should be treated as young ladies, will you test positive? I am not talking about STDs or being someone's baby daddy either. Will you test positive for the identity of manhood that they need to see in YOU?

MAKING HISTORY WITH THE
KING HOLIDAY LEGISLATION

FREDERICK WILLIAMS

When Senator Edward Kennedy invited my boss Senator Birch Bayh and me to his office in order to discuss the feasibility of introducing legislation to make Dr. Martin Luther King Jr.'s birthday a national holiday we immediately recognized the overwhelming task that would be. As I strolled into the Senator's office on the fourth floor of the Russell Senate Building and saw Coretta Scott King and Congressman John Conyers sitting there I knew I was about to be a part of making history. Peter Parham, who was my counterpart on Kennedy's staff, was also there.

As early as 1968, only four months after King's assassination on April 4, Conyers had considered the possibility of designating King's birthday as a national holiday. Since he first floated the idea in Congress, he had confronted relentless Southern opposition in the House of Representatives. The Southern coalition still dominated the House side of Congress and they were determined there would never be a holiday named for a Black man or woman.

Despite the efforts of the Congressional Black Caucus they still were unable to make any progress so Mrs. King and Conyers decided to ask Kennedy, as Chair of the Judiciary Committee, to introduce the legislation on the Senate side. Since Bayh was the ranking Democrat on the committee he was invited to participate during the initial stages of the process. Knowing my boss quite well, there was no doubt in my mind that he would gladly join in. Even though Bayh was from a very conservative state, which it still is, he could always be counted on to support legislation beneficial to the Black community. Black America credits Kennedy as being their best friend in the

United States Senate but Bayh deserves a place in the hearts of Black America also. In the years I worked for him I can not recall one time when he didn't support legislation beneficial to our communities.

As chairman of the committee, Kennedy agreed to introduce the Bayh Bill, S. 25 which was identical to the Conyers measure on the House side, H.R. 15., and hold a two day hearing. That marked the beginning of a four year struggle to get the legislation passed into law. It would also be one of the first times in the history of the United States Senate that two Black American staffers organized a hearing on a major piece of legislation. Working closely with Mrs. King and Conyers, Peter and I identified those leaders who would be invited to testify in support of the legislation. We placed notice of the public hearing in the record and then had to set the time for the opposition to testify.

One of the most important functions of a staffer is to write the floor statement for their boss. This is read into the Congressional Record when the bill is first introduced. The tone of that statement will also dictate the tone of the hearing. It was important that Kennedy and Bayh's statements reflect exactly why Dr. King was deserving of a national holiday in his name. That was a critical strategic consideration and we knew that the statement had to reflect the universal nature of King's work. It could not be limited to civil rights but had to encompass human rights. The speech with the best expression of universal love was that portion of Dr. King's 1963 delivery at the Lincoln Monument that has now become famous as his "I Have a Dream," vision. No one could possibly find fault with the message in those words. I also included King's message in his "Letter from a Birmingham Jail." The "I Have a Dream" talks about a world where color is no longer a factor, but instead God's love rules. The "Letter from a Birmingham Jail" speaks of the importance of justice over laws. Since laws are simply the will of the majority at the expense often of the minority, they must always be subordinate to justice, which is God's laws. I would have loved to include the earlier message in Dr. King's speech at the Lincoln Monument when he scolded America for their failure to live up to its promises to Black America. I would have also been thrilled to include a mention of his 1967 Riverside Church speech when he valiantly spoke out against the Vietnam War. But our goal was to pass the legislation and all other considerations had to take a back seat to that fact.

As we prepared for the hearings we knew the first obstacle we would confront was the tremendous amount of opposition from the southern senators both on the Judiciary Committee and within the full body of the Senate. We were not disappointed. After the elected officials who were in support of the legislation testified, they were followed by Senators Strom Thurmond, a Republican from South Carolina and Jesse Helms, also a Republican from North Carolina. They were the two leaders of the opposition within the Senate. The leader on the House side was Congressman Larry McDonald, a Democrat from Georgia. The key opposition outside the Congress was the Liberty Lobby and its spokespersons Stanley Rittenhouse and Julia Brown.

After Kennedy and Bayh read their opening statements they were followed by a number of the thirty-seven senators who had signed onto Bayh's "Letter of Support." At the beginning of the hearing it appeared that we were very close to the fifty-one votes needed to pass the legislation on the senate side. After a number of the senators testified in support, they were followed by many of the members of the Congressional Black Caucus, to include Conyers. Then many of the Black leaders spoke in favor, to include Mrs. King and Joseph Lowrey, President of the Southern Christian Leadership Conference. Mrs. King made a very passionate plea to the senate to pass this legislation as a tribute to a man who had sacrificed all his life to help make the United States a better place for all its citizens. She told the senators that more than any other man, King was committed to achieving the words set out in the Declaration of Independence, and that is all men are created equal with certain inalienable rights to include a pursuit of happiness through liberty. Lowrey's testimony was in support of Mrs.King.

Unfortunately, Mrs. King's words did not convince Thurmond, Helms, McDonald and the entire contingent of congresspeople op-

111

posed to the legislation. Thurmond was the first to testify against the bill. He argued from a cost perspective. His assertion was that it would be too expensive to the taxpayers to have another paid holiday for government workers so close after the Christmas and New Year holidays. His compromise was to have a recognition day on every Sunday before January 15, the actual day of King's birth. He argued that since King was a minister and that Blacks were an extremely religious people why not just have a special day for King on that Sunday. Kennedy and Bayh immediately requested a cost benefit analysis from the Congressional Budget Office (CBO). The results of that study indicated that the money spent on that holiday would bring in quite a bit of tax revenue for the government and easily offset the money lost in salaries to the employees. With the CBO figures we were able to dispel Thurmond's claim of the cost and that effectively quieted his opposition.

Jesse Helms and Larry McDonald's opposition was based on their assertion that King was influenced by communist and may have been a communist himself. This argument was a "no-brainer" to defeat. We simply asked them to prove that King had ever attended a communist meeting, had professed any allegiance to the communist doctrine and to reconcile how an ordained minister could possibly be a communist, which is an ideology that essentially denies the existence of God. They were unable to support their position.

However, Helms and McDonald did not give up the battle. Instead, they turned to Stanley Rittenhouse, chief lobbyist for Liberty Lobby and Julia Brown, a Black woman who had been an undercover agent for the Federal Bureau of Investigation in Cleveland, Ohio. My most disgusting experience while listening to their testimony was having to sit by and listen to Brown state that she couldn't say for sure that King was a communist, but in conducting her undercover investigation, "she knew him to be closely connected with the Communist Party." However, her testimony could not withstand the scrutiny of questioning from Kennedy and Bayh, and fell apart right at its core. Her strongest argument was that Stanley Levinson and Bayard Rustin, both advisors to King at different times, had communist affiliation. What they implied was guilt by association and it was a dismal failure.

Finally, Helms tried to bring up a morals charge against King. Helms was relentless in his attempt, actually passing around a file to other senators with alleged information about King. Senator Daniel Patrick Moynihan was sickened by this attempt to attack King's reputation. "The Congress of the United States has never been so sick as it could be today," Moynihan said on the Senate floor, "if few were to pay attention to the filth in this brown binder that has been passed around the chamber today." He then tossed the binder onto the floor and walked away.

Despite the inordinate personal attacks on King and the tremendous opposition to the legislation (there had never been a bill passed through Congress honoring a civilian with a national holiday), supporters for the King holiday never gave up. Even though our initial S. 25 was tabled in the Senate it did open the door for debate. We were able to place it on the congressional agenda and facilitate discussion. Once it was before a committee, we only had to listen to the opposition and one by one destroy their arguments against the holiday.

Mrs. King then initiated a massive lobbying effort facilitated by the King Center for Non-violence. The spokesperson for the holiday was Stevie Wonder. He would lead the rally at the Capitol every year on King's birthday and released the song "Happy Birthday to You," in King's honor. After a four year up and down battle, the legislation finally passed in the House of Representatives by a 338 to 90 vote and in the U. S. Senate by a 78 to 22 vote in 1983. It all got started that day in March when Senators Kennedy and Bayh introduced the idea of a national holiday in the Senate. A great deal of credit must be given to those two champions of causes supported by Black Americans in this country, to include the King legislation.

When Reagan finally signed the bill into law on November 2, 1983, he made the following statement. "Dr. King had awakened something strong and true, a sense that true justice must be color blind and that among Black Americans, their destiny is tied up with our destiny and their freedom is inextricably bound to our freedom;

113

we cannot walk alone." This represented a very strong statement committing our country to a destiny tied together from a man who did so much to drive us apart.

However, the most important remarks were uttered by Mrs. King right after Reagan spoke. She summed up the importance of Dr. King to this country stating that, "In his own life's example, he symbolized what was right about America, what was noblest and best, what human beings have pursued since the beginning of history. He loved unconditionally. He was in constant pursuit of truth, and when he discovered it, he embraced it."

THE AUTHENTIC AMERICAN CULTURE

CALVIN THOMAS

As I look back over my life as a Black man in America, one fact is certain: During all those years of growing up I never paid much attention to the whole notion of culture. I never gave much thought to its meaning or importance in my life. So, with that in mind, let's first define culture so the young people who are now like I once was, can be in the same place I am today. The word culture is often confused with the words myth, folklore, and legend.

A myth is a traditional story of a people or group with unknown origins. It is usually told in support of some phenomenon about the group that is beyond human comprehension and fills its members with wonder and awe. Folklore has sayings like, "Davey Crockett was born on a mountaintop in Tennessee, the greenest state in the land of the free, raised in the woods where he knew every tree, and killed him a bear when he was only three." That George Washington never told a lie is also folklore. Legends are tales such as the exploits of Billy the Kid, Jesse and Frank James, the Younger Brothers, Buffalo Bill, Daniel Boone, and Wyatt Earp. Even though these were real characters, their exploits were exaggerated.

Culture can be viewed as the total development, improvement, and refinement of the intellectual abilities, humanitarian contributions, and all art forms associated with a particular race of people. Their ways of thinking, communicating, acting, their ideas, artistic abilities, and customs are transferred or passed along to succeeding generations and can only be associated with that group of people. Our definition suggests that the most authentic culture in this country is the one that evolves from the African.

We must understand when referring to our history and culture, as it relates to being the descendants of Africans from the continent of Africa, that our ancestors were a stolen people, taken by force, from the land of their birth, brought to America, and forced into slavery. Slaves weren't allowed to openly practice any of their original culture and/or traditions. They were separated by many degrees, scattered throughout this country for the purpose of completely removing them from any reminders of their African past. They were denied the right to speak their original language, taught to speak a language foreign to them, fed a foreign food, and forced to practice many different forms of Christianity.

Although physically removed from all things remotely close to their original African cultures, the spiritual connection remained intact. Based on their natural spirituality, and the need to survive, they created, cultivated, and established here in America an incredible history and one of the most fascinating rich cultures, unparalleled by any modern civilization known to humanity.

The Black culture came about as a result of the need to survive the tyranny of slavery. Our proud ancestors never accepted slavery and fought against it every opportunity they had. Nat Turner, inspired by a vision from God, led a rebellion that was a warning of events to come; he preceded the Civil War. Harriett Tubman, by anyone's measure, had to be one of the bravest women to ever live. She not only struck out for her own freedom, but went back down into the South thirty-nine times and brought other slaves to the promise land. The last trip she made was to get her mother and father out of bondage.

Referring to that natural spirituality of the Black race, Ms. Tubman, in interviews later in life, claimed that God directed her and he safely protected her from any harm. She tells of the time when she received a vision from the Lord that she should not take her usual route out of the South. She altered her route and safely made it back up into New York. She later found out that a patrol of slave hunters had been lying in wait for her along that original trail.

Sojourner Truth, another strong Black woman, was guided by

her faith in God as she spoke out against the evils of slavery. We must also recognize the thousands of brave Black men and women who risked their lives working the many routes of the Underground Railroad that guided escaping slaves to freedom. Frederick Douglass, the greatest spokesman of the Nineteenth Century could mesmerize a crowd with his riveting stories about the de-humanizing nature of being property of another individual.

Finally, among these early Black heroes, there is a man that you will never read about in the history books and that is David Walker. As young students reading about the American Revolution and those men who spoke out for freedom, you will inevitably be introduced to Patrick Henry. All of us read his fiery speech that ends with his ultimatum to the British, "Give me liberty or give me death." But when in our same history classes did we get the opportunity to read from David Walker's Appeal, a much stronger statement about freedom than Henry? In his Appeal, Walker argued for the active resistance to slavery. He advocated for Black pride, unity, collective action, and liberation "by any means necessary." Walker concluded his Appeal with the bold words of warning:

I speak Americans for your good. We must and shall be free I say, in spite of you. You may do your best to keep us in wretchedness and misery, to enrich you and your children; but God will deliver us from under you. And woe, woe will be to you if we have to obtain our freedom by fighting.

Every child in America should have the opportunity to read of this man and his appeal for freedom, not only for one group of people, but for everyone. Walker was a true American who believed in the basic democratic principles articulated in the Constitution.

117

Tubman, Douglass, Truth, and Walker expressed their unique abilities as outstanding speakers and writers. Blacks also used the spiritual as a way to relieve their suffering and stay in touch with their spirituality. They created songs to work by, songs that kept them connected with their roots, and songs for happy times. They had songs that were codes loaded with hidden messages. Songs like "Swing Low Sweet Chariot," "Kam ba yah, Come By Here," "Nobody

Knows the Trouble I've Seen," "Run Mary Run," "Steal Away to Jesus,"
"In the Great Getting Up Morning," and many more. These spirituals
emanated right out of the slave fields and are as much American as
any other form of music. As such, they represent the roots of American culture.

By the turn of the Nineteenth Century, and under harsh Jim
Crow Laws, the Black culture rose to one of its highest peaks of survival. A culture born out of slavery was now responsible for creating
new art forms and popularizing many genres of music. In spite of
being denied the proper education, we also became outstanding en-
trepreneurs, entertainers, inventors, doctors, lawyers, and teachers.

Our forebears were leading land surveyors, and did work in the
scientific fields of astronomy, mathematics, engineering, and elec-
tronics. A Black man invented the cotton gin that brought the South
an economic boom in cotton. We developed the filament which ig-
nites the light bulb, and developed the mechanical oil lubricating
device which extends the life of the perpetual engines. It was a Black
man who designed the first three-way traffic device. A Black also invented the air conditioning unit we now enjoy on hot summer days
in our homes and cars; and refrigeration that preserves the nutri-
tious value and life of perishable items. A Black scientist developed
the method to preserve blood and made the process of transfusions
more efficient by separating the red blood cells from the white cells.

George Washington Carver produced over three-hundred prod-
ucts from the peanut, sixty from the pecan, and one hundred-and-
seventy five from the sweet potato; extracted blue, purple, and red
pigments from the red clay soil in Alabama; and created the process
by which stains and shades of textile dyes are extracted from paint.
From the short time span of thirty-five years, 1865 to 1900, our ancestors, the ex-slaves, were singularly most responsible for America's
emergence onto the global sphere as the most powerful nation on
earth.

This talent all sprang out of the Black culture that was not visible
because the dominant group kept it marginalized. Instead of allowing us to build the image of the great and magnificent people we

118

were at that time, the dominant culture found it necessary to tear us down. For the first one-hundred years after slavery and during slavery, white America dictated those images and identities of Black Americans and they were all negative. Culture is about image building. All races have built their images based on positive identification. We never had that opportunity until now. For the first time in our history, we can be in total control of portraying our heroes and heroines in a positive image, the way it should always have been done. When I was a young man, I never had the opportunity to read about the many great Black Americans who did so much to make this a great country. Young Black Americans are privileged to have that opportunity, but it is up to them to take advantage of what is before them.

Sports are another field in which Blacks have excelled. The Black athlete's ability and talent, as early as 1889 through the various Negro Leagues, was on display and often drew very large crowds. These athletes increased the level of excellence in all sports, the first being baseball with Jackie Robinson. Once he was called up to play for the Brooklyn Dodgers, the manner in which the game would be played was changed forever. Prior to Jackie, the game stressed only power, but with him it began to shift to base running, bunting, and other aspects of the game. Blacks had the same impact on basketball.

Before we were allowed to play in the National Basketball League (NBA), the game was extremely slow and the winning scores were twenty to seventeen and even eleven to seven. When a team managed to score fifty points, it was the shot heard around the world. The Black player's ability to run faster and jump higher gave rise to the jump shot and dunking. It took the game to a new level of finesse, excitement, and entertainment. In 1951, because of the superior athletic ability of the Black basketball player, the NBA took away the big man and the speed advantage by widening the lane from six feet to twelve feet.

119

Blacks also excelled in horse racing as early as the nineteenth century. In 1896, Monkey Simon, a Black jockey rode at Clover Bottom Race Track near Nashville, Tenn. In 1870, Ed Brown, another

Black jockey, won the fourth running of the Belmont Stakes. On May 17, 1875, in the running of the first Kentucky Derby, fifteen of the seventeen jockeys were Black. Among them was Oliver Lewis, whose winning horse, "Aristides," was trained by a Black trainer, Ansell Williamson. Over the span of twenty-eight years, eleven Black jockeys won fifteen Derbies. Between 1893 and 1898, Willie Simms, won in different years, all three legs of the Triple Crown, the Kentucky Derby, the Preakness, and the Belmont Stakes. Because of their incredible success in the sport of horse racing, Blacks were barred from riding in any of the three major races for seventy-nine years, from 1921 to 2000. However, in 2000, Marlon St. Julian broke the drought by riding in the Kentucky Derby. In that same year, a gentleman named DeWayne Minor became the first Black to ride in the distinguished gentleman's sport of harness racing.

Black Americans have also had a historical presence in rodeo shows. In 1911, fifteen percent of all rodeo cowboys were Black. In that same year, William "Bill" M. Pickett, performed all over the country and in Europe. His rodeo event was called "Bulldogging," also known as steer wrestling. Because of his distinct and unique technique, he was called by two different names, "The Dusky Demon" and the "Bull Dogger." Many have referred to him as the greatest cowboy ever to perform in the bulldogging event. In 1982, another Black cowboy, Charlie Sampson, became the national bull-riding champion.

I could easily write a book highlighting the positive impact of the Black athlete on the world of sports in this country. Blacks have become so dominant in major sports that a 1997 study conducted by Northeastern University Center for Sports in Society found that seventeen percent of Major League baseball players were Black, sixty-seven percent of football players and eighty percent of the NBA's players were Black.

In spite of all the problems that we as Blacks confront on a daily basis, the longer I live the more I appreciate my race, and I am totally mesmerized and incredibly proud of my culture. I make a sincere effort every day to look within myself and search for ways to be deserving of the struggles, sacrifices, and contributions of my ancestors to our culture. My drive for living is to do something of benefit for our youth in honor of those who have gone before us, and have given so much of themselves.

Our culture will always represent change for the good of all humanity. I want every young Black man and woman to experience this fire within my soul about my race and culture. Always remember that we Blacks, although still not considered by the dominant group as full American citizens, are as American as the old proverbial saying "Apple Pie." I titled this paper "The Authentic American Culture" because that is exactly what Black culture is. It is a fact that the majority never wanted to accept the Black race as equals in this country, but did embrace our music, art forms, dress styles, and even the slang. The most blatant theft came in the field of music. The pioneer rhythm and blues singers had their style stolen by whites, who didn't want to use the same name, so they changed it to rock and roll. Elvis Presley readily admitted to stealing dance routines from Chuck Berry. The popular song, "My Babe" was specifically written for Little Walter, but Elvis Presley made millions with his version.

It is also the Black culture that helps to give America genuine humanitarian standards of decency recognized by other countries. When President Barack Obama was elected, this country's negatives went down within the international world of public opinion. In fact the world embraced him more than many members of this nation. His first mission, once sworn in as president, was to travel to other countries and renew their trust in us. He has been quite successful in doing that to the chagrin of his enemies.

Over the decades, Black entertainers have served as ambassadors of good will to other countries. Louis Armstrong was considered the ambassador of music, Muddy Waters was well received in London, and Michael Jackson was loved all over the world. In the late 1970's it irked many from the white political structure when the Rev. Jesse Jackson was able to obtain the release of white hostages being held in countries at odds with the United States. Even President Obama was surprised when he received the Nobel Peace Prize. If any one

121

statesman has the ability to bring permanent peace between Israel and the Palestinians, it is Obama.

During the past century, Black athletes always represented America on the diplomatic front. For years the greatest ambassadors of humanitarianism were the Harlem Globetrotters. They traveled all over the world, showcasing their outstanding basketball skills to the world. Young people today know very little about the Globetrotters since the great players now have been integrated into the NBA. In 1947 and 1948, the Globetrotters beat the Minneapolis Lakers, with George Mikan, considered the best player in the professional ranks, in exhibition games. Reece Goose Tatum, Marques Haynes, George "Meadowlark" Lemon, Albert "Runt" Phillips, and Inman Jackson were players who easily would have dominated the NBA if not for segregation. Just imagine the line-up the Globetrotters would have today if all the dominating players in the NBA were forced to play for the Globetrotters.

In all aspects of American life, Blacks, when finally allowed to participate, have dominated. No wonder the dominant group attempted for over one hundred years after slavery to limit our participation. The government and media supported their racist customs and laws. The government at all levels condoned segregation and the media distorted our perception and importance in books, magazines, movies, and finally on television. Minstrel shows were an abomination against Blacks, and The Birth of the Nation was the greatest lie ever told and projected in a movie.

However, this exclusion could only last so long and with the successes of the Civil Rights Movement, Blacks were finally welcomed under the Big Tent of Integration. Blacks relished this newly acquired equality, and the more they experienced it, the greater their appetite and hunger for it became. Blinded by the prospects of inclusion into the ruling class, Blacks never realized that as a free people their culture is the only thing about the Black race of interest to whites. They stole from the culture and then marginalized us as a people. However, as a result of integration, Black communities as they existed during the segregated period, are all but extinct. At one time in our history we adhered to the belief that it takes a village to raise the children. In other words, the family structure stretched throughout the entire community. Ms. Henrietta, who lived at the end of the block in my neighborhood, would chastise me if she caught me doing something wrong. She would then tell Mamma who would whip me for the fact that Ms. Henrietta caught me being bad.

During our years prior to integration, the "n" word was forbidden in most homes, and there was always a high level of respect for ladies, from mothers to sisters, aunts, and cousins. Today the "n" word has been made into some kind of distorted term of endearment. How is it possible that a word that carries with it so much tragic history for our race, can be considered a loving term. Young men refer to each other as "dawg" which is rather strange to me. A dog is a pet and is considered part of the animal life below that of man. Why would they deliberately put themselves in that category when for so many years we fought whites for trying to do the same thing? It seems rather incomprehensible to me. You turn on BET network during a Saturday when our children are home and you see video tapes of women half dressed and in fact there was one specific tape that only showed the back ends of young Black girls keeping rhythm to some rap song. There was also the tape where a rap singer swipes a credit card between the cracks of a young female's rear end, I guess as some kind of indication that she could be bought.

I recall one incident back in 2007 when some white man on television referred to the beautiful Black sisters playing for the Rutgers University basketball team as "nappy headed whores." He was rightfully fired from his job with MSNBC. But when asked to comment on his derogatory description of these smart, talented, and beautiful Black sisters on The View, a Black comedian hesitated for a minute and slowly repeated the descriptions, "nappy headed whores," and then said, "Yes, they are." There were no repercussions against this so-called Black comedian. Another Black comedian, on one of the late night shows, said that, "they (the Rutgers Basketball players) may not be nappy-headed whores, but they were sure some ugly women." Have we become that callous and insensitive to our own image that we would allow this to

123

happen without the greatest of uproars and complaints?

What would be the response if this had been done against any other racial group? I wonder how many times a day do our children hear the "n" word or the saying "my 'n,'" my dawg, my O.G., my Hoe, or the "B" word on television, radio, or from the mouths of people who look like them? Just whom do they think of when they hear these words? How many Blacks have ever heard or know the meaning of words such as "Hymie", "Kike", "Sheeny," "Shylock," "Heeb," and "Yid"? My guess is none, and that is a good thing.

However, if they have heard them it probably was not on television or radio. If so, they were used in some historical contexts making reference to the Jewish Holocaust, and were not meant to be understood as terms of endearment or as a joke. The Jewish people do not use or direct those terms and words toward one another. Jewish people consider it a desecration when the word Holocaust is associated on any level with the Black struggle. In all reality, Holocaust is a sacred word used for the exclusive purpose of distinguishing the historical suffering of the Jewish people. Now, that is power.

Unfortunately, Black people as a collective group have very little control over how they are portrayed through the print, audio, and visual media in news and entertainment. However, that is beginning to change. There are a few Blacks today with the clout necessary to give the green light to some television shows and movies that have made positive statements and expressions of our people. Immediately, what comes to mind is the movie *The Great Debaters*. This movie is not about sports figures, but about thinkers, scholars, and great speakers. It highlights historically Black Wiley College, which before the movie, very few people even knew existed. It is a historically true story. Wiley College did debate University of Southern California and defeated them, giving more credence to my earlier point that when we break the racial barriers and compete against the opposite race, we are usually victorious.

I have written a lot, but nothing will exceed what I am about to address to the beautiful young Black men and women, the flowers of our wonderful Black race and culture. Know that you are the descendants of an African people who were brought to this country against their will. Your heritage evolves from a people who suffered immeasurable brutalities and then forgave the people who committed such horrendous crimes. Your ancestors made them see the errors of their ways, and brought forth the changes that have made this a better country.

The insistence and determination of your people to be free, ultimately made freedom an attainable dream for every oppressed person in the world. The spirit and faith, along with the resilient nature of your people, brought forth the Civil Rights and Women Rights Movements in this country.

The Black race has made so many unselfish contributions toward humanity that I could write for the remainder of my life and not be able to convey the real compassionate nature of your race and culture. I can only plead and encourage each and every one of you to read and study the accomplishments of your race. You should listen to the stories of the elderly members of your family and community and research the Internet to learn more.

Your beautiful history and rich culture stem from one of the most extraordinary civilizations in the world.. Look around at yourselves and appreciate that you are one important component of the universe of races.

Realize that everything about you is beautiful. Your hair, nose, lips, and skin tone are made in the image of God. Recognize that the negative words you may hear are false manifestations of what some may want you to believe about your race. Remember your presence among some is a constant reminder of the wrongs they and their fathers have committed against you and your fathers. Some cannot forget the debt they owe you, yet they refuse to pay it. They know they are wrong, yet their nature just won't allow them to make atonement for their indiscretions.

Understand that in the nearly three hundred years of building America, we have never done anything or committed any aggression against the ruling class on any level that comes remotely close to what was done to us. They know that at some point in the future,

125

world opinion will force them to do the right thing and atone for their many sins. I am sure they are well aware of this possibility and plan to do everything within their power to rid themselves of the burden of having to pay reparations, a debt they have no intentions of paying. I say to young Black men and women that no matter what happens, short of total destruction of the United States, they will not be successful in their attempts. Atonement must be made; the debt has to be paid if this country wants to remain the leader of the free world.

You must also recognize that the ruling class of this country does not like you. Not because of who you are, but rather for who they are not, yet want to be. I plead with you, young Black men and women, to have no fear in embracing your blackness, and the legacies and enslavement of your ancestors, their sacrifices, suffering, and losses. Stand up tall, look around you, and say boldly to yourselves aloud, "I am the sum total of those who came before me. I am and I represent their pain. I am their cry for freedom, the whelps on their backs left from the oppressors' whips. I am everything they ever were and yet more as a result of them. I am standing tall, representing the great attributes of a great culture and a mighty race of people. I will continue to build upon their legacy, for the good of mankind and the greatness of the God that lives within our hearts

I respectfully submit to you, young people, to fill up on the accomplishments of your people and your culture, speed off to self-determination, self-reliance, independence, and a renewed sense of self, created for the purpose of assisting people who look like us.

YOU CAN LEARN A LOT FROM DEAD PEOPLE

TOSCHIA

One of the most disheartening problems I have witnessed working, as a child advocate is the lack of understanding of history with regards to young people, especially in African-American children. There tends to be a great disconnect or rift between both old and young, rich and poor, and the other silly, trivial socio- economic barriers that people contrive to not work together. Many of the young people that I come across do not think that they can make a difference in the world.

They, like many adults, think the average minority young person isn't capable of much beyond hanging on the corner, having babies, or over populating the prison system. I think that people in general must understand that YOU have the power to change the world! It starts with YOU! The list goes on and on with things that are wrong in our communities: homelessness, apathy, lack of education, crime, hunger, AIDS. We usually look at these problems and decide they're too big for us to do anything about. Thus, by our lack of effort to even try to evoke change we are assisting in creating a permanent social underclass. Many young people think they will make a difference "one day" or "someday." We think things will be better when we get out of middle school and go to high school. Or it will be better the next grading period, or it'll be easier when we get to the next grade. Or we would be happier if we had a two-parent household or if we had more money. But we should live for today! Carpe diem; seize the day! Do the right thing today so that you will have a better tomorrow.

Many dead people changed the world when they were young just like you! Think about David from the Bible. He was just a teenager when he made a major accomplishment. He simply didn't fit in! He was too old to sit at the kids' table but too young to sit at the adult table. David was probably around the age of an eighth grader, which is a time when you really don't fit in anywhere. But that same boy, David who probably had pimples, smelly armpits, and trouble fitting in, was used by God to slay a GIANT! Can you imagine that?

Another example of a courageous youth was Mary, the mother of Jesus. She was just a teenager when she was chosen to bear the long-awaited savior. God could have chosen her cousin Elizabeth; certainly she would have been more qualified. She was much older and she actually *wanted* a baby. I'm sure all the messy, gossipy women that sit on the front porches with nothing to do probably judged Mary because she was an unwed mom. They probably thought Elizabeth was more qualified to be the mother of Jesus. I'm sure Mary wasn't from the suburbs but from the hood. She probably had the equivalent of Payless BOGO (buy one, get one half-off) shoes and not Nike or Jordan's. Nonetheless, God chose Mary, the teenager from the equivalent of the projects. Imagine that? Kids have always taken the lead in world change because young people rock! The Civil Rights Movement was just one of the many movements by young people that changed the course of history.

So if you're thinking "someday," think again. You can take the initiative to make sure your pants are pulled up young men, and influence others to do so. If you don't take yourself seriously, no one else will. Young women can take the lead by not engaging in sex! Make a young man respect you and your body. Many of the young men who will pursue you are suffering from their own personal demons and use sex as a way to dominate women. They go from girl to girl and as soon as they are gratified sexually they won't call you or take you to the prom, and many will cause you to be an unwed mother. It's not worth it. Young men, do not allow a conniving young woman to get you caught up in their games by pitting you against another young man. She isn't worth it. I have seen one too many young men die over a silly girl! Sex is a deadly weapon, literally and figuratively! Most teenage parents end up dropping out of school

128

and end up on welfare. Life doesn't have to be hard if you listen! Sex is not all it's cracked up to be but it's a great responsibility between two people that give themselves to one another, understanding that they are giving the very fiber of their soul. Believe me, it's worth the wait because it's complicated. Many young men sleep around because they have indirectly come to hate women and have never seen their father's love or cherish their own mothers. Subconsciously they use women for their physical fantasies. And like a candy wrapper, they get thrown away once they have been eaten. Many young women are looking for the love they never got from their fathers so that five minutes of touching that they receive from a man is a substitute for something greater. Sex is too complicated and emotional so just leave it alone! So many young people are rushing to grow up. For what? To pay bills, bills, bills.

Enjoy your childhood while you can.

Take your extra energy and put it into making good grades, making changes, being unique, and becoming a leader. All young people have the potential to be leaders! *You* can take the lead by speaking up when someone in your school is being mistreated or picked on. Or choose to remain silent before saying something derogatory to someone (I'm still working on that one in my thirties). You can take the lead by befriending kids that are having a bad time in school, or by not getting involved in cliques that look down on other people. It has taken me awhile to learn the qualities of a good leader, so I will pass these qualities on to you so that you can be successful in all that you do.

I'm no expert on leadership, but these few traits have helped me. They are discernments, which include wisdom (applying truth to everyday situations), confidence (not arrogance or cockiness) and determination (sticking to something). You don't have to be a certain age to be a leader or change the world. I'm sure David wasn't carded to make sure he was of age or asked to show ID as he walked away after killing Goliath. There is one important ingredient necessary for success and change, and that is the ability to listen to those who have achieved success before you. It is imperative that you

129

listen to your elders and respect them. Listening to those who have experienced what you are going through will save you a lot of heartache and pain. Life does not have to be hard, and listening to their parents, teachers, mentors, or clergy can alleviate a lot of issues that young people face. Then, you can help lead a new generation one day as well.

Remember that we all stand on the shoulders of giants that fought for freedom. There was a time when our people were killed for even thinking of picking up a book, yet when the yellow school bus (free…I might add) comes and stops directly in front of our home, some choose not to get on and take the magic bus ride to school. That magic bus will drop us off at the magic kingdom that is public school. The magic kingdom has the key to end poverty, apathy, and a lot of the myriad generational curses that can help lead our people to the promised land.

See, in that magic kingdom there is a sacred place called the library, where we can enter the supernatural realm and come face to face with our ancestors by using the enchanted and clairvoyant tool called a book. Once you enter the magic zone, there are so many different historical figures that will give you a different outlook on life and help you prepare to change the world. In the magic kingdom you have the privilege of learning from DEAD PEOPLE!!

When you learn from dead people, your life will seem mundane and very boring compared to those who have come before you. Sometimes young people feel like they are having a bad day because friends are gossiping about them or something happened in English class. Or it might be their football game is rained out or their parents don't allow them to play the Wii game on the plasma TV in their room, even though their grades are mediocre.

130

Once you enter the magic kingdom, you will learn from the dead that a truly bad day is when you are awakened to the sound of your slave owner yelling at you, telling you to get to work. Imagine every muscle in your body throbbing in excruciating pain as you hurriedly get off the hard ground you slept on. You grimace in pain as the fresh wounds from the night before sting from the sweat on your body. Quickly you wash the dust off yourself and try to hold down your breakfast of hard grits and dirty water. You try to remove the particles of dirt in the water with your fingertips. Next you dig out a few ants and a roach out of the bowl, praying it doesn't make you ill. You rush to make it to the field on time; you don't have a watch so you have to rely on the sun. You take several slow breaths to avoid having a panic attack because you know if you are late you will be beaten again. Your wounds are dripping blood and each drop of sweat that enters the cuts evokes horrific pain.

You hurriedly make it to your destination and crouch on the floor with the other slaves, your backs pressed up against the wall in a dark, dusty, smelly room. You pray that everyone in your family stays together and no one is sold today. After reading about tales of adversity and triumph from other dead people, I promise your bad day won't seem so bad. I know some people suffer greatly; I do not mean to minimize that. Some kids have to endure the loss of someone they love, the divorce of parents, not having money for adequate clothing, and sadly experience some abuse. But some of the petty things that bug us don't seem to matter as much once we visit the DEAD PEOPLE! One thing that I've learned from the dead people is that in life we have to face challenges. If you read about the life of any number of respected leaders, you will find that they all faced some significant challenges.

Reading autobiographies can change your life! They can motivate you to try to change the world; they can help you garner intellectual arrogance. After reading a few autobiographies you will feel compelled to graduate high school, go to college and not just receive the basic bachelors degree, but also seek more education. Heck, anybody can get a bachelors degree! But leaders, movers, shakers, and those on a mission know that you can't just stop at the minimum for, you see, education is one of the tools that you need to slay those dragons of poverty, apathy, and despair. For those of you who, in lieu of college, chose a technical trade, be the best that you can be! Receive as many certifications to propel you to be the best auto mechanic, barber, or any other trade you choose. If you are seeking

131

a career in the military, move up through the ranks as quickly as you can. Be the best soldier in the U.S. military. If you are a cake decorator or baker, take it to the next level; take a business class and open up a bakery.

By reading autobiographies you will feel empowered to move your butt! Empower others! Think outside the box and if you have to do it alone, you aren't scared because you know that others accomplished great feats before you, when the chips were down. They overcame and you will as well. Many young people throughout history from Paul Revere to Mother Teresa found ways to overcome and excel.

In the Bible, the book of Jeremiah 29:11 reads, "For I know the plans I have for you. Plans to prosper and not harm you, plans to give you hope and a future." Sometimes the obstacles we have to overcome can make us stronger, helping us to achieve our goal in life.

A lesson that you will also learn from dead people is that they made sacrifices in order to get to the next level in life, as will you if you want to succeed. A sacrifice can be as simple as taking the extra time to complete extra homework assignments in order to qualify for college scholarships. Sacrifices require laying aside something that matters to you. It might be television, video games, or hanging out with friends. Successful leaders like Dr. Martin Luther King Jr. and Malcolm X made sacrifices for equality. The biggest sacrifice of all was the death of Jesus Christ for our sins. These people were passionate and steadfast in their quest to change the world and they sacrificed with their lives. No one expects anyone to give his or her life for a cause. But I'm afraid there aren't enough people making basic sacrifices, like volunteering at a soup kitchen, mentoring others or even volunteering to help out the elderly.

132

Young people, you have the gifts of zeal, youth, and innocence on your side. So just do it! Young people whom only talk the talk can eventually become adults that talk but aren't willing to work to make their dreams a reality. I come across a lot of adults who want to make changes. There are countless organizations and people that are allegedly trying to help our youth. Some have failed because of their inability to listen, dive in, get "dirty," or follow up and talk to young people to see how they feel.

Life is not pretty for many, but that can't deter you from being the best that you can be. Are you willing to make sacrifices in life to help other people? Many Americans have a hard time under-standing what a sacrifice is. In our comfortable world, we don't take advantage of the opportunities to sacrifice for others. If possible, travel and see the world while you are young so that you can be a better, productive adult. If you can't afford to physically travel, that is still no excuse because your mind can travel within the magic kingdom--the library. As you travel and read you will be amazed at those that can guide you. Jesus Christ is the most spectacular because Harry Potter's wizardry has nothing on the man who sacrificed his life and rose from a tomb after being dead for three days! That same man would put Harry Houdini or David Copperfield's magic tricks to shame. Jesus turned water into wine. He performed all types of outstanding miracles. Then his haters killed him, but guess what? He let them hurt him but he got the last laugh. He rose from the grave and became the Prince of Peace and the ruler of the whole world. Talk about a sci-fi story, Jesus was the bomb.com. I'm telling you that once you start to study the DEAD PEOPLE, now, you will be armed, fired up, and ready to go change the world. These dead people are going to give you the keys to success. Eleanor Roosevelt, Jesse Owens, Harriet Tubman, Louis Braille, Clara Barton, Marian Anderson, Fannie Lou Hamer, and so many more that have changed the world for the bet-ter. These people, along with contemporaries in your life, like positive adults, can help you gain strength, courage, and confidence. You will be changed by every dead person you meet which will help you look fear in the face. Some dead people like Shakespeare have even written books, poems, and short stories to enlighten, entertain and sharpen your imagination. The books by Dr. Seuss, the poetry of Robert Frost or Gwendolyn Brooks, and a personal hero of mine Mary Shelley are others who have made changes.

Mary Shelley was a young teenage writer who lived in an era when women had no rights and were expected to write only about love. She defied the odds and said, "Anything boys can write, girls can write better." Yes, she was a young girl that scared the "bageebies" out of everyone with the very first horror tale, *Frankenstein!* Subsequently other women like George Eliot stopped writing under male pseudonyms to sell books. Dorothy Wordsworth stopped writing her brother William's stuff and wrote her own Grassmere *Journals.* African American and Asian American writers like Alice Walker and Amy Tan exploded on the literary scene. See what one teenager did? Mary Shelley, Phyllis Wheatley, Dorothy Wordsworth all started a precedent of women writers that transcended race and literary era, and even stretched across continents. Mary Shelley proved that she could scare the heck out of you just as well or better than any boy! Talk about courage? Eleanor Roosevelt said, "You gain strength, courage, and confidence by every experience in which you stop to look fear in the face. You must do the very thing you think you cannot."

Courage is not the absence of fear. Courage is when you choose to acknowledge your fear and look it dead in the face! Many people, young and old alike, are afraid of failure. They are afraid of what people will think if they get an "F," afraid of people making fun of them if they found out their family was on welfare, or that their father hits their mom. Or if one of their parents was an alcoholic or went to jail. Always remember that it doesn't matter where you come from; it's where you are going! All that

we experience in life is merely preparing us for the greatness that is to come. So the next time you feel abandoned because you are in state protective custody, write about it. How do you feel? What do you want for your future?

134

The next time your parents are fighting and you put the pillow over your head to block out the noise and fear that you feel, pull out paper and pen and write about it. If you have a child out of wedlock as a teenager and people look down on you, write about it. If you have the misfortune to read this from behind bars, write about it. Remember all that is for your good is coming! You must always remember that a good leader shows others how to lead. So when you write your feelings, emotions, and experiences down you must share them with others. You never know who could benefit from your experience or who can rely on your words as strength to overcome, just as you will. Write, share, and write! God doesn't allow you to go through circumstances and overcome obstacles to be so selfish as to not share with others. Just as we learn from dead people we want others to learn from us.

Please utilize the magic kingdom. Read fiction, nonfiction, and magazines anything you can get your hands on and write as well. It may not look cool to be caught reading and you may even be called a geek. But take it from me and many people who have done pretty well in life; always remember we learned a lot from dead people and you will too. You can still play video games, participate in sports and have fun. In addition to your daily routine, try to incorporate the "secret place" called the library into it. I promise you will be better for it; you will lead a better life and will be able to affect others in a positive manner as well.

KKK: THE REAL BOOGEYMAN

By Jayme L. Bradford

Growing up, I was always afraid of the boogeyman. But for me, the boogeyman wasn't Michael from the movie Halloween, or Jason from *Friday the 13th* or even *Freddie Krueger,* the charismatic dream slasher from Nightmare on Elm Street.

My boogeyman wore a white robe and hood. He could be a neighbor, businessman, or even my teacher. He was a member of the Ku Klux Klan. I knew that he hated the thought of me just because I am African American. My character and intelligence didn't matter, simply because of the color of my dark skin.

One of my earliest childhood memories was that of a 19 year-old boy named Michael Donald, who was lynched in my peaceful hometown of Mobile, Ala., in 1981. This incident had a major impact on my life and changed my perception of race relations. Donald was the target of a Ku Klux Klan initiation. Randomly chosen, he was abducted while on his way to the gas station to purchase a pack of cigarettes. Two Klansmen Henry Francis Hays and James "Tiger" Knowles, Jr. beat the teenager unconscious with a tree limb. Then they slipped a noose around his neck and strangled him. Hays slashed his throat three times to ensure that he was dead *(Jet,* Dec. 26, 1983). They later hung him in a tree near downtown for the entire community to see. Those pictures continue to haunt me.

My family had recently moved back to Alabama after living in Atlanta. We left the big city in part because of the Atlanta Child Murders, which took the lives of 28 African American youth. My parents were very concerned about raising three young children under those conditions, so they decided to move back home to Mobile, where they thought their children would be safe. Despite Wayne

137

Williams, a young African American male being convicted for the serial murders, the African American community thought otherwise. We believed that it was the work of the Klan.

Then, everything changed. When Donald was lynched, I realized that my parents did not have the power to protect me. The boogeyman was real, and he could kill me and get away with it if he wanted too. Even as a child, I was outraged. I wanted the people to do something, but I failed to realize that they were frightened too. If it could happen to Donald, it could happen to anyone.

I remember participating in my first protest march with my father, who taught me to be politically active at an early age. It was a big deal because two local attorneys, Michael and Thomas Figures, were taking the lead and the Rev. Jesse Jackson, a civil rights leader who later ran for president of the United States, came to town. I recognized him because my father proudly hung his large portrait in the den.

In 1984, Hays and Knowles were found guilty of murder/lynching and sentenced to death and life imprisonment respectively. Frank Cox, Hays' brother-in-law was sentenced to 99 years in prison for providing the rope to hang Donald. Hay's father, Bennie Jack Hays, was also charged in the murder, but died before his trial. I believe that God judged him accordingly.

In 1997, the year I finished graduate school at the University of West Florida, Henry Hays was executed. I had never favored the death penalty until then. I wanted to go to the prison the night of his execution, but my father thought it was too dangerous. I listened to him and monitored the local news for updates.

138   The Exalted Cyclops was 42 years old when he died. His death was significant in the state of Alabama because he was the first white man to be executed for killing a black man in 84 years. His death proved that white men could no longer lynch African Americans for sport without just punishment.

That same year Beulah Mae Donald, Donald's 67-year-old mother, sued the Klan with the assistance of the Southern Poverty Law

Center. Back then, I did not understand the courage it took to do something like that. Like Mamie Carthan, the mother of the famous lynch victim Emmett Till, she wanted the world to know what the Klan had done to her innocent son. Donald won her civil lawsuit with the wrongful death verdict of $7 million. Unfortunately, the Klan filed for bankruptcy and gave her a fraction of that amount. However, they were forced to give her the deeds to their headquarters in Tuscaloosa, which she sold for $52,000. Just the thought of her owning their building always made me laugh.

Michael Donald, who worked in the mailroom of the *Mobile Press Register* where I later interned, had always dreamed of building his mother a home. Ironically, she used the settlement money to do just that. He was a devoted son, who was able to provide for his mother, even in death. Although she did not gain much financially, her point was made. Her son's life was valuable and his killers would not go unpunished this time. Sadly, she died shortly after. Her life's work was done.

Since then, the street where Donald was lynched has been renamed in his memory. He is also remembered in exhibits at the American Black Holocaust Museum in Milwaukee and the Civil Rights Memorial Center in Montgomery. And I remember him by sharing his tragic story with my students when I teach about Ida B. Well's anti-lynching campaign in History of Journalism. Whenever the teaching opportunity presents itself, I talk about him. And the more I say his name, Michael Donald, the boogeyman goes away.

THE GENERAL AND THE CHITTERLINGS

Dr. George Hilliard

While reflecting on black history month this year, I thought about the first Black History Week celebration at a local military hospital in San Antonio, Texas, forty years ago. I was a senior resident, training in OB/GYN, on a very busy gynecologic oncology service when the hospital Commander's Executive Aide approached me, and stated that the General wanted to know if I would volunteer to organize and implement the First Black History Celebration for the hospital. Without hesitation, I informed the General's Aide that I was too busy to take on such a challenge. I most respectfully declined.

Approximately thirty minutes later, I received a page on the public address system to report to the hospital Commander's Office. When I arrived there, General's Aide informed me that the General would like to discuss with me the plans for the black history celebration. The aide very politely informed me that the request allowing me the opportunity to volunteer was really an appointment to carry out that activity. Essentially the request was an order.

After an awkward moment of casually knocking on the General's door and asking if he wanted to see me, he invited me in and I sat in one of the chairs in front of his desk. He gave me his thoughts on what the celebration should be about. He also gave me the name of five other African-American active-duty enlisted personnel, and suggested they might want to volunteer to be on my committee.

The committee, consisting of the other five volunteers and me, met and drew up a very comprehensive celebration. We wanted it to be our program and not necessarily what the General wanted, although he had made it clear that it was his program. We wanted the

141

celebration to include politics and social activism. After the meeting I called a local minister who was then a Black city councilman and mayor pro tem for the city of San Antonio, as well as an avid civil rights activist himself. I requested that he give the luncheon speech and he accepted the invitation.

With the speaker confirmed we then contacted the hospital food service and requested a menu to include soul food which could be available for those who attended the activity as well as hospital patient's if they so desired. The menu included what some would expect, including chitterlings, collard and turnip greens, yams, fried and baked chicken, cornbread, and all of the trimmings associated with such. We knew that food service would have a very difficult time providing the chitterlings.

Our hunch was correct, they informed us that the military base meat inspector had refused to allow for the delivery of such a large amount of chitterlings, since it could not guarantee the product's safety. The food service further informed us that the menu would be what the food service wanted to prepare. Furthermore, the administrative services did not approve our choice speaker for the event. We also wanted to print a program with speeches, writings and special sayings from some of the recent civil rights activists. The base's printing office informed us that our 16 to 20 page document would have to be reduced to just two sheets of paper for front and back printing due to a paper shortage. During that time there indeed was a paper shortage in the United States, and military supply had been importing paper from Canada.

At this point, the committee became quite frustrated. It seemed that we were not getting the support to carry out a meaningful celebration of black history week. During a private meeting of the committee, the chairman of the committee threatened to leak to the local black newspapers about this anticipated failed event. The General was not informed. However, less than 24 hours after the meeting of the committee, I was summoned to the General's office and informed by the General himself on the rules of press releases regarding activities of the hospital and the military. He stated that any release of military information could only be provided by the hospital's Information Services. How did he know? Only six committee members were aware of the plans.

The General then wanted to know if there were any problems associated with implementation of all of our plans. When informed that there were problems, he personally called the base's printing press and ordered them to prepare ten pages per program for as many as we needed. He called the base's food service and informed them that they would provide 300 pounds of chitterlings for the luncheon. When told that we wanted the city councilman as our speaker, he exclaimed, "great idea".

And so, the First Black History Week Celebration at the military hospital took place. We would prepare for 50-75 people at the black history luncheon celebration, but the General had other ideas and every seat in the 300-plus seat auditorium was taken. This was now the General's program. When the city councilman arrived, we took him to the auditorium. The General's aide arrived and informed me to call the General at once. When I reached the General by phone, he informed me that protocol had been broken and that the distinguished city councilman should have been presented to his office. I hurried back into the auditorium and asked the councilman to follow me. We exited the auditorium and hurried over to the General's office. The councilman walked in and stated to the General it was a pleasure to be there because the last time he had visited a high ranking official, he was required to arrive at the back door.

After a rousing lecture on black history and civil rights activities by the councilman, the General thanked our committee for a very successful inaugural Black History Celebration. The city councilman, our committee, the General and other members of the General's staff left the auditorium and made our way to the General's dining room where he demonstrated his approval and camaraderie by eating a plate full of chitterlings, to the delight of all present. His staff and other military personnel ate by example. The soul food dinner was available for all hospitalized patients who desired such. After lunch, the General again thanked the black history week committee and stated that his program could not fail because he had volunteered us for what he considered was a worthwhile activity in his hospital community. And in our own rather devious way, we introduced our leader to a new delicacy that he, undoubtedly, had never eaten before.

THE MATHEMATIC MAKE-UP OF SELF:
THE SELF WITHIN OR AN EXAMINATION
OF OUR BEING THROUGH NUMBERS

BROTHER FATTAH

Our community is one community, very similar to the human body. We have billions upon billions of cells, yet our body is one and functions as a unit. The concept of the "many" as an expression of "the one" is an ancient principle that carried the Original Man and Woman through many hardships.

The Black community in America is a string of disconnected organizations, mostly churches and other religious cloisters, with no constantly visible vehicle of unity. For the most part, the faith community of different denominations remains incestuous. Our European oppressors could never have enslaved us without attacking the natural tendency to see *ourselves* as one. Today, they maintain their brutal, psychological and pathological oppression by keeping us perpetually separated.

Self-hatred is the root of our problem. I can think of no other people who affectionately refer to themselves with negative terms like "nigga." We are so used to being oppressed, other nationalities within North America who are witnessing our poor conditioning feel free to use this term among themselves. The time is now for us all to begin to love ourselves and reclaim our dignity.

Dignity can only come when we love and activate the Divine gifts we were given. We must tap into the power of God within Self.

The Number 26:
The English Alphabet and the Power of "God" Within Self

What we yearn for is self-acceptance and knowledge. But what is the "Self?" I hope you will have a deeper understanding of that question after you finish reading this short essay. I will define "Self" according to its numeric component, or what we call its letters. A "letter" is not just a symbol representative of a single sound in the English language. To add an **"er" to** a verb is to make a noun. Without it, we have the verb **"let"** which means **to allow or permit,** according to most dictionaries. Implied is the idea that power to do so is present within the **"letter."**

There are "26 letters", or I say "26 powers" we can use to initiate our ability to communicate. Sound is the medium through which we bring into existence our creativity. According to the Book of Genesis, God's first word was **"...Let...."** The creator fashioned you and me in His and Her own image and we have the same ability to be divine producers. Psalm 18:21 says, **"death and life are in the power of the tongues: and they that love it shall eat the fruit thereof."** Do not underestimate the power of God within (your positive words) to shape your own reality.

The Many Numerical Definitions of the word "SELF"

Below is a simple chart defining the numeric value of each letter according to its position in the alphabet.

A	B	C	D	E	F	G	H	I
1	2	3	4	5	6	7	8	9

J	K	L	M	N	O	P	Q	R
10	11	12	13	14	15	16	17	18

S	T	U	V	W	X	Y	Z
19	20	21	22	23	24	25	26

The Full Numerical Value of "Self"

146   **My concept of the Full Numerical Value of "Self"** of any word is its comprehensive purpose as expressed in numbers. The resulting numbers for "Self" will unlock the value each individual person has to the community. Although "Self" is singular, we all have one and we even share the same "Self". Using the chart above, the numerical correspondence of "Self" is **"19+5+12+6"**. This equals a Full Numerical Value of **"42"**. These two digits speak volumes of the comprehensive purpose of "Self".

- Four (4) symbolizes *the inquisitive mind, asking questions, the capacity to search and discover all that is out here to find.* Think about it. There are four cardinal directions. We use these four directions to guide us in a time of confusion. It is the "inner compass" and it is manifest in our desire to *read, write, and define* our reality. We can also say it is *Literacy* and *Logic.*
- We have 4 physical elements (fire, air, earth, and water). As such, four (4) symbolizes *foundation* or *the state of preparedness,* which allows us to build on *stable ground.* Without these elements we would not have substantive matter. It also means understanding because just as a physical foundation of a house is the support for its infrastructure, so does understanding support our wise choices in life.
- Two (2) symbolizes *the state of dependence.* We know that "2" comes right after "1." This *dependence* is expressed fully in terms of the parent-child relationship, wherein children depend on the strength of their parents to provide nourishment and protection from the environment. We even see this principle in the concept of *faith in the divine, the community* and *brotherhood/sisterhood.*
- Two (2) also means *reflection.* Just as the moon (having no light of its own) *reflects* the light of the sun at nighttime, we have the mental capacity to *contemplate* or *reflect* on what we learn from our everyday experiences, family, and community.

As a unit **"42"** symbolizes the person actively engaged in the process of **"defining and discovering themselves through all sorts of literary pursuit"** in order (4) to make themselves an **"interdependent part of the community."** Discover your purpose and make your contribution to the uplifting of our people.

The Simplified Numerical Value of "Self."

The simplified Numerical Value of a word is its fundamental and basic purpose particular to the person, rather than the whole. Here, we unlock what the word's numerical value means for itself.

"**Self**" according to its Full Numerical Correspondence is "**19+5+12+6.**" It is simplified into "**1+5+3+6**", making all digits single. The Simplified Numerical Value is "**15**". One (1) symbolizes *leadership, focus*, and *determination*; it is our ability to make a decision in response to what must be done. We can also say it symbolizes the *gifts, skills* and *talents* we have to offer the world. Five (5) symbolizes *connection, relationship*, and the *ability to sense/observe*.

Together, "**15**" represents a person who knows what he has of value and is connecting him or herself to some avenue to express their value. We all desire to share what we have with the larger community; this is the nature we are created with. Join an organization that addresses your particular gift and express the beauty that God has put within you for our community.

The 4 Components of "Self"

S
"**1**"

One (1) symbolizes a healthy self-esteem. Being the first number, it symbolizes the initial component of self that allows every brother and sister the opportunity to mature into completeness. Having a healthy self-image or worth gives us the confidence to "step out on faith" toward any goal we set. We all have an "Inner Leader" who seeks to motivate us to do what must be done. The leading voice within just happens to sound like we do, except we do not hear it with ears; we hear it in our minds.

We can also say One (1) represents our gifts, skills, and talents we possess from the Divine. With your particular set of gifts and talents, you are recognized and praised for the wonderful things you do with them. Whether it is the ability to speak, run, calculate numbers, or even build fine structures, each one of us has something that makes us special and different. Properly cultivating your talents will give you the praise and admiration of your family and friends that naturally feeds a growing self-image.

The negative stereotypes our people are indoctrinated with are designed to damage our self-image. Whether it is our popular language (like "Nigga"), unnatural hair or hair color, or even images of unproductive or childish behavior ("sagging pants"), we are constantly being bombarded with unhealthy reflections of our own self-image.

E

"5"

Making Sense of Yourself and What You Have

Five (5) is a numerical symbol for the faculty of observation. We observe through the sensory data received by our "5" senses. It represents all that can be known or perceived. As such, it is Knowledge; and like food, it sustains and satisfies our natural desire to grow intellectually as well as socially.

Five (5) also symbolizes the realization of what activities correspond to the gifts, skills, and talents we possess. It implies experimenting without talents to fully know who we are. From this deep sense of self, we pass from knowledge into intuition, which guides us into the path of what we desire without really knowing where we are going. Experimentation is the science of learning how to make "sense" of any subject. In this case the subject under study is you.

Just as our 5 senses connect us to the physical universe, five (5) also symbolizes our desire to form healthy relationships with others. Being among a true brother or sisterhood is food for the soul, keeping us grounded in times of confusion and doubt. Our families and friends offer guidance and satisfy the natural feeling of belonging. IN this sense, it can represent being a teacher or being taught, being consulted or being a counselor. We all must learn how to be friends to one another.

The word **"Five"** has a numerical correspondence *of* **"6+9+22+5"** and equals **"42,"** the same numerical value of **"Self."** This is a sign that the meanings we gather from the number Five (5) are the most important numeric components of Self. The willingness to translate our abilities into concrete action by coming to know ourselves is vital. The same is equally true of forming healthy relationships among one another.

149

L
"3"

The Warrior Within

Three (3) symbolizes the ability to handle difficult or stressful situations. There is an old saying, "Two is company and three is a crowd." Another is,"If at first you don't succeed, try and try again." The beauty in both is they symbolically teach that difficulty is associated with the number Three (3). Overcoming the stress of an external or internal threat is necessary to win the battles we face in life and is another vital component of "Self."

We can also say Three (3) represents harnessing control of the mind, body, and soul. Notice the letter "L" is like unto a leg that holds any structure up. Having the courage to fight, protect, and to stand up or defend communities and ourselves makes one ready at all times to defeat negative aspects that exist within us. As children we were encouraged by our elders to stand up for ourselves when we were getting picked on. The same still holds true as we mature.

Every one of us must learn to be militant. Pain and suffering is natural and inescapable—there is no way around it. Only when we are ready to pass the threshold of pain will freedom to express ourselves grow. Out of this freedom comes an artistic sense that is the basis for the inner beauty we have within. Living without fear is like the sun, it shines regardless to whom or what. We must be the same.

A positive characteristic of fear or the presence of stress is its ability to make us aware of the necessities of life. Self-preservation is the first law of nature and—as the old saying goes, "necessity is the birth invention." Being pushed into a corner gives us the opportunity to show our creative and artistic capacities.

150

F
"6"

The Power of Attraction

The creator made us all Beautiful and He placed a demand and a command to work to express our Divine Beauty by applying our talents to attract all the necessities and righteous desires we seek from this Universe. Six (6) is a "1" that is pregnant with life, or is like a "1" whose belly (necessities and desires) is fully expressed. Everyone has the potential to put his or her ideas into material form. From creative productivity comes an internal sense of psychological security from leaving something of us on the earth, bearing witness to our presence.

Conclusion

My dear brothers and sisters, life is too valuable to go through it unaware of who you are. Make a list of the talents and skills you have and make a courageous attempt to find your place in the world. Regardless of your age, the Creator made you intelligent enough to make sense of what you have. All you need is the courage to be who and what God created you to be.

MAYA ANGELOU
"HER VOICE RINGS ETERNALLY!"

AARONETTA PIERCE

For decades now the words and wisdom of Maya Angelou have been changing lives. Few mortals have so openly and repeatedly unveiled their deepest truths and honest life stories as have the many poetic and autobiographical volumes written by Maya Angelou. From her early bestseller, *I Know Why the Caged Bird Sings*, her writings have bridged racial, social, language and cultural divides. Her universality as a writer has convinced us of her eternal message that as people and especially as women, "we are more alike than we are not alike." Her poems connected our ordinary lives to extraordinary possibilities. Aspirations were aroused through her luscious description of women in the poem, "Phenomenal Woman," and hopes became promises in her poem, "Still I Rise." Her incredibly crafted phrases have enriched our lives, captured our hearts, raised our self-esteem, uplifted our hope and faith, and made us friends of poetry. The audiences that have filled her performances over seasons of appearances have been moved by her artistry, her dignity, and her veracity. Often Black women have read her poems and identified themselves as her primary inspiration, yet time has revealed that there was a profound commonality in the message that allowed women and men of many races, countries and cultures to identify with her writings. Single-handedly, she has advanced cross-cultural communications as profoundly as did the Civil Rights Movement.

Rarely does one get to witness the enormous transformations that their ideas inspire in others as consistently as did Maya Angelou. Thousands of women and men sought her out at every appearance or book signing to let her know that she had changed their lives.

Changing lives requires divine intervention or certainly divine inspiration and that was her gift. Writing was also "her gift" and it is one of the reasons we revere her. She had the special ability to weave words into phrases, which became sentences that told stories. These stories created clear mental pictures to which we could so comfortably relate. Her prose and poetry taught us to love ourselves—our shapes, our mates, our sisters and our journeys.

As great as is the literary legacy of Maya Angelou, almost as memorable is the impact of her significantly compelling oratorical skills. Blessed with a voice as uniquely identifiable as her finger-prints, she used her voice to ignite within us a love and respect for, not only her poetry, but also for the poetry of other great poets like Paul Laurence Dunbar and Langston Hughes. By reading their poems to us, she made certain that we inhaled the wisdom, sanctity, and purposefulness of the messages embedded in their artistry. She reminded us that art reflects life, and that these sagely written words actually speak to our cultural experience, and mirrors the historical conditions that we have both endured and celebrated. Much like the melodies and lyrics of "The Blues," artists use their chosen art disciplines to make known their inner most thoughts and feelings.

Writing about Maya while sitting at home in San Antonio is so comforting to me and so appropriate as well. This is a city for which Maya had a sincere fondness and where we shared many happy times. Her love for San Antonio grew gradually as she made trips here to visit our family, to perform here, or during those times when she was passing through in her "designer motor coach" on IH 10 as she headed west for speaking engagements or to visit her beloved son, Guy Johnson, in California. Her arrival in San Antonio always took priority with my husband Joe, and our sons, Joe and Michael, and me. We knew how blessed we were to have her in our lives. Our family joined her on many exploratory adventures in our unique city and she accompanied us to art and civic events. Though the Spurs' games were a huge part of our family's activities, she was never in town at the right time to see a home game. Many times her visits included small and large dinner parties and always there were

stimulating conversations and fascinating exchanges. Very simply,
her visits gifted us with laughter, joy, love and wisdom. Maya's
attachment to San Antonio crystallized after she spent a summer
living in an apartment on the banks of the San Antonio River. It
all came about after the city was recommended to her by another
famous writer, Alex Haley.

In 1988, Maya was invited to be the guest of honor at a weekend retreat at Alex Haley's bucolic farm in East Tennessee. This was
no ordinary invitation nor was this an ordinary farm. When Alex
designed the farm, he envisioned hosting numerous long, slow, private and exclusive weekend round-tables centered on a special honoree. Maya was the first such honoree selected to hold court at Alex's
unique retreat. He asked her to select twenty people with whom she
would like to spend the weekend. She invited Joe and me to join
what proved to be a wondrous group of friends, writers, painters,
historians, educators and musicians; and we will forever be in a state
of gratitude for this precious experience.

The farm was tucked away off the main interstate, down an in-
tersecting highway, and along another winding road. Finally, you arrived at the guard-staffed entrance gate. Once inside the complex,
the principal and seemingly the oldest dwelling greeted you. It was
a stately, white wood-framed farm house that was conservatively
adorned with gingerbread-architectural embellishments. A spacious
man-made pond, complete with ducks and a variety of fishes, was the
grand centerpiece easily visible from the front porch swing and the
second floor veranda. The pond was also easily accessible by a few
canoes resting on the banks. If a stationary vantage was preferred,
guests could walk to the center of the pond over a sturdy, white-
washed wooden bridge which ended in a circular pagoda, with a few
well-placed, padded, wooden recliners and taller perches for fishing.

Surrounding the pond were four or five elegantly-rustic cottag-
es which afforded one all of the comforts of a tastefully appointed
apartment. Each cottage had a name and Joe and I were assigned to
the Duck House, where our telephone was a perfect replica of a duck
decoy. Not far from the main house, but politely hidden by a slight

155

incline and a grove of trees, was a tack house and a tool and equipment shed. While touring the grounds, I discovered that these ancillary structures were well stocked to support the productive use of several acres for raising pumpkins and other small crops. I nervously crossed the swinging bridge that led to one of the fields abloom with pumpkins and plucked a few of the orange trophies to share with my parents back in Nashville.

Some of the most supreme conversations I have ever heard occurred during this gathering. It was easy for me to be impressed amid such vibrant mental conversing. It was inspiring to witness the concern for others, the commitment to grow, and the breadth of knowledge that these participants shared. It was also the first time that Joe and I met Maya's amazing mother. Vivian Baxter, Lady Baxter as she was named by her daughter, was everything and more as Maya revealed her in, *Mom and Me and Mom*, the last autobiography published during Maya's lifetime. It was clear, as we watched them together, that Maya adored her and that her mother adored and admired her even more. There were times they seemed to hang on each other's words as genuine friends—the six foot daughter and the five foot mom. Lady Baxter was always stylishly dressed and navigated easily in three inch heels.

One night at dinner, Lerone Bennett, Jr., Ebony Editor, asked everyone to tell how they first met Maya. At our turn, we shared that our story began in San Antonio in 1983. The city was mounting its first major music festival under the leadership of the renowned art patron, Gilbert Denman, and under the direction of internationally respected, artistic director Parvan Barkardjiev. Great music, opera, and dance were programmed at every San Antonio venue, park, mission and a few churches. The Carver Cultural Center, under the leadership of longtime director Jo Long, was presenting the poet and author Maya Angelou; her first appearance in the Alamo City.

The highlights of the society scene were the great parties that were planned in honor of each visiting celebrity artist. The night before Maya was to perform her hosts had to cancel her party, honoring her visit to our city. I never knew whom the hosts were or why they had to cancel. What mattered was that Jo Long called to ask if Joe and I would host the party for Maya. It was with great joy, humility, jubilation and giddiness that we said, "Oh yes, you bet we will!"

Maya was the star attraction from the moment she entered the house and held court at what would become her perch, (other than the head of the dining room table) whenever we entertained her at our home. She charmed the guests and filled the house with grace. Ralph Waldo Emerson wrote that, "The ornaments of a home are the friends who frequent it." Rarely ever had our home been better adorned. As the evening passed, while I was busy with hosting duties, Joe took Maya on a tour of our beginning art collection and his growing collection of books by African Americans. He told her the story that one summer when I took our sons to Nashville to visit my parents, he had traveled to Houston to visit with his parents' friend John Biggers, a great Texas artist, who taught at Texas Southern University. Without planning, Joe purchased our first four artworks by John. That sealed the deal. It turned out that Maya loved the work of John Biggers and owned one of his greatest works, "Kumasi Market." We exchanged contact information, began corresponding and the rest of that story is history.

It was during the retreat at Alex's that he told Maya about his fascination with San Antonio and that for several months he had cherished his own private retreat, living and writing in the city. He had chosen an apartment in the Casino Building right downtown where he enjoyed the buffets at Las Canarias, meeting curious tourists and residents and learning more about San Antonio. He suggested the she might find it a great place to write also. Maya loved the idea. She already liked the city as a result of her many visits, had local friends (as she would call it, family-friends), relished seeing more shows at the Carver Cultural Center, envisioned enjoying plates and plates of Mexican food and practicing her fluency in Spanish.

After she gave us some parameters, Joe and I returned to San Antonio and selected a condo on the river and then had it furnished. Once Maya arrived, we spent a day shopping for everything from towels and sheets to colanders and champagne glasses. In addition

157

to spending time on her number one priority which was to write, there were two additional priorities during her stay. One of those priorities was cooking and the other was to entertain in-town and out-of-town guests. Maya was definitely serious about cooking. Not only was her food unimaginably delicious, but she could masterfully mix, bake, boil, and fry foods that, when presented to guests, were picture perfect. She could manage all of this while still conversing and entertaining the entire time. She made cooking an art form. You must read, *Hallelujah! The Welcome Table* to truly comprehend her love of cooking and her mastery of the techniques.

Joe and I became fellow-tourists during Maya's summer here. Even familiar sites were more exciting when experienced with her. She especially loved going to the Mexican Market where her favorite restaurant was La Margarita. She would sing song after song in Spanish with the Mariachis. I was lost after "La Bamba" and "La Cucaracha," but she greatly expanded our repertoire. Everyone present on these occasions knew that they were witnessing something very special and would come closer to enjoy the frivolity. Maya knew how to have a good time and she knew that it was important to have a good time as often as possible—daily if you were lucky.

During that summer, we were fortunate to see one of the earliest plays by local playwright Sterling Houston. Maya and Sterling became friends and a few years later, she made a special visit here to see his play, "High Yello' Rose." It was an added treat that her friend, Cleo Parker Robinson, had a dance company that was performing at the Carver. Maya gave a party for Cleo and the dancers and prepared all of the food herself. It was a full meal. As a former dancer, she knew they would be properly hungry. And they were.

Maya enjoyed visiting antique shops everywhere she traveled, and San Antonio was no exception. One day while visiting her, I was admiring a shelf of gorgeous antique wine glasses she had purchased at a local shop. She confessed that she had not planned to purchase so many of them but when she inquired as to their cost, the storekeeper responded that, "actually these glasses are quite expensive." Without requesting the exact cost again Maya simply told her, "Fine,

I will take all of them." As is still too often the case, the storekeeper failed to see the wonderful, powerful, dynamite six foot tall woman standing in her shop. She only saw what her history had taught her to see.

Visiting Maya's apartment in San Antonio was often a chance to view works-in-progress. I remember on one occasion seeing a body of photographs of famous African American women strewn about the dining room table, as Maya sat before them studying one after the other. I would later learn that these iconic images were created by the renowned photographer Brian Lanker, and would appear in one of the best-selling photography books ever published. The book is a history lesson featuring African American women who changed America and is entitled, *I Dream A World*. It bears the name of the 1929 powerful, though short, poem by Langston Hughes in which he shares his vision for a more perfect world. Maya was selected to write the foreword for this landmark book, and the impact of *I Dream A World* is legendary.

At the end of Maya's stay in San Antonio, we co-hosted a party at our home so she could say good-bye to her new friends and could meet some of our friends. Maya made only one menu request; she wanted barbecue from Bob's on Roland Street. A few days before the party, she told us that she had invited Oprah and Stedman. Our guests knew that they were coming to a party honoring Maya Angelou and that was exciting news. We made no additional revelations. Maya and Oprah arrived early (Stedman flew in later) and allowed the family a precious time to get acquainted with the super star. Our sons had met Ms. Winfrey earlier that day while they helped "Auntie Maya" and her packers close her apartment. They also had gotten to meet two of Maya's other "nephews"—one a young Ghanaian college student and the other, her friend James Foreman's son, Shaka, who had come to drive Maya's Mustang back to North Carolina (she had enjoyed the freedom of driving her own car around San Antonio). To the great credit of our friends, as they arrived and met all of our honored guests, they remained as cool and as cordial as was their nature. There were many stories shared during the evening, lots of singing,

159

Mariachi music and finally, dancing. We took a great picture of our son, Michael, dancing with Oprah and he could hardly wait for the photographs to be printed, so he could share them at Churchill High School as soon as the fall semester began. What beautiful memories we have from that night.

Whenever I watched Maya interacting with friends and acquaintances, it reinforced two of her many life lessons passed on to me and others. First, as she often encouraged in us, "You have to be where you are at the time." Sometimes she said it differently, "You have to be in the moment." Her plate was always so full, yet she seemed to master the art of concentrating on what was immediate. She encouraged us to be totally present and to relish the activity in which we found ourselves. From my perspective, she offered quality time to her friends. She made us feel that her time with us was meaningful and that showing someone that you valued them could be as simple as listening to them. It reminded me of times when I have talked with someone, while they looked over their shoulder to find that more desirable person with whom to visit. If truth be told, I have also been guilty of this same inhumane transgression.

Lest I misrepresent the truth, Maya's respect for others was never a blanket invitation to ramble on and on. She can best be described by the following phrase; "She did not suffer fools lightly." While she enjoyed learning about and celebrating the accomplishments of others, she was quick to yawn when someone's self-praise turned from informational to conceit. She was unequivocally intolerant of conversationalists who made disparaging racial, religious or gender remarks in her presence. It did not matter to her how important the person may be, or thought they were, she would first verbally announce her outrage and if there was not appropriate contrition, she would ask that person to leave, or if more appropriate, she would leave.

Her loyalty to her friends knew few bounds. Even though the demands on her time every single day were gargantuan, she supported her friends whenever humanly possible. Several times, she made video cameos in support of my community projects, and in 1988, while Maya was living here she was of immense assistance to me on a major undertaking. I was completing an assignment from then Mayor Henry Cisneros. He had appointed me as chairperson of a Blue Ribbon Committee, charged with making recommendations to improve the city government's role in supporting the arts. After nine months of working with a stellar committee of city-wide art and business leaders; holding meetings with all the art disciplines and organizations in the city; holding hearings in every council members district, we published our findings. Our major recommendation required a new Department of the Arts be created within the city government. Since this would require a line-item expenditure in the city budget, a formal process had to be followed. Before a special session of the San Antonio City Council, with lots of artists, art patrons and art organizations in attendance, we made our case. Additionally, we had a secret "weapon" in the room. Maya Angelou had come with Joe and me to provide moral support and to speak, if necessary. At the appropriate time, Mayor Cisneros invited Maya to the dais, introduced her ceremoniously and invited her to recite her iconic poem, "Still I Rise". She recited eloquently and with the gratitude of everyone, the Department of Arts was born.

In 1994, she also recited her poem, "Alone" at the wedding of our son Joseph to Kama Lynn Bethel at the Rutgers Chapel in New Brunswick, New Jersey, and fifteen years later, she added them to her Winston-Salem Thanksgiving Dinner when the two moved to Charlotte, North Carolina. In 2005 when I chaired the Texas Medal of Arts Awards in Austin, Texas, she taped a video for the show, proclaiming her advocacy for the arts and her plea for continuous and increased financial appropriation for the arts from the state legislature.

Maya probably showed her greatest friendship and loyalty in 2007 when during the Democratic Presidential Primary she supported her friend Hillary Clinton, while the majority of the African American voting public supported Barack Obama. The Clinton's had a long association with Maya. Who could forget that President Clinton chose his fellow Arkansan to write and recite a poem at his inauguration in 1993, and that she electrified the nation and raised her profile even higher when she gave voice to, "On the Pulse of Morning." My younger son, Michael, was living in Dallas at the time and I remember him calling me in dismay. He had heard a radio ad made by "Auntie Maya" (pronounced aun-tie, the name that her young mentees called her) supporting Hillary Clinton. I suggested that he call and visit with Auntie Maya and ask her about the ad. Soon after, we both had the chance to talk with her when we traveled to Houston to hear her speak. After her mesmerizing presentation during dinner, the conversation turned to the presidential contest. Mind you, Maya had the strongest faith in her opinions than anyone I have ever known, and I never heard her equivocate about them. Therefore, I was prepared to be educated and enlightened regarding her position on the subject. And thus, she shared with us simply and briefly that, "Arkansas was a mean, mean place for Black people when I grew up there," she said. "The Clinton's made major changes in the face of Arkansas and I will always be grateful to them for those changes."

Since Maya had so many friends, the amount of time she devoted to advancing our personal and public causes cannot be underestimated. When she hosted large parties, she encouraged everyone to mix. She essentially created a level playing field where her friends could meet like-minded souls, be mentored, participate in spirited conversations or debates and discover ways to help each other as she already helped us. Through her, our family made life-long friends.

As for Maya's circle, her greatest loves were in her immediate family, especially those who survived her; her son, Guy, her daughter-in-law, Stephanie, her grandsons, Colin and Elliott and her great grandson and granddaughter, Brandon and Caylin. Her traveling companion, Ms. Stuckey, became like a daughter to her, and of course everyone knows her beloved famous "daughter" Oprah Winfrey. Her small office and home staff, including Mrs. Clay plus her bus driver and extra hand Mr. Bryant, were her extended family. (Maya gave up flying in the early 1990's. Thereafter, she traveled on a designer bus with most of the comforts of home, from a big screen television to a pretty well-stocked kitchen and a circular king-sized bed.) They spent so much time together just traveling, laughing, eating, and living. Each of them was an essential part of her journey.

162

Maya also had three best lifelong friends. One of them survived her, an art historian, Dr. Mary Jane Hewitt, who lives in Los Angeles. The others were a university English professor to whom she dedicated many of her books, Dr. Dolly McPherson, and a British author, Jessica Mitford. Watching her, I learned why she said, "Only equals can be friends." They don't have to measure up in riches, in intellect, or beauty; but they must bring the same commitment to the friendship.

Bondage, discrimination, disrespect and invisibility describe the legacy that has burdened so many African Americans. Yet, Maya was that rare spirit that defied obscurity. She seemed innately to possess a spirit of liberation. She embraced her own values, demanded respect and she was a beacon of wisdom. At a time when the voices of many African Americans were denied, squashed and compromised, she seemed secure in her right to define and explore her principles in her own journey. She certainly set the bar high for us to follow.

Maya's passing leaves a huge vacuum in the world. Other monumental forces will come along, but there will never be another Maya Angelou, as there will never be another like her good friend, Dr. Martin Luther King, Jr. But you know, there does not have to be another because we will always have them. They will be with us as long as we read their books, consider their suggestions and reach for their goals. Maya left us poems that are indelible. She left us immortal poems like "A Brave and Startling Truth", the tribute she wrote for the Fiftieth Anniversary of the United Nations that is like a road map to peace and understanding. She left us her sage ideas in phrases like, "One isn't necessarily born with courage, but one is born with potential. Without courage, we cannot practice any other virtue with consistency. We cannot be kind, true, merciful, generous, or honest," and, "Nothing can dim the light that shines from within," and, "If you have only one smile in you, give it to the people you love," and my favorite, "When someone shows you who they are, believe them the first time."

Maya left us so many lessons, if only we make the connections. She challenged us to take responsibility for someone other than ourselves. She also held us accountable and that I will sincerely miss. We

163

all sat up a little straighter when we were in her presence, minded our "p's and q's" and thought before speaking because we knew she would call us on our manners. She was in no way a disciplinarian she was simply a presence like no other. Maya left us a grand body of work to study—for vision, inspiration and consolation. She wanted us to live with some grace and allow it to temper our relationships, our negotiations and our differences. She wanted us to develop a belief in ourselves so that we could find the truth and let it be our guide. She wanted us to speak truth to power, so that we could look ourselves in the mirror and feel blessed with whom God had created. When we engage with the resources she has bequeathed, we may become just a little better and we may just make this a little better world. To Maya! Joy!

ACHIEVING VICTORY THROUGH COURAGE, FAITH, AND DETERMINATION

NEVIL SHEDD

I was one of those five young Black men who walked on the basketball court at the University of Maryland Sports Arena on March 9, 1966, and confronted a hostile America that did not believe we could defeat the almighty, all-white University of Kentucky basketball team. We were playing for the national championship, and it was predicted that we would lose. After all, the great and legendary coach Adolph Rupp had made it known that five "coons" could not beat five fine white boys. That one game had more meaning outside the basketball arena than any other in the history of the sport. Its importance was a manifestation of what was happening in this country; it was linked to the civil rights struggle underway particularly in the southern part of the country. Black Americans, under the able leadership of Dr. Martin Luther King Jr. were demanding their most deserved and proper station in this country, and white Americans were determined to deny them their rightful place, based on some irrational notion of superiority. It had been that way for decades, and their argument was that it should not change.

As we went through our warm-ups, each of us had reasons why we could not lose. My reason was deeply etched into my memory bank and carried me back to my childhood days in New York City. For a moment I took my eyes off the court and looked up into the stands at my parents and knew they were my reason. Through their suffering I learned to respect courage. Both parents made extreme sacrifices that made it possible for me to be on that court, before a national audience, with the opportunity to make history, and in many ways become a legend in my time. How could I not win? What my teammates and I had to do was vindicate the hundreds of years of suffering juxtaposed against the same number of years filled with hope. We were their hope, and it was mandatory that we deliver a physical and measurable victory. Our victory would make it possible for millions of our people throughout this country to know they could win and that they were somebody.

Sitting on the bench, listening to the screaming fans and the bands playing from both schools, my mind flashed back on a time and incident that tore me apart when it happened and haunted me right until the moment before the tip-off. Once that ball went into the air and the game began, I knew I would erase the pain of that memory forever. With the beginning of that game, the past and the present merged and dictated a major change was coming for the future of Black people in this country. But it all goes back to that afternoon when I went down to Pennsylvania Train Station in New York to meet Dad who worked as a Pullman porter on the railroad.

As a Pullman porter, Dad would spend a lot of time traveling from New York to Chicago and from New York to Miami. When he made runs to Miami he would always bring back a lot of fruit, and I would meet him at the train station to help carry it home on the subway. When the trains would arrive, Dad, along with a number of Black red caps, would assist the white people off the train. First, however, they had to unload the luggage and move it far enough from the train so the steam that periodically exploded from the train wouldn't hit it. I would often help move the luggage away from the train while Dad helped the white folks off. It irked me to hear how they talked to him, calling him boy and all he could do was say "yes ma'am," or "yes sir." I finally couldn't take it anymore when one white man literally cussed him out for something that was not his fault. And that was the incident I momentarily thought about as I sat waiting for the game to start.

I stood there and watched Dad move the man's luggage away from the train; then I returned to the exit to help more people off. But for some reason one of the white men walked over to his luggage, picked it up and put it right next to the train. Within minutes, a blast of steam totally inundated his luggage with moisture. With a shocked and angry look on his face, the man ran over to Dad and began to blame him for the damage. He called him "nigger," "boy," and was all in his face. Instead of smacking that fool right in his mouth, Dad pulled out a towel, strolled over to the luggage and began to wipe it down. That wasn't good enough for the man. He followed Dad over to the luggage and continued to call him out of his name. Just about that time I wanted to go down there and slug the man in his mouth. But I didn't; instead I got angry with my father. I just couldn't understand how the man I most admired in life, the person who was my role model, could allow those men to talk to him that way. I respected him as a man, but he was testing that respect when he took that kind of abuse.

On the train ride home, I felt ashamed of my father. I turned my head and stared out the window because I didn't want to talk to this man who would allow that white man to talk to him in that manner. Finally, when we were all sitting in the living room, I exploded.

"Dad, how could you let that man talk to you like that?" I shouted with tears streaming down my face. "I love you Dad, and I don't want nobody talking to you like that. You're a man just like him and you shouldn't have to listen to that."

He let me finish blowing off steam, then got up, grabbed me by both my skinny arms, and pinned me against the wall. I knew he was angry by the manner in which he grabbed me, but I also knew he was hurt by the tears that streamed from his eyes.

"Boy, you think I like that man talking to me that way?" he asked, but did not wait for an answer. It was his turn to talk and mine to be quiet. "I'm your daddy and I got to take care of you. I got to put food in your stomach, clothes on your back, and a roof over your head." He paused because his emotions had him all choked up. He clenched his teeth and continued. "And I'll take that abuse as long as I know that my payoff is you'll have opportunities I never had and you'll take advantage of them so you'll never have to take that kind of abuse from no man, ever!"

Fast forward ten years later as the horn blew for the start of the game. I was in a position not to have to take that kind of abuse. The

167

night before the game, Coach Haskins came into our rooms and repeated what Coach Rupp had privately told some friends.

"Ain't no way five coons can beat five white boys."

Before he could finish those words, I thought about that time Dad held me and with tears said his effort should pay off and I shouldn't have to take that abuse he took. But that racist coach had done just that. The difference was that we could retaliate by winning. That would be more rewarding than punching him in his racist mouth. Mama drilled in our heads all the time that being successful was going after something you want to be and pursuing it until you got it. Right at that moment, I wanted to be a part of an all-Black basketball team that in forty-eight minutes would be crowned the national champions. Four other young Black men felt the same way. Kentucky really never had a chance. We could have beaten them with determination alone, and essentially not having to be the better basketball players, which we were, to the man.

Proper preparation was the primary reason we were destined for victory. The five of us had been preparing for that day for years. Even though we didn't know each other until we arrived at Texas Western University, we had an inevitable connection. We were destined to carry the weight of the entire Civil Rights Movement on the night of March 9, 1966. We were carrying the weight for Medgar Evers, gunned down outside his home on June 10, 1963; we carried the weight for four little beautiful Black girls killed in the Sixteenth Street Baptist Church bombing on Sept. 9, 1963, in Birmingham, Ala.; we carried the weight for three civil rights workers murdered in Philadelphia, Miss., in 1964; we carried the weight for Malcolm X, gunned down in a Harlem theater in February 1965; and we carried the weight for young heroes at the time like John Lewis, now a Congressman from Atlanta, Ga., James Clyburn, a current Congressman from South Carolina, Stokely Carmichael, who called on Blacks to organize because through unity came power; and we carried the weight for Robert Moses, who was beaten many times traveling throughout the South registering Blacks to vote. That night we carried the weight of over thirty million Blacks who had finally

168

said enough is enough and were ready to lay their life on the line for freedom. They needed our victory as a physical manifestation of their struggle.

Through some distorted view of themselves, white people believed they were invincible when dealing with Black people, even though they had been proven wrong time after time. Jack Johnson proved them wrong when he beat their "Great White Hope" in 1915. Jesse Owens proved them wrong when he beat the best German racers in the 1936 Olympics. Thank God that we, as Black people, don't have to prove our value by diminishing that of another race. Our basketball team felt that way from the beginning of the game until the end. When Coach Haskins told David Latin, our overpowering and dominating forward, to slam-dunk the first opportunity he had and he did it, then the result was inevitable. But in all honesty, we dominated another basketball team and not a white basketball team. We saw opponents and not color. Once that whistle blew and the game started, the opposition could have been blue people from Mars. They were in for a whipping, because we had already made up our mind that the championship belonged to us.

I can practically replay that entire game in my mind. It was such an honor to be able to participate, and there is no way I will ever forget how we took on the powers that be and won. But the moment I remember most is when I walked to the free-throw line with the game tied and a chance for me to put us ahead. When the referee handed me the ball and I knew the entire Black community was watching. My biggest thrill was knowing that the man who had taken abuse for me was also sitting right there in the stands watching. It would have been too much out of character for a player at that moment to turn, look into the stands and shout, "Dad, this is for you." Instead, I bounced the ball a couple of times then sank the foul shot. After that we never did give up the lead. David dominated under that basket and Bobby Joe Hill dominated the rest of the court. He was so good that even a racist like Adolph Rupp had to acknowledge his superior skills that night.

When the final horn blew and the score read Texas Western 72 and Kentucky 65, our fans let out a loud cheer, and the celebration

169

was on. I pointed to Dad and Mama. He knew exactly what I meant. He immediately stretched his arms in my direction. His years of abuse at the hands of men who believed the color of their skin gave them the right to do whatever they wanted were now vindicated with that score. All those years he had shown the courage to endure, and the reward was worth the pain and tears, many, I knew, he shed alone.

Both Grandma and Mama had prayed that the world would change and God would deliver Black people from the abuse and suffering they endured all those years. Grandma was no longer around to share that delivery from God, but Mama swore up and down that He had been right out there with us and because He was, there was no way we could lose. Because of the mornings that she would go without eating so that my brother, Dad, and I could, she is due the privilege to believe God was on our side. However one wants to view that victory is fine, but what is not left to interpretation is that Black America shared a night of rejoicing that would carry on for years and culminate with election day in November 2008, when a Black man was elected President of the United States of America.

I can assure you that five young Black men were honoring their race, their culture, and their people's future with the victory that still resonates today within the Black communities throughout this country.

REVEREND FRED SHUTTLESWORTH:
LION OF THE CIVIL RIGHTS MOVEMENT

SEPHIRA BAILEY SHUTTLESWORTH

Reverend Martin Luther King Jr. called him "one of the most courageous freedom fighters in the South." In the 1961 documentary, *Who Speaks for Birmingham*? Howard K. Smith, a young CBS reporter called him "the man most feared by the southern racists." No annals of American history are complete without encompassing the contributions of this great man. He is, without doubt, an authentic American hero. His name is Rev. Fred Shuttlesworth.

He was born in Montgomery County, Ala. on March 18, 1922, to an unwed mother and the local watchmaker. His maternal grandfather moved the family to Birmingham when Fred was three years old. In Birmingham, his mother, Alberta, met and married William Nathan Shuttlesworth who adopted young Fred. An inquisitive, gifted learner throughout his schooling, popularity surrounded him like a spotlight. In his community, at church, and in school, he regularly heard, "Boy, I see something in you." He heard it so often that soon he thought he saw something in himself.

As a teenager, Fred showed extraordinary learning ability. He once read a four-page oration three times and committed it to memory. His fellow students and the teacher were awe-struck when he stood and recited it verbatim. Fred went on to graduate valedictorian of his high school class. By then, he had narrowed his choices of professions to doctor or minister. He has often said to me that while growing up, he knew more about what he *could not* be rather than what he *could* be. He married at age 19 and became a father at 21.

In his early twenties, Fred began to feel a call toward the ministry, studied the scriptures daily in preparation, and became a minister in 1943. However, for years something had been nagging him. He could not help wondering why, if God made us all in his image, Black people (then called Negroes) had no rights that white people had to respect. His wondering would later lead him to openly challenge the unjust laws of segregation that ruled the South.

Birmingham, Ala was considered the most segregated city in the South, where segregation was not only accepted as a way of life, it was the *law*. Rev. Shuttlesworth began challenging those laws in the 1950's, first by asking that the city hire Black police officers to patrol the Black communities. His open challenge of the system quickly made him a target for the Klan and other hate-driven groups. History should be careful to record the dramatic exchange that unfolded from 1958 to 1963 between Fred and his nemesis, Eugene "Bull" Conner, Birmingham's notorious Commissioner of Public Safety. That public challenge eventually led to marches in the streets, boycotts, fire hoses and police dog attacks, bombings, arrests, mob beatings, murders, but finally the Civil Rights Act of 1964.

Shuttlesworth was the target of three bombings, including an explosion of his home in 1956 from which he miraculously emerged unscathed. He also survived a mob beating in 1957 as he attempted to enroll two of his children at an all-white high school. He was arrested more than 35 times and sued for millions because of his valiant attempts to lift his people.

Perhaps the most extraordinary thing about this man's work is the spirit in which he insisted on carrying out his tasks. In a document called the *Birmingham Manifesto*, co-authored by Shuttlesworth and Rev. Wyatt Tee Walker, they vowed, "not one hair on the head of one white person will be harmed in our struggle to be free." Although Shuttlesworth was a fiery preacher, who often times irritated both his friends and his foes with his sharp mind and his sharper tongue, he became respected as the courageous, grass-roots leader of the Birmingham movement.

During the spring of 1961, Rev. Walker, then the Executive Director of the Southern Christian Leadership Conference (SCLC), alerted Rev. Shuttlesworth that the Congress on Racial Equality (CORE) had organized the Freedom Riders to challenge the segregation laws on buses and in waiting rooms throughout the Deep South. Walker arranged for Shuttlesworth to be the primary contact for the Riders as they traveled throughout Alabama.

On Sunday, May 14, the drama began to unfold when Shuttlesworth received a phone call from James Peck apprising him of their arrival in Birmingham. The bus never made it to the city. Upon arrival in Anniston, Ala., some 65 miles away, the group was greeted by an angry mob that taunted and threatened the riders and slashed the tires on the bus. Eventually, the driver exited the bus, locked the door, and went for help. With the riders locked on the bus, the crowd began to break windows and tossed an incendiary device through one. The fire caused an explosion which blew the back section of the bus open allowing the riders to escape the fiery furnace right into the grips of the angry crowd.

When Shuttlesworth heard of the violence in Anniston, he organized a nine-car caravan to journey to the aid and rescue of the Freedom Riders. He housed the riders at his church, Bethel Baptist, and in the parsonage. He saw to it that the injured, including James Peck, received treatment. Over the coming days, he engaged in a series of negotiations with local and national authorities, including then Attorney General Robert Kennedy, asking the government officials to provide protection for the riders.

Rev. Shuttlesworth was arrested five times for his participation with the Freedom Riders. In his book, *A Fire You Can't Put Out*, Andrew Manis credits Rev. Shuittlesworth with playing a significant role in the Freedom Rides, acknowledging that the riders spent more time on his turf (Alabama) than any other place along the route. Manis wrote that Fred's role of "encouraging, housing, providing medical care for, and ferrying the riders to the bus station was indispensable."

Those were the days when Black men knew how to fight and who to fight. The enemy was the system that held so many of our people back, that kept the poor, always poor. The laws of the land

173

even upheld the idea that a Black man was less than a man. And for once in our extended history, we came together to organize and force the doors of change open. *Why did we do it?* We did it for the children. Like Fanny Lou Hamer, most of us had gotten sick and tired of being sick and tired. We wanted, if not for ourselves, for our children to be able to pursue our dreams in the land of the free; for future generations to have the chance to self-actualize and become who they were intended to be. Like the greatest of our patriots, we too, longed for life, liberty, and the pursuit of happiness. And we were willing to pay with our very lives. And pay we did.

Fast-forward fifty years.... What about the children today? How are they faring. Did the sacrifice pay off? I suspect that our leaders of the ages would sing, in chorus, the praises of many of our young people for their tenacity, their stewardship, their scholarship, and their character. But together they would also cry out from the agonizing truth that too many of our young people have taken their eye off the mark.

I am reminded of the Biblical story of David and Goliath. David represented the youthfulness that often produces change. Where countless others feared the adversary, he was full of courage. Goliath represented a way of life, a system hinged on fear and destruction, anchored in evil. That system had existed since the beginning of time and it is still alive and well. More of our young people must remove their self-serving blinders in order to see the real challenges that beset our communities and families. From poverty to health care, education, sexism, economic disparities, injustice, crime, drugs, environmental issues, and our old enemy racism, the world is full of formidable foes to fight rather than to perpetuate the lingering attacks on each other. Where is the courage to lead the fight against the systems that threaten life as we know it as well as for generations to come?

174

I am convinced that it does not take courage to fight and/or kill your brother. Instead, it takes courage to slay life's giants. The bold truth is that when you take someone else's life you give up your own along with it. Multiple lives lost and multiple families in anguish and almost always over something frivolous. And all the while, the real Goliaths are running amuck. Too many of us have taken our eyes off the prize.

When we fail to harness our energies to address the needs of our fellow man (the community as a whole) we leave ourselves vulnerable to ultimately make decisions that hurt or destroy us. This is one of the tenets that our forefathers understood well. For men like Shuttlesworth and King, preparation for their life's work began early, and commitments were made to either kill the system or be killed by it for the good of the masses.

So what if with the same tenacity and determination that we attack each other and vow to get even, we attacked injustice and disparity, vowing to even the playing field? And what if our young people could somehow see that having babies outside the family structure sets our race up to be slaves to another system that insures that our children are born weaker, learn slower, perform poorer, and struggle to the extent that they too, become wards of the system, perpetuating this cycle again and again to the destruction of our people? Is that what our ancestors gave their lives for? Is it really how we want our history to be written? A proud people who emerged from royalty and evolved to...what?

What will your legacy be? Are you a thug with a gun and proud of it? Or are you a leader, full of the kind of courage that won't let you sit idly by and watch the world destroy itself? Are you able and willing to find an unjust cause and apply your best efforts to rectify it? What we've learned from the past is that violence begets violence and courage begets courage.

On behalf of those very courageous men, women, and children, including my husband and many of his colleagues, we are asking you to prepare yourself in your youth for a cause greater than yourself. Learn all you can while you can. And if you really want to establish a legacy of courage, take others along with you. Inspire someone you know to improve their lives and plant seeds of prosperity and change in their community. Repeat this practice again and again. Remember, courage begets courage. The world is counting on you to make it better. Get on your mark! Keep your eyes on the prize! Stay the course! And run your race with grace and integrity! If you do that well, not even the wind can touch you.

"WE WHO BELIEVE IN FREEDOM CANNOT REST": WHAT THE LIFE AND WORK OF ELLA BAKER MEANT TO ME

MARGARET RICHARDSON, M. A.

"Until the killing of Black men, Black mothers' sons, becomes as important to the rest of the country as the killing of a white mother's son, we who believe in freedom cannot rest."

Today, Ella Josephine Baker is forgotten. Her name is spoken only in circles of current leaders on the national stage. She is seldom written about in a history book, her profile in courage barely recorded among the many works detailing the Civil Rights Movement. Most of the work she did is attributed to others, some a little too eager to reap praise for work they did not have the stomach or fortitude to do.

Ella Baker's towering presence in the Civil Rights Movement has been made into a footnote after being taken over and consumed by the profiles of Martin Luther King Jr., Jesse Jackson, and others who captured the eye of the television camera. Maybe it was because Ella Baker worked from the sidelines, always in support of someone else. Or maybe, just maybe because that is the way she wanted to work. Ella Baker was a force of nature and touched every facet of the civil rights movement, from grassroots work to collective organization to social activism. She selflessly mentored and nurtured emerging young leaders like Diane Nash, Bob Moses, and Stokely Carmichael. Even though she is forgotten, Ella Baker made a definite impression on me.

As odd as it sounds, I was introduced to Ella Baker while I was looking for material for Kathleen Cleaver and Pauli Murray, other forgotten "sheroes" of the movement. While reading *Freedom's Daughters: The Unsung Heroines of the Civil Rights Movement From 1830 to 1970*, by Lynne Olson, I was impressed that Baker, who had been married from 1940 to 1959, had not taken the name of her husband. You ask: Why did this stand out to me? In a time when women were being told that their femininity was connected to a certain perception of womanliness, hour-glass silhouette, and staying at home to take care of house and home after World War Two, the fact that a Black woman could be married yet refuse to take the name of her husband symbolized to me that she was her own person. Not only that but many of those close to her never knew that Baker was married. I was fascinated by the example she set – she would not let herself be defined by being her husband's wife. Indeed this symbolized a greater significance because it is how Ella Baker lived her life, on her terms, refusing to be relegated to inferior status, even by those in the struggle who were not used to taking orders from a woman.

Ella Baker challenged and then helped to support Martin Luther King Jr. in establishing the Southern Christian Leadership Conference (SCLC). Created in the days after the Montgomery Bus Boycott, Baker seized the opportunity to take the momentum of the boycott and continue to the work of trying to register Blacks to vote. Even though King was the head of the SCLC and needed Baker for its day-to-day operations, he was uneasy having to depend on Baker. She was often the only woman in the room during discussions of organizing and planning, the only female in the sea of Black men who had assumed the front ranks of the Civil Rights Movement.

Baker was the SCLC's main organizer, secretary, and staff. She was the main reason for its effectiveness and success with registering Blacks to vote in the South. Also, she was the leading force behind the Student Nonviolent Coordinating Committee (SNCC). Now remembered primarily as the launching pad for the young Stokley Carmichael and for the controversial call for Black Power that predated the creation of the Black Panther Party, SNCC was a leader in empowering students to action, to participate in the struggle that was also theirs to shoulder.

SNCC was formed in the days after the beginning of the sit-ins that took the world by storm. Quietly organized and executed by college students, the sit-ins were the very definition of the Baker philosophy of participatory democracy. The students themselves were doing the legwork of their organizing while assembling the leadership from their ranks to answer the call for direct action. Baker, while not their direct leader, was their unofficial godmother, providing guidance and supporting the students' efforts for them to provide their own direction. The Freedom Rides, also spawned as a result of the work by SNCC, found its origins in the example of direct action while retaining their independence of thought.

I can go on and on about the many decisions that were influenced by the presence of Ella Baker. But in the examples I have mentioned are perhaps two examples of how significant Ella Baker was to the Civil Rights Movement, to Black women in general, and to me in particular. Not only was she determined to control her own destiny but she was did not let anyone define who she was. She challenged anyone who attempted to put her in a box, not only through words but deeds. In fact, it would seem as if she worked harder just to prove that she had a place at the table and worked even harder to make sure others could benefit. In each of the organizations she worked with, Baker was the foundation that kept them grounded. She was the clay that held the mold together and she was the glue that kept many of these organizations together.

Ella Baker's body of service in the civil rights movement will never be chronicled as it should and certainly not given the space in this essay that it should. She devoted her life to the struggle and to the countless people she mentored, mothered, protected, and sheltered. That is perhaps, her legacy to me as an emerging leader in my community. The devotion Baker showed to the people she took responsibility for is a dynamic that I have only begun to understand and share. It is up to anyone who answers the call of direct action to understand the sacrifice, responsibility and blessing that comes with the job. It is also up to anyone who answers the call to remember that they have an obligation to share their resources with those coming in behind them. We as a community will never rise as long as some refuse to pass the torch or fail to take under our wing someone who needs nurturing. I may not ever have the opportunity to devote my resources as completely to the cause for uplift as Ella Baker did. But as God orders my steps, I realize that part of my path has already been prepared for me by the life and service of Ella Josephine Baker.

THE TUSKEGEE AIRMEN AND AMERICAN EXCEPTIONALISM

C A R Y   C L A C K

The eagle gets its name for the color of its plumage. The word "eagle" is a derivative from the Latin word, "Acquilus" which means, swarthy, dark-colored, or blackish. In the early 1940's there were a group of eagles down in Alabama who wanted to test their wings. These eagles were men whose plumage was swarthy, dark-colored, and blackish--men who other men didn't believe possessed the talent, the temperament, the intelligence, the reflexes, and the courage to fly.

From childhood, we are told that the sky is the limit. But for these swarthy eagles in Alabama, these men known as the Tuskegee Airmen, the cliché was a lie. The sky wasn't the limit. Like many places on the earth to which they were bound, the sky was off-limits because their skin, their plumage, had been darkened by the sun's kiss.

But one of the attributes of eagles is their vision. They possess extraordinary eyesight and can see things far into the distance. They have the ability to see things others can't. The Tuskegee Airmen, confident in the God given gifts, looked into the distance and saw themselves in flight, imagined themselves taking to the air in the finest aircraft in the world and fighting for their country, even as it denied them the freedom for which the country was at war to preserve.

They began World War II as outcasts whose talent was denied and not given a chance to flourish and ended it as heroes on their way to becoming legends. Officially known as the 332nd Fighter Group of the United States Army Air Corps, they received their training at the historically Black Tuskegee Institute in Alabama. Nearly 1,000 pilots were trained in the program and the Tuskegee Airmen became world-famous as the United States' only all-Black unit of the war. They became subjects of lore, books, and movies, lionized as men who overcame obstacles of law and custom to achieve heights that surprised only those who doubted their gifts.

In 2007, President George W. Bush awarded the airmen the Congressional Gold Medal. The youngest of the airmen was in his 80's. In his remarks to the airmen, Bush said "Even the Nazis asked why African-American men would fight for a country that treated them so unfairly…these men in our presence felt a special sense of urgency. They were fighting two wars; one was in Europe, and the other took place in the hearts and minds of our citizens. That war taking place in the hearts and minds of Americans proved to be the more difficult of the two, but they won both wars.

For decades the amazing feats of the Tuskegee Airmen were coated with perfection. Perfection is an ideal dreamed about and pursued but rarely captured. It is so rare and out of reach that its elusiveness is used as an excuse for mistakes. When someone errs, it is dismissed with the reminder, "Well, nobody's perfect." Because most claims of perfection such as "He's the perfect husband" or "It's the perfect job," are subjective and exaggerated, the only things truly perfect are those that can be quantified by objective numbers. In bowling, a perfect game is a score of 300. In baseball, a perfectly pitched game is retiring 27 batters without allowing a base runner. (Although a truly perfect game would be getting 27 batters out on 27 pitches.)

For more than 60 years, the Tuskegee Airmen's perfect number was "0" as in the number of bombers lost to enemy fighters. But the day before they received the Congressional Gold Medal, an Air Force report was released that revealed that enemy aircraft had shot down at least 25 bombers escorted by the 332nd Fighter Group. The report proved just one thing: nobody's perfect, not even the Tuskegee Airmen. It didn't diminish their achievements, heroism, or trailblazing or remove from the record that they were so good that their services as escorts were requested by white bomber pilots who didn't know or didn't care that they were Black.

The report corrects numbers but can't rewrite the history of what these great aviators accomplished. Anyway, losing 25 planes in more than 15,000 sorties on 1500 missions made them close to flawless. The Tuskegee Airmen, those eagles out of Alabama, were men of extraordinary vision. They saw things and imagined possibilities others couldn't see or imagine.

When their government and fellow countrymen and women doubted them, they saw the bountiful gifts that God had blessed them with. When their country, the land of their births, treated them like second-class citizens and denied them justice and equality, they saw the immense promise of the Declaration of Independence and the Constitution. When society and custom demanded that they bow their heads in shame and submission, they lifted their heads, raised their eyes, and fixed their gaze on a far horizon that they knew was their destination.

And they took flight, made history, and became legends.

The night before he was assassinated, Dr. Martin Luther King Jr. cried out that he'd been to the mountaintop and seen the Promised Land. The Tuskegee Airmen flew over that mountaintop and carried all of us closer to that Promised Land. Perfection is in an ideal rarely achieved. The Tuskegee Airmen weren't called to be perfect. They were called to be heroic, they were called to be trailblazers, and they were called to fly into history.

The eagles answered that call magnificently.

REFLECTIONS ON SHIRLEY CHISOLM

IVY TAYLOR

For the last few years, I have felt increasingly frustrated around MLK Day and leading up to Black History Month. We give such short shrift to this complex and important issue. Dr. King's "I Have a Dream Speech" and Rosa Parks and Frederick Douglas do not comprise the extent of Black or African American History. In addition, ALL Americans can learn from the history of Blacks in America.

Shirley Chisolm's story is a page that is not often referred to during our stilted celebrations of our history. Her page is one that has always been known to me for two reasons: 1) I grew up in New York City and therefore remember as a child that she served in Congress and 2) she was a member of Delta Sigma Theta Sorority, the organization that I became part of in 1991.

When I learned about Ms. Chisolm during my new member initiation into Delta Sigma Theta, I never would have dreamed that our lives would have any parallel paths beyond New York City as well as the Delta's.

Shirley Anita St. Hill Chisholm (November 30, 1924 – January 1, 2005) was an American politician, educator, and author. She was a Congresswoman, representing New York's 12th Congressional District for seven terms from 1969 to 1983. In 1968, she became the first African-American woman elected to the United States Congress. On January 25, 1972, she became the first major-party Black candidate for President of the United States and the first woman to run for the Democratic presidential nomination. Ms. Chisolm was a driven and respected political figure and someone who paved the way for people like me.

I like to call myself the "accidental politician", as I never aspired to be in elected office. I was an urban planner focused on inner city revitalization issues. Some community leaders asked me to run for a city council seat representing a district dominated by neglected inner city neighborhoods and I saw it as a chance to make a difference. Five years later, when San Antonio's mayor was tapped to join President Barack Obama's cabinet, my colleagues selected me to fill his unexpired term becoming San Antonio's first Black mayor in modern history (San Antonio had a mayor of African descent before Texas became a state). The only other woman mayor had served over 20 years earlier. At the time of my appointment to the office, another San Antonio history maker, Henry Cisneros, pointed out another interesting twist. Mr. Cisneros was the first to note that no other American city with a population over one million had ever had a black woman as mayor.

Of course it is exciting to think that in future years my child and grandchildren will see my name in the history books. But from my perspective, it is more important to reflect on the trailblazers that made this possible and think about all the territory that still has to be conquered. Frankly, to still hear "first black...." in the 21st century challenges us all to address the issues that continue to hold back the potential of so many Americans.

Ms. Chisolm was a trailblazer on a huge scale and in my new unexpected career path, I feel comforted in knowing her story. Over the years, I have subscribed to the biblical philosophy, "to whom much is given, much is required." Ms. Chisolm stated it this way: "Service is the rent that you pay for room on this earth."

Ms. Chisolm often vocalized that she felt being a woman was more of a barrier to her chosen path than being African American. While that has not been my experience, I certainly believe that women bring a different leadership style and skill set that is needed in many forums, but especially in elected offices today. Even during her era, Ms. Chisolm noted "At present, our country needs women's idealism and determination, perhaps more in politics than anywhere else." I wholeheartedly agree and invite more women to serve in unexpected ways to help fulfill the promise of our communities and our nation.

IDA B. WELLS-BARNETT,
THE CRUSADER FROM MISSISSIPPI

RHONDA M. LAWSON

———————————

There are some who throw up their hands in the face of adversity, feeling powerless against the wrongs of the world. Some might even ask, "What can I do? I'm only one person. I have no money. I have no influence. Who would even listen to me?"

Those words may possibly have crossed the mind of Ida B. Wells-Barnett at one time but instead of succumbing to those thoughts, she did the seemingly impossible—she overcame them. Today, she is most remembered for her journalistic efforts against the horrors of lynching and her crusades for women's rights.

Born in 1862, the daughter of two activists in Holly Springs, Miss., Ida rarely had time to dwell on being powerless. By the time she was sixteen, both her parents had died of yellow fever, leaving her on her own to take care of five brothers and sisters. Despite being a former slave, she had learned to read at a young age, so she was eventually able to find work as a schoolteacher. Later, she and two younger sisters moved to Memphis, Tenn., where she again taught school while attending nearby Fisk University. This move would soon change the course of her life.

Shortly after moving to Memphis, Ida planned a trip to Nashville, Tenn. The United States Supreme Court had just overturned the 1875 Civil Rights Law that banned discrimination in hotels and in transportation, ruling that the national government lacked jurisdiction where the facilities and transportation were under local and state laws. The state of Tennessee, as well as most southern states immediately began to enforce segregated quarters for Blacks on trains, and that was the case when Ida bought her ticket for first class travel.

Having taken her seat in the first class car, the conductor promptly informed her that she would have to move to the Black section of the train, which was always in the front car because it was the hottest and where the smoke from the train settled. Ida adamantly refused to move. The conductor then tried to forcibly remove her, but she defended herself, biting him on the hand. He got help and with two other grown men, forcibly dragged her out of the car to the applause of the white passengers.

Because of the altercation, Ida sued the Chesapeake and Ohio Railroad, winning a five hundred dollar settlement, which was immediately overturned by the Appeals Court. She ended up paying two hundred dollars in costs. Ida's disappointment only lasted a moment. She began writing a series of articles about race and politics in the South under the pseudonym, "Iola." These articles spurred her career change from teacher to journalist.

Her articles attacked the unlawful lynching of Black men and women. When two prominent Black men were lynched, Ida put it on the front page of her newspaper. She advised Blacks to leave Memphis because it, "will neither protect our lives and property, nor give us a fair trial in the courts." She further encouraged Black citizens to avenge the lynching even if they had "to burn up whole towns." Ida encouraged all Blacks to arm themselves and protect their families. Her articles were so incendiary they caught the attention of both Black and white journalists. In 1887 the lady from Mississippi was named the most prominent Black correspondent at the National Afro-American Press Convention. She also bought one-third share in the newspaper, *Free Speech and Headlight,* becoming part owner and editor.

Soon, tragedy hit close to home when three male friends of hers, all successful businessmen, were accused of a crime and subsequently lynched. This so outraged Ida that she began an anti-lynching campaign through her newspaper. Her articles encouraged Blacks to boycott the city's transportation system. Her personal investigations uncovered other lynching injustices. She was so successful in motivating the southern Black populace that her newspaper was destroyed and her life threatened if she ever returned to Memphis (she happened to be visiting the Black publisher T. Thomas Fortune in New York when her press was burned). She stayed in New York and went to work for Fortune but continued campaigning against the atrocities of lynching in the South in New York and England. "Having lost my paper," she wrote in her autobiography, *Crusade for Justice: The Autobiography of Ida B. Wells Barnett*, "I had a price on my life, and been made an exile from home for printing the truth, I felt that I owed it to my race to tell the whole truth now that I was where I could do so freely." Her articles became so popular that Ida B. Wells' clubs sprung up in Chicago and other northern cities. Their goal was to eliminate lynching.

Her work brought her face to face with some of the most prominent figures in African American history, including Frederick Douglas, Booker T. Washington (she was very critical of Washington's accomodationist policies), and Dr. W.E.B. DuBois. She stood against both racial and gender injustices, helping to found the National Association of Colored Women. Even after moving to Chicago and marrying Ferdinand Barnett and giving birth to four children, her work for equality continued. She even ran for state senate in 1930, although her campaign was unsuccessful.

Ida died the following year of kidney disease, but her work in the pursuit of equality has never been forgotten. Today the Ida B. Wells Memorial Foundation and the Ida B. Wells-Barnett Museum in Holly Springs stand as a memorial to her work. Today, African American politicians and journalists, including President Barack Obama stand on the shoulders of giants like this young girl from Mississippi who dared to stare adversity in face and not back down.

A SHARECROPPER'S DAUGHTER

B R E N N E R   S T I L E S

No one possibly could have anticipated that a forty-one-year old uneducated sharecropper from the Mississippi Delta town of Rueville, Fannie Lou Hamer, would become one of the real heroes of the 1960's Civil Rights Movement. Fannie Lou was the youngest of twenty children born to her fiery mother who always carried a gun while working in the cotton fields. Early on in life she preached to Fannie Lou, "If you respect yourself enough other people will have to respect you also." To her mother the gun she carried in the cotton sack was the equalizer and brought her respect.

In order for the family to survive their miserable sharecropper's existence, Fannie Lou was forced to work the cotton fields right along with her siblings. Three quarters of all the Black residents in the Delta before 1970 lived below the poverty line. There was no time for school or a formal education. All the knowledge came in the fields trying to survive. But what Fannie Lou had more than most of the others was a strong "mother wit," and very low tolerance for injustice. These qualities would serve her well as she took on the forces of segregation and political oppression at the height of the Civil Rights Movement.

Rueville was a rural plantation town where the sharecropper population was the majority and if allowed to vote could have held every one of the elective offices. That is why the white landowners used every form of intimidation to make sure they never got the right to vote. One of the most effective forms was to evict any recalcitrant sharecropper who tried to vote, off his land. That method was quite effective with the farmers. Most of them refused to participate with Robert Moses and the Student Non-Violent Coordinating Committee when they showed up to register them to vote. That wasn't true with

Fannie Lou when she first met Moses at a voter registration meeting held at the only Black church on the outskirts of the town.

Moses explained to the reluctant Blacks that the only way they could possibly break down the old tradition was to go with him to Indianola and apply for registration. Fannie Lou and a few other workers accepted the challenge and went to Indianola to register. Their registration request was not granted and she knew that the landowner would be right there to meet her with an eviction notice. She was right and he was waiting for her. The white owner told Fannie Lou that the Ku Klux Klan and White Citizens Council were harassing him because his field hands had been messing in politics. She had a choice, according to him: She could stop her meddling in politics or leave the land and cabin she had called home for the past eighteen years, which also meant leaving her husband, Pap Hamer. That night she left her family and found shelter in the home of a SNCC supporter.

There was no looking back for Fannie Lou. She was totally committed to the battle for justice. According to her, the refusal to vote and the denial of basic human rights in Mississippi may have been legal by the white man's standards but unjust by God's standards. She enrolled in SNCC's literacy classes under the leadership of another dynamic woman, Anne Ponder. Once she graduated from Ponder's class, she and four other students traveled to Tennessee to attend Septima Clark's intensive one-week teacher training class. It was when Fannie Lou and the other women started back to Mississippi along with Ponder, that she encountered the real brutal nature of racism.

194   They were traveling by Trailways Bus and when they stopped at the station in Winona, Miss., Ponder decided that she would test the new Interstate Commerce Commission regulation outlawing segregated facilities in interstate travel. She exited the bus and proceeded to walk into the white waiting room. Ponder and the others were arrested and taken off to jail, even though the students hadn't gone inside the waiting room. One of the arresting policeman promised that they would make the girls "wish they were dead."

Once inside the jail, they dragged Fannie Lou into a separate and empty cell. The police then forced two Black prisoners to beat her with a Billy club. One of the men held her down while they other inflicted the blows, then they switched and continued until her fingers went numb and skin on her back swelled up. But the beating did not have its intended effect. In fact, it did just the opposite; it made Fannie Lou more determined to change a system that allowed grown men, pledged to uphold the law, to break those same laws free from any punishment.

That beating in a Mississippi jail served as a catalyst to propel Fannie Lou forward. Afterwards she didn't want to just vote, but wanted control of the political apparatus in her county and town. With that in mind she helped to form the Mississippi Freedom Democratic Party (MFDP). A year prior to passage of the Voting Rights Act, these courageous Black sharecroppers joined forces with the SNCC and other Black civil rights leaders in the state of Mississippi to challenge the legitimacy of the established Democratic Party. Under the leadership of a sharecropper's daughter, the MFDP argued the moral imperative that they be seated at the National Democratic Convention in place of the established party.

To the chagrin of President Lyndon Baines Johnson, the MFDP took their case right to the convention when they were denied seats by the state delegation. Leading the charge was that sharecropper's daughter. They set up a boycott right outside the convention and were soon joined by such notables as Dr. Martin Luther King Jr., Stokely Carmichael, and the great Washington, D.C. civil rights lawyer Joseph Rauh. Dr. King argued that it was crucial that the convention recognize the MFDP because the entire free world was watching. It was an opportunity for the United States to demonstrate to oppressed people struggling for their own freedom "that somewhere in this world there is a nation that cares about justice."

195

The boycott in Atlantic City caught the attention of the entire world and infuriated President Johnson. When it was time for Fannie Lou to testify before the credentials committee, all television cameras zoomed in on her. She used this as an opportunity to strike back at the Winona Police Department by telling the world about the beating she took in a cell simply because she dared exercise her Constitutional right to vote. The apex of her testimony came when she pointed out that she was actually in jail being beaten at the same time that Medgar Evers was murdered in front of his home in Jackson, Miss. At that point, this sharecropper's daughter became the hero and everyone flocked to her after she ended her stirring rendition of a terrible example of America's injustice toward some of its people. *Jet magazine* reporter at the time Larry Still captured the scene in his column, "I felt just like I was telling it from the mountain," he reported Fannie Lou saying. "That's why I like that song, 'Go Tell It on the Mountain;' I feel like I'm talking to the world."

From that point on, this beautiful Black sister, who represented the tragic story of many of our women and men stuck in the mire of poverty, became a spokesperson for her race. In late 1964 Fannie Lou was invited to be the principal speaker at the Williams Institutional Christian Methodist Episcopal Church in Harlem. Malcolm X was present on the stage with her. Afterwards Malcolm X invited Fannie Lou to attend a rally of his new Organization of African American Unity, thus creating a bond between an east coast organization with a southern-based peoples' movement. For a very short period of time (Malcolm was assassinated two months later) Fannie Lou, an oppressed sharecropper from the South joined in coalition with an oppressed poverty stricken Black man from the North. They both had risen from the depths of what could be defeat to the heights of victory for their people, and thus demonstrated the excellence that is innate to African American people in this country.

196

Today, the heritage and legacy of Fannie Lou Hamer is carried on every morning, five days a week, on Sirius XM Radio on the African American talk show station by Joe Madison. He begins every hour with a quote from the sharecropper's daughter, thus assured that we will never lose the wise words of this knowledgeable woman. The quote is an excellent way to end this tribute to her. It goes as follows:

"You can pray until you faint, but if you don't get up and do something, God ain't going to put it in your lap. And there's no need of running, no need of saying honey, I ain't going to get in the mess.' Because if you're born with a Black face in America, you're already in the mess."

REVEREND CLAUDE BLACK DEFENDS AN ICON AND CHALLENGES A GIANT

Taj Matthews

Writing as a young African American, I am very much aware of the tremendous responsibility that my generation will soon inherit from our elders. Now reaching the twilight years of their lives, they are the generation who stood their ground in the 1960's and 70's and fought against an entrenched, well-oiled racist machine throughout the South and in the North. After decades of humiliating social injustice, the Black men, women, and children of the civil rights years said no more.

Frederick Douglass, the great orator and abolitionist told Black people of his generation that "Power concedes nothing without a struggle. It never has and it never will." That was the case in the South when men like Dr. Martin Luther King Jr., Rev. Ralph Abernathy, and Rev. Fred Shuttlesworth took on Eugene Bull Connors, Commissioner of the Birmingham Alabama Police Force, and Governor George C. Wallace during that turbulent summer in 1963.

The one important quality these men possessed was courage. They faced the immense power of the racist machine and did not back down. But it wasn't only in Birmingham that this kind of courage existed. It was also present in San Antonio, Texas, manifested through my Grandfather, Rev. Claude Black. He never received the national recognition of a Dr. King or Rev. Abernathy but he displayed the same kind of courage as those other brave Black men. "He stood up during times that positions (on civil rights) were not safe and the politics not popular," is how Martin Luther King III described my grandfather.

Rev. Black's life was constantly threatened. A number of times he was accosted by hostile racists and his church was burned down, but he never wavered in his staunch commitment to equality for his people. "A person that can talk about justice should fight for it," according to Dr. Nick Carter, President of Andover Newton Theological Seminary. He went on to say, "In the Hebrews scriptures, that is what we call a righteous man and that is Reverend Black."

On two separate occasions, Grandfather put his courage right next to his convictions and did not back down from his detractors. The first time he was tested happened in 1952 when the famous cultural icon, Langston Hughes, was invited by local Blacks to read some of his poetry at the Colored Library Auditorium, which is now the Carver Community Cultural Center. The Black community was very excited about Hughes coming to San Antonio. On the other hand, there were quite a few in the white community that resented him because of his committed struggle against racial inequality. They did not want him to visit for fear that he would incite the Black population to take a stand against the city's segregated facilities.

Within days of Hughes's scheduled appearance the city attorney, with the assistance from the police department, forced the sponsoring group to cancel the event. Yes, if you can believe that in America, where freedom of speech is supposed to be protected under the First Amendment of the U. S. Constitution, a man was blocked by the awesome power of the local government from exercising that very guaranteed right. The reason given by the city officials was that he would incite a riot with his speech, supposedly tainted with a Communist message. That infuriated my grandfather. Against the advice of less courageous individuals, Rev. Black decided to address the all-white and segregationist city council to demand an explanation.

200

My grandfather entered the chamber at City Hall and was met with contemptuous looks from the whites attending the council meeting in anticipation of his appearance as well as the seven city council members, including the mayor. Despite the sneers and ugly stares, Grandfather took his seat and waited his turn to speak. He listened as the man testifying, Austin Hancock of the segregationist organization, The American Heritage Group, accused Hughes of being anti-American. He claimed that his appearance would cause an uprising among the local "Negroes."

When he finished his vicious attacks on this great Black American, Grandfather walked to the podium ignoring the jeers and taunts of being called "Communist, Communist." It was quite ironic that these people would accuse a man of God of being a Communist. I guess these fine citizens didn't understand that Christianity is anti-ethical to the Communist doctrine. Grandfather would later admit to me that he felt nervous standing there and vulnerable to a bunch of racists, who would just as soon see him hanging from a tree as standing there acting like an "uppity nigger." But he stood his ground and demanded that the council provide concrete proof that Langston Hughes ever had any Communist affiliations.

Members of the city council never addressed Grandfather but left that job to the city attorney. He provided Grandfather with no concrete evidence but simply stated that he was fearful that Mr. Hughes would incite a riot. He refused to further elaborate or to answer any of Rev. Black's questions in order to clarify his charges. During the entire deliberation not one city council member spoke up.

Just as Grandfather finished speaking, real trouble, in the form of five large white men, walked into the chamber and walked right up to the front, blocking Grandfather from leaving the chambers. It took five of them to confront one pacifist preacher. They showed their cowardly nature while, on the other hand, Grandfather brushed right around them, showing his courage. As he made his way to the back of the chamber, he heard one of the men shout, "Now what you all must understand is that not all the 'niggers' in this city are like this uppity 'nigger.'"

It was not surprising to Grandfather but somewhat appalling that the city council allowed this man to insult and demean a man of the cloth without one member objecting. But Grandfather did not back down. He marched out of that chamber and city hall with his chest stuck out, proud that he had stood up for one of the most basic Constitutional rights given to all Americans, and that is freedom of expression. In doing so, he also stood up for a great

Black American icon, the poet, Langston Hughes.

Rev. Black's tremendous courage was on display again in 1958 when he single-handedly challenged the entire city's religious community and Rev. Billy Graham. The Black ministers of the city were asked to encourage their congregations to attend the Billy Graham crusade coming to San Antonio. Grandfather supported what Rev. Graham was doing in building a strong soul-saving ministry and he was willing to support his efforts. But that all changed when he found out that Price Daniel, a man who was running for Governor of Texas on a segregationist ticket, would introduce Rev. Graham at the revival. He felt that if he participated in the event, it could be interpreted that he supported the segregationist for governor. Grandfather went one step further than not participating in the event. He contacted the organizers for the Billy Graham crusade in San Antonio and complained about a segregationist being a part of a Christian service. Their response was that Grandfather needed to be a better Christian. He countered, saying it seemed being a Christian, according to them, did not require that we all fight for equal rights.

The committee continued to ignore his concerns so Rev. Black decided that he would mount a boycott of the crusade unless Daniel was dropped from the program. His question to the organizers, who all considered themselves dedicated Christians, was how could they possibly talk about God and love but accept racism, discrimination, and segregation? At that point, he believed that Rev. Graham had to take a stand against segregation. Grandfather contacted Dr. Martin Luther King Jr., A. Phillip Randolph, and Adam Clayton Powell Jr. and asked that they contact Rev. Graham in an attempt to persuade him to drop Daniel from the program. They all did contact him but to no avail. The only concession Rev. Graham made was to integrate the audience. He went one step further and found a Black minister willing to appear on stage with him and Daniel. They needed a "token," according to Grandfather, to show that all Blacks were not supportive of Daniel being dropped.

The crusade went on as planned and Grandfather refused to participate as did most of the other ministers. But their one Black minister stood on the platform with the segregationist and made a mockery out of what Grandfather and the others attempted to accomplish. Years later that same minister admitted to my Grandfather that it was a mistake on his part. An interesting aside is a few years later that same minister was beaten up by a group of racists and turned to Grandfather for help.

During that entire ordeal, the white ministers of the city attacked Rev. Black. They felt that his efforts were harmful to Rev. Graham's crusade for Christ. But just as Dr. King wrote in his "Letter from a Birmingham Jail" to a group of ministers who thought his actions in breaking laws were not Christian, and explained to them that being Christian called on all men of the cloth not to support unjust laws, my Grandfather told these ministers that it was his God-given duty to oppose any segregationist wherever he might appear, and that included a Billy Graham crusade.

On many other occasions, Rev. Claude Black put his life on the line as he constantly fought against the forces of evil in San Antonio and other parts of Texas. He was cut from the same cloth as other courageous Black leaders during those times of immense danger. These were men and women who stood for what was right and wouldn't let anyone back them down from their position. Just as the Black race has always had heroes to rise up to the crisis of their time, these brave men did the very same during the civil rights crisis. For that reason we must place them all in the category with such heroes as Nat Turner, Frederick Douglass, Harriet Tubman, Sojourner Truth, Dr. W.E.B. DuBois, and Ida B. Wells.

It is now important that my generation, the future leaders of the race, step forward like the brave men and women of the past, and take on the crisis facing us today. We must fight against all the negative influences in our community. Those of us who are the potential leaders must reach out to our peers and speak out when they are abusive to each other. We are compelled to tell our brothers to treat our sisters with respect; we are compelled to tell our brothers to leave the drugs alone, get an education and become productive participants in society. We are compelled to tell our brothers to pull up their pants, straighten out their attitudes, give up the gang mentality, and stop killing each other. If we do anything less, then we have dropped the ball and do not deserve to inherit the future of our culture and our people.

MOVING FROM OBSCURITY TO PROMINENCE

R EVEREND J AMES W. S ANDERS , S R .

I was born on September 17, 1929, in Union, S. C., a small, rural town located in the northern part of the state. The year I was born, over two hundred thousand people throughout the world died from an outbreak of influenza, the soft drink 7-Up was created, and two years earlier, Charles Lindberg had made his historical flight across the Atlantic Ocean in the Spirit of St. Louis. Most Americans had adopted the new age technology called the radio. It was a time when writers like William Faulkner, F. Scott Fitzgerald, and Ernest Hemmingway began to showcase their talent while the Harlem Renaissance was coming to an end. Harlem had seen the discovery and growth of immense African American talent readily on display in its music, art, poetry, and novels. A group of artists, led by the Harvard trained, Dr. W.E.B. DuBois, the Howard University Philosophy Instructor, Alain Locke; and by the young Bohemian writers, Langston Hughes, Wallace Thurmond, and Zora Neale Hurston, denounced the Euro-centric belief that all good literature must have a European connection and explored the African American culture in ways never done before.

Although I have traveled all over the world, I have never lived more than thirty miles from my birthplace. About the time I was born, Blacks were leaving the South in large numbers as a result of the push/pull phenomenon. The push was the escape from the horrendous conditions under which we were forced to live. Many Blacks refused to accept segregation and left for the North. The pull was the attraction of finding work in the north. Henry Ford had just introduced the Model T Ford, Andrew Carnegie had steel mills in Pittsburgh, and Blacks headed North to find work in these industries. Despite the poverty and racism, my family decided to remain right there in Union because that was our home and we refused to give it up to anyone for any reason. We were the Sanders family and that meant a lot to us.

Our pride emanated from Granddad, who was the greatest influence in my life. William Sanders was a no-nonsense man. He had a mill job as a painter. He was strong-willed, very tough, and because of his firm belief that all men should be treated fairly, he often took stands that put him in danger from the white establishment. One time he had an altercation with his supervisor on his job and the man called Grandpa a "nigger." Granddad punched the man right in the face and stood his ground in case any of the other workers wanted to take him on. They chose to leave him alone. In another confrontation he took on a lynch mob. His youngest brother was about to be lynched in the county courthouse yard for looking the wrong way at a white woman. Someone told Granddad and he went up to that place and asked what the problem was. After being told, he grabbed his brother by the arm, walked right through the crowd and said, "Come on let's go." Nobody did or said anything to him. That took a certain kind of courage that men possessed back then. This myth that all our Black men were cowards and ran from danger just isn't true. Granddad was proof of that.

Granddad also taught me about honor and pride among Blacks caught up in that horrible system. He told me early to always let your word be your bond. If you promise somebody something keep your promise. If you find you can't keep it, don't wait for them to come to you, go to them. If Granddad was your friend he would tell you, "I'm with you when you're right because you are right. And I'm with you when you're wrong to help get you right."

Every Sunday during my youth, he took me to church with him. As Superintendent of Sunday school at Corinth Baptist Church he was never late and would take me every Sunday during my youth to church with him. He was truly my role model, and every young boy in this country should have a role model just like him.

From him as well as my father, who was also my role model,

206

I learned the importance of hard work. Poppa worked for the government during the Great Depression. President Franklin Roosevelt's administration established the Works Progress Administration, designed to provide employment for unemployed workers. Although he only made $15.00 every two weeks Poppa managed his money so that we could make it. He taught me to never live above my means. He would often say, "If you desire something wait until you are able to pay for it." That advice stuck with me throughout my life. Mamma worked for several white families every day from 8:30 in the morning until 1:30 in the afternoon. She would wash and iron for five different families and still come home to take care of her family. She was a strong and beautiful woman.

School and education was an absolute necessity in our family. I was taught that our education should help us as well as others who would need our help. My parents wanted their children to accomplish more in life than what they had. Poppa would often say, "James, if you don't go any further than I did, I will consider myself a failure." I believed both my parents and after graduating from high school, I attended Benedict College in Columbia, S. C., from 1947 until 1951. Benedict College has a very rich history. Its first class consisted of ten emancipated slaves and one teacher, Reverend Timothy L. Dodge. He was a college-trained preacher from the North, who became president of the institute. The college had very humble beginnings. It was housed in a former slave owner's mansion in 1839 to train teachers and preachers.

By the time I began my college career, I had already given my life to the Lord. While in the tenth grade I began my public ministry. I was only sixteen at the time. Prior to my calling I had worked a number of jobs around Union. At twelve years old I worked in the afternoon and on Saturdays for Cleveland Five and Ten Store. I made $7.00 a week. I also worked a variety of jobs as dishwasher and janitor. In 1943 I got a job at the only hotel in Union. I worked as a dishpan washer and as a bell hop. But I had to give it all up when I received my calling. I had to dedicate all my time to the Lord. I preached my first sermon on June 9, 1946, at my

207

home church, Corinth Baptist in Union. I continued the study of ministry at Benedict College.

I met my best friend whom God strategically placed in my life while attending Benedict College. He was a World War II veteran who had returned to college in order to better his life. He was not a bitter man over the racism that Blacks in uniform faced but was determined to take advantage of all opportunities presented to him as a result of fighting for democracy overseas only to return home and be denied those same democratic values. He had a car, and I was able to ride back and forth to school with him. Our friendship was a blessing from God, and what we shared as two Black men is what all Black men should share. We would never have called each other by the "n" word or "dawg." And we certainly would never have dreamt of taking a gun and aiming it at each other like these young kids do today. Loving each other as Black men struggling to survive in an oppressive world was a greater virtue than the hatred our youth feel today.

I was called to my first pastorate while still in college. I became minister of a very little church in Union County, eleven miles from my home. It was 1948 and I was only eighteen years old. The following year, while still in college, I was called to be the pastor at Bethel Baptist Church in Gaffney at the age of nineteen.

I didn't restrict my work to just the ministry. I worked for the Union County Educational System for nineteen years and eventually became Vice-Principal of Sims High School, my alma mater. My experience as an educator was interesting and challenging. When I became principal of a rural elementary school, there were three teachers including me. The schoolhouse consisted of two buildings. Children and teachers had to make fire from wood gathered from wooded areas around the school. Our pay was always much lower than that of the white teachers, our books were used, and the conditions for teaching were deplorable. After the Brown vs. Board of Education Supreme Court decision in 1954, conditions began to improve. But they were never equal to that of the white schools. Despite these obstacles, we were determined to teach our children because we all understood that education was the key to our future. We loved our children and believed they could achieve only if shown the love and commitment necessary for them to live healthy lives. This is missing with so many of our children today, and we must all make a commitment to change that problem. Regardless of all other problems our communities may confront, there is one thing no one can stop us from doing, and that is love our children.

The guiding hand in my life has always been God, and He has allowed me to soar to heights of success I never dreamt possible. Although I have never lived more than thirty miles from where I was born, I have accumulated a wealth of experience. I must proclaim that the Lord has blessed me immeasurably. One piece of advice I would like to leave with the young who read this anthology is that the road to success is always paved with commitment. One must be committed to God, to one's self, and to the job that one intends to do in life. There must be accountability, and you must always measure how well you are fulfilling your duty as a man or woman, father or mother and member of the greatest culture ever to come out of this country.

It is my sincere hope that this work will be an inspiration to those in need, those who are hurting, and those who want to learn from a man who has dedicated his life to the betterment of his people. It is through faith in God that I have persevered over the past eight decades and know that what I have accomplished has been as a result of hard work. We must all strive for excellence so the quality of what we do superseded the quantity of our works.

Postscript from the Editor: We lost this wonderful man on July 6, 2010. As he suffered with his illness, he was determined to finish his contribution to the anthology. He talked often with Toschia Moffett who is working on a biography of his life. During their talks he would constantly tell her not to worry because his works on earth had been blessed by God. His ministry at Bethel Baptist Church for over sixty-one years and as Senior Pastor at Island Creek Baptist Church for thirty-eight years had earned him a place in Heaven. But what he didn't articulate was that his works here in this world and for his people earned him a place as a legend among his people. His life is a compilation of all the stories that preceded his. Dr. Sanders is gone but not forgotten and will always remain a hero for all of us to emulate.

THE LOVE THAT FORGIVES

F REDERICK W ILLIAMS AND C ARRIE W ILLIAMS

On Sept. 15, 1963, less than a month after Dr. Martin Luther King Jr. delivered his historical "I Have A Dream" speech in front of thousands at the Lincoln Memorial and millions watching on television, four innocent, beautiful, and precocious Black girls entered the Sixteenth Street Baptist Church in Birmingham, Ala., for Sunday School services. Little did they know on that day they would enter martyrdom as a result of the most evil and atrocious act carried out against a race of people since Hitler's concentration camps.

Four young girls who didn't seek martyrdom, but only wanted a normal life, were denied that right because Birmingham in 1963 was anything but normal. It is difficult for us, now living in the 21st Century, to fully comprehend what it was like to be Black at the time these young ladies were killed. We take for granted what they, as well as thousands of other Black teenagers and adults, were forced to confront and challenge every day of their lives. For them something as mundane and simple as shopping in downtown department stores was an ordeal. For us it is a pleasure trip. They were not allowed to try on clothes unless they planned to buy the items; they were forced to endure the humiliation of drinking out of water fountains and using restrooms marked "For Colored Only," as if whites would catch some kind of disease if they shared those facilities with Blacks.

It was against these abuses that the Black children of Birmingham decided to do something that the adults refused to do which would ultimately lead to the brutal bombing incident at the Sixteenth Street Baptist Church. When many of the adults turned their backs on Dr. King and Rev. Fred Shuttleworth's call for massive demonstrations against apartheid in what many considered to be the most racist city in the country, the young folks showed up for the job.

On May 21, of that same year, three months before the fatal attack on the children, and a little after nine o'clock in the morning, over fifty young Black warriors marched out into the street ready to do battle with the white menace of apartheid. Those young warriors were determined to take their rights and freedoms guaranteed them in the Constitution. They were willing to stand tall and tell the world they were proud Black Americans, ready to confront the evil that would three months later prove just how demonic its forces could be toward other human beings.

Once the first fifty marched out of the church, were arrested, and thrown in the back of wagons to be hauled off to jail, another thousand followed close behind them. Once they were arrested, a third line, then a fourth line of young Black fighters, some only 6 years old, valiantly confronted the police knowing they would be arrested. There were so many demonstrators that the police literally had to bring in school buses to keep up with the flow of students.

Across the street in Kelly Ingram Park, Black adults watched in amazement as the children made a bold statement about freedom and liberty. Also looking on in a state of anger, to the point of insanity, was Eugene Bull Connors, Commissioner of Police and the personification of southern-style segregation. Unable to dissuade the children to disperse and end the demonstration, Connors finally gave the order to fire hose the young demonstrators, and also turned the vicious police dogs loose on America's children.

The more the dogs tore into the children and the more the power of the fire hose knocked them to their knees, the more determined they were, as they continued to show up in overwhelming numbers. A Black principal at the local high school actually locked the gates in an attempt to keep the students inside. But they would not be deterred by any obstacles, be it Connor's dogs or the principal's locked gates. They trampled the chain-like fence in order to be with their friends and allies.

The young Black Americans in Birmingham were essentially

doing what young Blacks had been doing for decades. They were doing what a sixteen year old girl did in 1951 at R.R. Moton High School in Farmville, Va. Young Barbara Johns, the niece of the firebrand minister Vernon Johns, had summoned all 450 Black students to an assembly in the auditorium on the morning of April 23, 1951. Against the protest of the faculty, she stood in front of the student body and rattled off a series of complaints about the condition of their school. When the faculty attempted to remove her from the stage, she ordered them out of the auditorium. Just like the children in Birmingham, twelve years later, recognized the futility in trying to get adults to do what they should, she was determined not to let them stop her and the other students from eradicating evil.

She told her fellow students that Plessy v. Ferguson was nonsense and the white apartheid system would never comply with the decision that separate must be equal. Again, it was the children who became the warriors for justice. They made it known that they would no longer attend classes in tarpaper shacks, having to wear coats in the winter just to stay warm. They objected to being forced to ride in hand-me-down buses from the whites to schools that were not in their neighborhood. The buses often would not even start and if they did, would break down on the road. She told the students that they all should be outraged that their history teacher also had to drive the bus and had to gather wood and start the fire inside the school in order to keep them warm.

Barbara Johns shouted loudly for all to hear that young people demanded their rights as Americans. Since the adults couldn't get the job done, then the young people would. The white school board had rebuffed the demands of the adults to improve the conditions in the classrooms and reneged on a promise to build a new high school. The adults appeared impotent in their negotiations with the whites, so Barbara and her fellow students decided they would strike. They marched out of the school building and downtown, prepared for a confrontation with the power structure. The students then appealed to the National Association for the Advancement of Colored People for their legal help. A week later when officials from the NAACP

213

arrived in Farmville under the assumption that it was the adults who had requested their assistance. They were surprised when they walked into the room full of students. The lawyers informed the students that their strike might be illegal, and they could be arrested. But just like the students in Birmingham twelve years later, they challenged the police to arrest them. They boldly stated that there was too many of them for the small jail in their town. But they were willing to be incarcerated in defense of their God given freedoms and liberties.

History inextricably connected these young Americans in a common bond over time. They were all marching toward freedom in their own time in their own country with a clear understanding there might be repercussions. They never dreamed just how vicious the forces of apartheid could be and the extent to which they would go to inflict pain, even on innocent young people.

When the bomb exploded at 10:22 a.m., four young ladies were in the basement lady's room talking about the beginning days of the school year. That particular Sunday happened to be Youth Day at the church and they were preparing to run the main service at eleven o'clock. The four girls, Denise McNair, Addie Mae Collins, Cynthia Wesley, and Carole Robertson, all dressed in white, were excited about the adult roles they would play in about twenty-five minutes. In a bitter twist of irony, a Women's Sunday School class, upstairs in the sanctuary, was discussing the topic for the week, "The Love That Forgives."

Actually, six young people died on that tragic day, the four little girls in the church and two young Black men who were shot dead for no apparent reason than riding on their bicycles. Virgil Ware was shot in the back by a racist policeman and Johnny Robinson was shot by a good old Eagle Scout, Alabama version, vintage 1963. The brutal killing of these two young men did not receive the same coverage as did the four little girls. But it was just as dastardly an act as was the killings at the church.

At the funeral days later for three of the girls (Carole Robertson's parents decided to have a separate funeral for her), Dr. King would reiterate and elaborate on what the women's group had been

214

discussing when disaster struck. He would stress the value of love and forgiveness as requisite for the Christian church. Love and forgiveness were also critical components in Black America's struggle against evil. Why four beautiful young Black ladies and two vibrant young men had to die seemed to be a test of Black America's ability to love and forgive. The fact that an aggrieved Black population did not strike back and had the willpower to forgive the murderers is a testament of the goodness we possess as a people. It is a very special spirituality that is endemic to the Black race. Dr. W. E. B. DuBois wrote about it as a unique quality that Black America has given to all civilization. Our family members who were sacrificed at the altar of evil are a true personification of the forgiving nature of our people.

Their deaths served to connect the entire Black experience from the time our forebearers first arrived in this country in chains until today and far into the future. Theirs was an awesome sacrifice that serves an awesome purpose. The four young ladies and two young men's legacy in death is our challenge in life so their existence will live on. It is quite obvious who occupies the moral high ground in this country, and the rest of the races can learn from our experience on how to be forgiving and actually believe that by loving your adversary, you also love yourself. For a few years after the tragedy at the church, Black folk turned inward and discovered who they were and how God had blessed them with an inordinate amount of courage and dignity through times of suffering.

We must never lose that special quality that is the foundation of our culture. We owe it to Denise, Carole, Addie Mae, Cynthia, Virgil, Johnnie, and all the other martyrs who have gone to their death at the hands of the evil that constantly tries to destroy the good that our race represents. It is now time for a new renaissance among our people. Like the great sphinx rising out of the ashes of destruction, we must rise once again and reject those forces of greed, narcissism, and nihilism that would bring us to a point of cultural annihilation. We owe it to our martyrs, our heroes, and ourselves.

EPILOGUE

FREDERICK WILLIAMS

Black America is at a crossroads as two distinctly different forces vie for control of its culture. The next twenty to twenty-five years will determine which set of forces will win out. If our culture is strong and unified behind the grace, beauty, and proud heritage of our past, then we will have confronted the negative forces of self-destruction and defeated them. Just like our ancestors confronted adversity and won, so can we also. But it is imperative that the youth take a stand against the prevalent nihilistic attitudes that are selfish and individualistic with no concern for the greater good of the race. Each author you have just read has, in their own way, delivered a message of hope for all our people. We have endured the worst in the past, and now it should be much easier as we move forward into our future. However, it will only be a smoother road if we remember that our ancestors brought us up "the rough side of the mountain" and opened doors they never were able to walk through. Our young people are freer and have more opportunities to achieve success than ever before in our history.

We must first, however, recognize that Black Americans are an excellent people with an excellent track record of achievements in the past. We must not allow certain forces, let loose in our communities, take advantage of the freedoms our ancestors suffered for us to have for their own individual and selfish gain. Those who make a fortune by producing music and literature that portrays our race and culture in a negative light must be rejected.

It is imperative that we all understand that our culture is on loan to us for a specific number of years and then is passed on to a new generation. While keepers of the culture we must continue to improve on the beauty, grace, and strength that our ancestors left as our heritage and legacy. A short trip down memory lane reveals just how skilled, talented, and determined were the many who went before us.

Blacks have excelled in sports for over a century. Soon after the end of slavery, Black excellence began to shine. In the sport of boxing, Jack Johnson forced white men to seek a "Great White Hope" to save their dignity. In the 1936 Olympics, Jesse Owens embarrassed the German dictator who had claimed the German runner was invincible, by defeating all of them in the 100-yard dash. In fact, Owens won four gold medals in the Olympics that year, proving that Black excellence was unstoppable.

A sport in which Black excellence in performance has been ignored for years is horse racing. For example the first winner in the Kentucky Derby was Jimmy Winfield, a Black man. In fact, 15 of the first 28 Derbies were won by Black jockeys. And the greatest jockey in the history of the sport was Isaac Murphy who won three Kentucky Derby races and 44% of all his races throughout his career.

Black exceptionalism does not end with sports, but can be found in academic circles also. There is no question that Dr. W.E.B. Du Bois was the country's most gifted scholar of the 20th Century. He was the first Black man to receive a Ph.D. from Harvard University. He was a historian, sociologists, philosopher, novelist, and all around brilliant thinker. Dr. Alain Locke, also a philosopher, attained Phi Beta Kappa status and graduated magna cum laude from Harvard University. He was the first Black Rhodes Scholar at Oxford University and editor of the first Black anthology chronicling the changing nature of Black people in America, *The New Negro*. Jesse Fausett, was the literary editor for *Crisis Magazine* during the Harlem Renaissance. She was the first Black female to graduate from Cornell University and the first Black woman to achieve Phi Beta Kappa status. Dr. Ralph Bunche became the first African American to win a Nobel Peace Prize for his work toward bringing peace in the Middle East in the late 1940's. Today, we have Dr. Cornel West who is one of the most sought after scholars in the country. Dr. Condeleezza Rice was and still is an accomplished pianist and a scholar who has served as National Security Advisor and Secretary of State. Dr. Angela Davis is an accomplished scholar who has taught at the University of California at Los Angeles and wrote many political tracts critical of the oppression Blacks have suffered in this country.

In the field of music, Black Americans have excelled from their first arrival under the most horrendous conditions in this country. Spirituals became the slave's comfort and relief from suffering and as a code that a planned escape was imminent. Within those lyrics were the hopes and dreams of millions of men and women for release from bondage. Spirituals drew their parables from Biblical references. Moses' demand to the Pharaoh to "Let my people go" became the foundation on which spirituals were based. From out of those slave fields, our ancestors produced America's first original music in blues, ragtime, jazz, gospel, rhythm and blues, and rap. It is all American music, created, produced, and performed in the rural areas of the South as well as the cosmopolitan urban communities of all our major cities.

Black Americans have also excelled in the classical genre of opera. Marian Anderson was one of the most recognized stars from the 1930's until the apex of her career when she appeared with the Metropolitan Opera Company in New York, performing the role of Ulitca in Verdi's *Un Ballo in Maschera*. In 1939 after the Daughters of the American Revolution refused to allow her to perform in Constitution Hall because she was Black, Ms. Anderson, with the assistance of First Lady Eleanor Roosevelt, performed on Easter Sunday that same year on the steps of the Lincoln Monument where 75,000 people came to hear her. According to Conductor Arturo Toscanini, Marian Anderson possessed a voice that "comes only once in a hundred years." She was another example of how Black Americans have never given up when faced with adversity but instead have risen far above the problem and came out the winner.

There is a genius of creation inherent within Black Americans that allows them to write music affecting the entire world. Michael Jackson was loved as much in Europe and Asia as in the United

States. Before Michael, there was W.C. Handy, Eubie Blake, Louis Armstrong, Bessie Smith, Billie Holiday, Duke Ellington, Count Basie, and many more. Many female vocalists, Sarah Vaughn, Dinah Washington, and Etta Jones were precursors to Dianna Ross, Aretha Franklin, Gladys Knight, Tina Turner, and Patti Labelle, all who have in turn set the precedent for the contemporary female vocalist, Beyonce, Fantasia, Jennifer Hudson, and Kelly Roland. These ladies all represent a continuum of excellence in music that has always existed within the Black culture.

There are talented men also who have traveled that same continuum. Roland Hayes, the son of a former slave, became one of the first Black men to sing classical music. Following in his legacy were greats like William Warfield, Paul Robeson, Ray Charles, Marvin Gaye, Lou Rawls, Luther Vandross, and Teddy Pendergrass. This is only a small representation of the men who have excelled and set a very high standard of excellence in the performance of Black music, which is American music.

Dance is also an expressive art form in which Black Americans have excelled for centuries. Our ancestors would dance to relieve the frustration and pain associated with slavery. Contrary to the misinformation found in many school history books, our ancestors did not dance to entertain their oppressors, but instead they danced because it was a natural way to find some joy in life. The Cakewalk was the first dance performed by our ancestors on plantations throughout the South. As often would happen with original works by Blacks, the white population adapted the Cakewalk and began to have competitions for best performance. Ragtime music was influenced greatly by the steps involved in the Cakewalk.

There is such an outstanding list of extraordinary dancers throughout American history it would take pages to name them all. But let us begin with the person who received awards for her performances both in the United States and France. Josephine Baker's career spanned over a fifty-year period and two countries, France and the United States. Katherine Dunham was both a performer and choreographer. She was so respected that in 1987 other dancers paid tribute to her when they performed, "The Magic of Katherine Dunham," at the Alvin Ailey American Dance Theater in New York. Besides her career as a dancer and choreographer, Ms. Dunham found time to earn a Bachelor of Arts, a Masters Degree, and a Ph.D. from the University of Chicago in Cultural Anthropology.

John William Sublet began dancing at the age of eight and created a dance routine, "Walking the Dog," that was emulated by Sophie Tucker. The Nicholas Brothers and Bill "Bojangles" Robinson set the stage for such great dancers as Sammy Davis Jr., Jackie Wilson, James Brown, Chuck Berry, and the late, great Michael Jackson.

There is a long list of Black Americans who have excelled in the field of literature. The early poets, novelists, and those who wrote slave narratives initially wrote about our ancestor's struggle to survive under the most horrendous system of oppression any people have been forced to endure. Most of the slave narratives were written by men and women who escaped bondage and were determined to tell the world how vicious slavery actually was and that no one was happy living under those conditions. Among the great writers were Olaudah Equiano, Frederick Douglass, William Wells Brown, Henry Box Brown, Harriet Jacobs, and William and Ellen Craft.

The Crafts' narrative reads like an exciting novel detailing how she, a very light skinned woman, disguised as an invalid, and her husband William, acting as her loyal servant, made their way through the South from Macon, Ga., to Philadelphia and finally Boston. They wrote of their exciting escape from slavery in a book, *Running a Thousand Miles for Freedom*. Henry Box Brown's escape story is just as exciting. He writes of how he and two white brothers, J.C.A. and Samuel Smith, who assisted him in his escape, constructed a pine box that was three feet long, eight inches deep, and twenty-three-and-a-half inches wide for Brown. They packed him into the box and mailed him to the Pennsylvania Anti-Slavery Society office in Philadelphia, Pa. He was in that box for more than twenty-four hours and arrived safely in Philadelphia.

William Wells Brown, who escaped bondage on New Years Day, 1834, also published the first novel by an African American, *Clotel*,

221

in 1853. However, his was published in England. The first novel published by an African American in the United States, *Our Nig; or, Sketches from the Life of a Free Black, in a Two-Story White House, North. Showing that Slavery's Shadows Fall Even There*, was written by Harriett Wilson in 1859. Despite the laws prohibiting slaves from reading and writing, the sheer desire of our ancestors to educate themselves could not be curtailed. Regardless of the punishment that was inflicted if a slave was caught reading, they still pursued their God-given right to become literate. Their willpower prevailed and their natural acumen shined.

There were a number of significant and well-talented essayists, novelists, and poets in the years following slavery and into the beginning of the Twentieth Century. The prevalent theme among these writers was no longer the brutality of slavery and the quest for freedom but the brutality of apartheid and the fight for equality. Literacy was viewed as the gateway to social and economic equality. Still, there was an attempt on the part of the white dominant society to block these writers. But like their earlier predecessors they would not be denied. Ana Julia Cooper, an educator who taught at the famous Washington Colored School in Washington, D. C., wrote, *A Voice from the South: By a Black Woman of the South.* Charlotte Forten Grimke was educated in the North, but after the Civil War went South to help teach the ex-slaves to read and write. She chronicled her experience in, *The Journals of Charlotte Forten Grimke.* Frances W. Harper, an active promoter of equality for her people, wrote, *Iola Leroy, or Shadows Uplifted* in 1892. Elizabeth Keckley in her autobiography, *Behind the Scenes; or, Thirty Years a Slave, and Four Years in the White House,* covers her years as a slave and her burning desire to be free, as well as the four years she worked in the Lincoln White House as a free woman, but still plagued by a racist and sexist America. Finally, Pauline Hopkins, born in Maine just prior to the Civil War, introduced the subject of color prejudice, sexism, and uplift of the race in her novel, *Hagar's Daughter: A Story of Southern Caste Prejudice.* Ms. Hopkins was a strong advocate for self-determination and racial equality. She argued and fought against the debilitating affects of apartheid on her people.

222

Two writers who initially excelled in poetry and short stories, and later in life with novels were Charles Chestnutt and Paul Laurence Dunbar. Chestnutt, who had trained as a lawyer, wrote *The Conjure Woman* in 1899, which is a series of short stories highlighting the Black folk culture of the South. *The Wife of His Youth and Other Stories of the Color Line*, written in 1899, was very critical of race relations in the country. Two of Chestunutt's best works were *The Goophered Grapevine* and *Po' Sandy*.

Born the son of slaves, as were many of the early writers, Paul Laurence Dunbar became the most recognized writer of African American descent in the country at the turn of the century. Dunbar not only composed poetry in a southern dialect but also in traditional English. Dunbar was primarily recognized as a poet but also wrote novels, musical comedies, and short fiction. Some of his poems in dialect include, "An Ante-bellum Sermon," "When Malindy Sings," and "The Party." His most famous poem not in dialect and critical of how Black writers were blackballed if they wrote positive works on the race was, "We Wear the Mask." Late in his life, Dunbar turned to short stories to include such classic as, "The Strength of Gideon and Other Stories," "In Old Plantation Days," and "The Heart of Happy Hollow."

James Weldon Johnson bridges the gap between the early nineteenth century writers and those of the Harlem Renaissance. He was productive as a writer during both periods. Johnson was the trailblazer of a most versatile group of men and women who had a very positive impact on our culture. Many have called him a Renaissance Man because of his numerous talents. He was a writer (*The Autobiography of an Ex-Colored Man*), a poet ("The Creation"), a songwriter ("Lift Every Voice and Sing"), a chronicler of Black history (*Black Manhattan*), and also the first Black Executive Secretary of the National Association for the Advancement of Colored People. Johnson became one of the major figures of the Harlem Renaissance because of his many different accomplishments.

It was the Harlem Renaissance that witnessed an explosion of Black poets and novelists. Such greats as Langston Hughes, Claude

223

McKay, Jesse Fausett, Walter White, Wallace Thurmond, and Zora Neale Hurston wrote about the "New Negro" evolving as a result of the great northern migration of the Black population. The Harlem Renaissance, a period that lasted from 1920 to 1929, represents the flowering of the African American culture. It was a time when Black writers, musicians, poets, artists, political activists, and intellectuals came together in one small section of New York city and refined the heart and soul of Black America.

Richard Wright, Ralph Ellison, and James Baldwin followed in the footsteps of the talented authors from the Harlem Renaissance. Toni Morrison, who won a Pulitzer Prize for literature, Terry McMillan author of *Waiting to Exhale*, the novel that launched an avalanche of Black novelists, and Walter Moseley, have continued the long tradition of outstanding novelists right up to the present day.

The creative nature of Black Americans is apparent in the art of writing poetry. It has the longest history of literary expression taking us back to the 18th century and Phyllis Wheatley's poetry. Her poetry was written at such a high level of excellence that it was presented to Thomas Jefferson as evidence to disprove his assertions that Africans were inherently mentally inferior to whites. Other early poets included Jupiter Hammond, Lucy Terry, Prince, and George Moses Horton. Early 20th Century and Harlem Renaissance poets include, Paul Laurence Dunbar, Langston Hughes, Countee Cullen, and Claude McKay. Gwendolyn Brooks, Maya Angelou, and Nikki Giovanni followed in the footsteps of the earlier poets and continued the tradition of poetic excellence.

The natural creative talent of Black Americans is on display at many of the country's most prestigious art museums. Again, there is a long list of African Americans who have excelled in all fields of art. Romare Bearden began painting in the 1930's as a member of the Harlem Artists Guild and over the years gained the reputation as one of the leading 20th Century abstract painters. The one artist most associated with the Harlem Renaissance period was Aaron Douglas. In collaboration with the writers, he coordinated visuals to the messages in their novels and essays. In 1926, he worked with

Langston Hughes, Wallace Thurmond, Zora Neale Hurston, and Bruce Nugent to do illustrations for the one time published magazine *FIRE!* It is now a classic publication. Douglas did illustrations for the *Crisis* and *Opportunity Magazines*. His most famous work is the murals, "Aspects of Negro Life," now housed at the Schomburg Center in Harlem. He also painted murals for Fisk University that dealt with African American identity and history. Douglas was often referred to as "the father of African American art."

Henry Ossawa Tanner was one of the first recognized African American photographers/painters. Tanner became famous for painting moving religious scenes and images of what he called the common man. Tanner's papers are now maintained in the Archives of American Art, Smithsonian Institution.

The essence of the African American culture has been captured over the centuries and decades by many other talented artists, of which Richmond Barthe, May Howard Jackson, Norman Lewis, Laura Wheeler Waring, and Charles Wilbert White are only a few.

Black Americans have also excelled in theater, movies, and television. *Shuffle Along*, featuring Florence Mills, Josephine Baker, and introducing the world to Paul Robeson, written and produced by Eubie Blake and Noble Sissle, is credited with jump-starting the Harlem Renaissance. Langston Hughes, after seeing the performance, knew he had to live in Harlem and be a part of the great outbreak of cultural identity stimulated by the musical, *Shuffle Along*.

Long before Denzell Washington won an academy award, Charles Sidney Gilpin won national acclaim for his portrayal of the lead character in Eugene O'Neil's play, *Emperor Jones,* in 1920. Rose McClendon also was recognized as one of the most accomplished and respected actresses of the 1920's and 1930's.

225

Cicely Tyson was nominated for an Academy Award for Best Actress in 1972 for her critically acclaimed performance in the film, *Sounder.* And who can ever forget her brilliant role she portrayed as a 110-year-old ex-slave, Jane Pittman when she made that historic walk up to the water fountain, marked for whites only, and graciously, with class and history on her side, took a drink of water. Ms.

Tyson epitomizes the message in this anthology. She refused to play roles that did not portray strong, positive images of Black women. Unlike many other actresses she did her race proud by putting image above profits and fame.

Hattie McDaniel became the first African American to win an Academy Award. She won the best supporting actress award for playing a maid in the movie, *Gone With the Wind*. She was roundly criticized by some groups for playing the role of a maid that tended to stereotype Black women. Her response was, "It is much better earning $7,000 a week playing a maid than $7.00 a day being one."

Black filmmaker, Oscar Micheaux, produced more than 40 films, including the first all Black feature films, both silent and sound. Disgusted with the stereotyped portrayal in the plantation literature, Micheaux was determined to produce films as a counter-attack to Hollywood. His film, *Within Our Gates*, was a Black man's response to the racist film, *Birth of a Nation*. Micheaux did with his films what the writers of this anthology have done through literature and that is to paint a positive image of the race as counter to much of the urban street fiction that exists today.

The actor, intellectual, and political activist, Paul Robeson, represents Black excellence at its highest plateau. He excelled in every endeavor he undertook. At age 17, he won a four-year scholarship to Rutgers University. During his years at Rutgers he excelled in sports and academics. He was an All-American football player for two years in a row. He won letters in baseball, basketball, and track. Academically he was elected to both the Phi Beta Kappa Society and Cap and Skull. Robeson served as the Valedictorian for his 1919 graduating class. He went on to become an actor on stage and in movies, and an outstanding singer and spokesperson against a segregated military and against lynching.

Garland Anderson, with only a fourth grade education, became the first African American playwright to stage a full-length drama on Broadway, *Don't Judge by Appearance*, later shortened to *Appearance*. Anderson's play had its debut at Broadway's Frolic Theater on October 13, 1925. It had a two-year run throughout the United

States, re-opened for a second run in New York on April 1, 1929. The play had its international debut in London, England, in March 1930.

Black Americans have also excelled in motion pictures. One of the greatest all-Black movies was the classic, *Stormy Weather*, featuring Lena Horne, Bill "Bojangles" Robinson, and included such outstanding performers as Fats Waller, Katherine Dunham, Cab Calloway, and the Nicholas Brothers. Another outstanding movie was *Carmen Jones*, featuring Dorothy Dandridge and the great Harry Belafonte.

Black movie makers Spike Lee and Tyler Perry have continued the legacy of Oscar Micheaux with outstanding film productions. Both Lee and Perry have given us movies that create positive and strong images of African Americans. There is no doubt, Lee's classic production, *Malcolm X,* should have received an Academy Award.

Over the past fifty years, Black Americans have been extremely successful in television programs. Diahann Carroll in *Julia,* Esther Rolle in *Good Times*, Bill Cosby in *I Spy* and *the Cosby Show,* and Will Smith in *Fresh Prince of Bel-Air*, are only a few of the many Blacks who have excelled on television.

There is no question that the most successful television personality in the history of the industry is Oprah Winfrey. When writing about Black and excellence, she stands out above all others.

There are many fields of endeavor that I haven't even touched on that Blacks have displayed their genius. In the fields of medicine and science Blacks have excelled even before the turn of the 20th Century. This is reserved for another anthology.

Finally at the end of Lee's *Malcolm X*, a number of young children stand before their class and proclaim they are the descendants of some classic heroes of the Black Diaspora. Essentially what they are telling the world is the identical message in the pages of this anthology: We are Black and we are Americans, and that is an excellent combination.

CONTRIBUTING AUTHORS

Dr. Loren Alves

is a Clinical Associate Professor in the Department of Pediatric Dentistry and Orthodontics at East Carolina University School of Dentistry. He is presently writing his autobiography about his rise from poverty and living in the DeSoto Public Housing Projects in Dayton, Ohio to a successful dental practice. He served twenty-one years in the United States Dental Corp., retiring as a Colonel. He retired with the Distinguish Legion of Merit Medal. Dr. Alves has lectured internationally and within the United States on "How to Meet Special Needs and Challenges in Life," and on the TEAM Approach to Success." He devotes much of his spare time as a mentor and a volunteer for the Omega Psi Phi fraternity. A chapter from his autobiography, "Coming of Age to Manhood," is included in the anthology.

Jayme L. Bradford

is an assistant professor and mass communications coordinator at Voorhees College in Denmark, South Carolina. She began her teaching career as a communications professor at Florida Community College in Jacksonville, Florida. In addition, she taught English and Journalism at William M. Raines Senior High School. She is the former communications chairperson and assistant professor at Edward Waters College, the oldest historical black college in Florida. She also worked as a features/entertainment writer for the Florida Times-Union and an education writer at the Muskegon Chronicle. She was voted "Journalist of the Year" by the Florida Rehabilitation Association and served on the Board of Directors for the National Association of Black Journalists. She has written a short essay, "KKK: The Real Boogeyman," recalling the brutal murder of a young Black man in Mobile, Alabama.

CHRIS CANNON

author of *Winning Back Our Boys* has become nationally recognized for his award-winning interactive youth presentations. Once labeled an at-risk youth, Chris spends countless hours training, transforming, and speaking to teens across the country regarding the pressures of sex, relationships, drug/alcohol and self-identity. He skillfully shows young people how to go from tragedy to triumph, from pitiful to powerful, and from regrets to rewards. His essay, "Testing Positive: What I Did to Have Sex with Her," is a cleverly constructed essay for the young that delivers a very different message than what the title might suggest.

CARY CLACK

received a Bachelor of Arts in Political Science from St. Mary's University in 1985. He then worked as a Scholar-Intern at the Martin Luther King, Jr. Center for Nonviolent Social Change, in Atlanta where Cary wrote CNN commentaries for Coretta Scott King. He began writing a column for the *San Antonio Express-News* in 1994 and later joined the *Express-News* Editorial Board before becoming a metro columnist. Cary was the first African-American on the editorial board of a San Antonio daily as well as the first metro columnist. Cary won the Dallas Press Club's Katie Award for Best General Column and in 2008 he won the Friends of the San Antonio Public Library's Arts and Letters Award for his writing. For six years in a row, until his departure from the paper, he won the *San Antonio Current's* Reader's Choice poll for Best Columnist in the city and was also selected Best Columnist three years in a row in the *San Antonio Magazine's* Editors' and Readers' Choice Poll. Cary's last column for the *San Antonio Express-News* ran on October 9, 2011. The next day Cary began work as the communications director for the Congressional campaign of Joaquin Castro. From January 2013 through Aug. 20, 2014 he was Congressman Castro's District Director. Since Aug. 21, 2014 he has been the Director of Communications for San Antonio Mayor Ivy R. Taylor. In 2009, Trinity University

Press published a collection of his columns, *Clowns and Rats Scare Me*. Cary has written a short essay on the Tuskegee Airmen for publication in the anthology.

DR. MATEEN DIOP

is a sought after speaker and motivator. He believes that without a quality education, our nation's future is in serious trouble. An advocate for inner-city education, Mateen never forgets his roots as it relates to how he managed to overcome hurdle after hurdle to achieve academic success. He has written extensively on the subject of motivating Black males in school and life. His books include, Inner City Public Schools Still Work, Unlocking the Successful Instinct in Black Boys and Single-Gender Schooling in the Inner City. Mateen is also Executive Producer and publisher of All Things Educational—The Magazine, along with an accompanying video podcast under the same name. As a product of a single parent home, Mateen stresses the need for fathers and father figures to become "actively" engaged in the lives of their children. A section from his book, Inner City Public Schools Still Work is included in the anthology.

DAVID FLOYD

was a full-time faculty member at Austin Community College. He taught courses in accounting for freshmen and sophomore students. He received his Bachelor of Science Degree from Huston-Tillotson College in Austin, Texas, his Masters of Science in Accountancy from Bentley University in Amherst, Massachusetts and his Doctorate Degree from Argosy University. He is the author of *Through My Mother's Tears*, a heartfelt story about growing up in poverty and achieving his goals in life against insurmountable odds. His contribution to the anthology is an excerpt from his autobiography.

GEORGE D. HILLIARD

attended Tuskegee Institute where he received a B. S. degree in Biology in 1966 and a M. S. degree in Biology in 1968. He received his Medical Doctor's degree from Meharry Medical College in Nashville, Tennessee in 1972. His Internship and Residency in Obstetrics and Gynecology was performed at Wilford Hall USAF Medical Center, Lackland Air Force Base, Texas, from 1972-1976. After twelve years of active duty service in the United States Air Force, he entered private medical practice in 1981.Dr. Hilliard remains in private practice in Obstetrics and Gynecology in San Antonio, Texas. He is the author of a number of scientific publications and a contributor to textbooks in his field and areas of interest. He is the past Chief of OBGYN at various San Antonio hospitals. He is a member of Bexar County Medical Association, and Texas Medical Association. He is a fellow of the American College of Obstetrics and Gynecology and a member of the National Medical Association. He is board certified in Obstetrics and Gynecology. Dr. Hilliard is involved in a number of professional organizations and community projects. He is a recipient of the 2013 Brotherhood/Sisterhood Humanitarian Award, presented by the United Communities of San Antonio (founded as the National Conference of Christians and Jews). His essay tells the story of how he was able to include chitterlings as part of the dinner served at the first African-American History Week at Lackland Air Force Base in San Antonio, Texas.

RHONDA LAWSON

is the award winning author of *Cheatin' in the Next Room, A Dead Rose, Putting It Back Together*, and *Some Wounds Never Heal*. Rhonda is a United States Army Journalist and has garnered several journalism awards, including the 1997 Training and Doctrine Command Journalist of the Year Award. Currently she is serving in Belgium. She is an active member of Zeta Phi Beta Sorority. Rhonda has a brilliant essay on Ida B. Wells Barnett,

The Crusader from Mississippi, included in the "Legacies in Courage" section of the anthology.

TAJ MATTHEWS

is author of *Grandpa was a Preacher: A Letter to My Grandson*. It chronicles the life of Reverend Claude Black Jr. who was one of the greatest and most respected civil rights leaders in the state of Texas. Taj currently serves as Executive Director of the Claude and ZerNona Black Development Leadership Foundation, which works to revitalize inner-city communities and provides special services to at-risk teens, senior and needy families. He has contributed an important essay about the courage his grandfather showed when he challenged the San Antonio City Council's banning the great poet Langston Hughes from reading his poetry in the city in 1960, and when he challenged Reverend Billy Graham's support of a segregationist governor to appear on the podium with him during Graham's visit to San Antonio in 1952.

TOSCHIA MOFFETT,

an attorney and author, is undoubtedly one of the brightest young African American females in America. She graduated from Duke University in three years and passed the bar exam by age 24. She is also an entrepreneur and marketing guru. Toschia has many hats and wears them all well. She has written one novel, *You Wrong for That*, and is presently completing her second novel. Toschia has contributed to several anthologies and written a number of magazine articles. She has an outstanding offering, "You Can Learn a Lot from Dead People," in the anthology.

233

FATTAH MUHAMMAD

is a brilliant young Black man who has mastered the use of mathematics as a method to understand human behavior and historical events. Brother Fattah co-founded a very progressive student organization seeking to unite all the Black students at the University of Texas at San Antonio. During his three years as a student at the University he addressed issues of race, religion and garnered support for the implementation of Black Studies classes at the school. He presently lives in San Antonio where he is authoring several articles and books analyzing the meaning of numbers, human relationships, and human history. Brother Fattah's essay is, "The Mathematic Make-Up of SELF: The Self Within."

Aaronetta Hamilton Pierce

has over forty years of serving as an advocate for the arts and cultural achievements of African-Americans. She recently has begun to write essays and speeches in order to make an even stronger case for extolling the genius that is our legacy. She has served on numerous art boards including the San Antonio Museum of Art, the San Antonio Performing Arts Association, the Witte Museum and the Las Casas Foundation. Aaronetta has also served on numerous panels for the National Endowment for the Arts, has chaired a Blue Ribbon Committee for then Mayor Henry Cisneros to determine the role of city government in the arts which resulted in the city's creation of the Department of Arts and Culture. She was the first Black woman appointed to a six year term as a commissioner for the Texas Commission on the Arts. She served ten years on the Board of Trustees at Fisk University. She is currently chairing a special committee for the African-American Studies Department at the University of Texas at Austin. Aaronetta has two outstanding essays, "Letters to My Grandchildren," and "Maya Angelou: 'Her Voice Rings Eternally,'" included in the anthology.

234

ANTHONY PRIOR

played seven years in the National Football League and four years in the Canadian Football League. Anthony still holds the speed record, having run the 40-yard sprint in 4.2 seconds for the New

York Jests. He is now an author of three series of essays criticizing the manner in which Blacks are treated in professional sports. For this anthology, Anthony has provided a short autobiographical account of his pursuit of his dream to play in the National Football League. "Forty Yards in 4.2 Seconds" has a deeper message about responsibility. One must always be aware there is something more important than sports in life and that is a need to be a good person.

MARGARET RICHARDSON

has a Masters Degree in Political Science and a Masters in Criminal Justice from the University of Texas at San Antonio. She was awarded a Ruth Jones McClendon internship to work in the Texas State Legislature in 2005. She is presently working on her Doctorate Degree in Political Science. She has written an essay titled, "We Who Believe in Freedom Cannot Rest: What the Life and Work of Ella Baker Meant to Me." In her essay she brings to light the important role Ms. Baker played in the Civil Rights Movement.

DR. REVEREND JAMES WILLIAM SANDERS, SR.

was the Senior Pastor at Bethel Baptist Church in Gaffney, South Carolina for sixty-one years. He was also an educator and served as Moderator for the Thickety Mountain Baptist Association. He was a member of Omega Psi Phi Fraternity, a Mason and a recipient of the National Association for the Advancement of Colored People Hall of Fame Award. The Governor of South Carolina presented him with the Order of the Palmetto, the highest award that the state gives to a civilian. He was a member of many esteemed boards and associations. He passed away on July 6, 2010, shortly after completing his short essay which is an excerpt from his forthcoming autobiography, *The Spiritual Journey of a Legend: The Life of Reverend Dr. James W. Sanders, Sr.*

NEVIL SHEDD

was a member of the historic Texas Western basketball team that won the National Collegiate Athletic Association Men's Division One Basketball Championship in 1966. Their team made history for being the first to start five African-American players in the final four. Nevil was one of the players featured in the Disney movie, *Glory Road*, which was about that victory. The team was honored at a White House ceremony in 2007. After playing for Texas Western, Nevil went on to play briefly for the Boston Celtics until he suffered a career-ending injury. He now tours the country as a motivational speaker and conducts a summer league basketball camp for the San Antonio Spurs. Nevil's contribution to the anthology is the second in a series of essays under the heading, "Legacies of Courage."

SEPHIRA BAILEY SHUTTLESWORTH

is a former teacher and elementary school principal of twenty-three years. In 1966, Sephira and two of her siblings integrated their county's school system. She began college at Union University in Jackson, Tennessee while still a high school student. She earned a Bachelor of Science Degree in Elementary Education in less than three years. In 1986, she met the civil rights icon Reverend Fred Shuttlesworth, and they remained friends for over twenty years, finally marrying in a candlelight ceremony at the church he founded in Cincinnati, Ohio. Following Reverend Shuttlesworth's stroke in the fall of 2007, the couple returned to his Birmingham, Alabama home in early 2008. She now dedicates her time to securing his legacy as one of the big three of the Civil Rights Movement, with Dr. Martin Luther King, Jr. and Reverend Ralph Abernathy. Her essay tells the reader of the courage that her husband possessed in order to confront the racist Birmingham police in the 1960's.

BRENNER DEE STILES

currently serves as a Veterans Peer Counselor with the U.S. Department of Veteran Affairs in the Mental Health & Behavioral Science Programs, assisting veterans not only in mental health, but also veteran's plagued with homelessness, financial, and other economic needs, which often deters psychological recovery. Brenner served in the United States military and takes pride in providing and assisting other service members. Previous to assisting service members, Brenner worked for the San Antonio Housing Authority, assisting those in the community in the capacity of housing, education, and self-sufficiently for economically disadvantaged households. Brenner served as a housing manager and as a program manager for more than six years providing these services. Brenner received a Bachelor's degree and Master's degree from the University of Incarnate Word, and is currently working toward her Doctoral degree. Brenner has been a strong advocate for those needing a voice in the community and those needing assistance to overcome life's everyday challenges. Brenner provided the anthology with an essay on the great Fannie Lou Hamer.

IVY R. TAYLOR

was appointed to serve as Mayor of San Antonio on July 22, 2014. Prior to her appointment, Mayor Taylor served as the District 2 City Council Representative. Ivy R. Taylor was elected to serve as the District 2 Representative on June 13, 2009 and served two and a half terms for a total of five years. Mayor Taylor began her career working for the City of San Antonio in the Housing and Community Development Department and the Neighborhood Action Department. After six years, she left employment with the City of San Antonio to become Vice President at Merced Housing Texas. At Merced, she worked to create and implement programs to improve family stability for apartment community residents. Mayor Taylor is currently a lecturer at UTSA in the Public Administration Department. Mayor Taylor currently

237

serves on the board for Healthy Futures of Texas and Big Brothers Big Sisters of South Texas. She has served on the City's Planning Commission and as a Commissioner for the City's Urban Renewal Agency (SADA) and on the advisory board for Our Lady of the Lake's Center for Women in Church and Society. Mayor Taylor obtained a Master's Degree in City and Regional Planning from the University of North Carolina at Chapel Hill in 1998. In 1992, she received a Bachelor's Degree from Yale University. Mayor Taylor has written a short essay on the life and times of Congresswoman Shirley Chissolm.

CALVIN THOMAS

grew up in Helena, Arkansas during the era of segregation. As a young man he often heard older men and women say, "Out of every five Blacks maybe two would succeed in life because life's odds were so stacked against them." He grew increasingly aware that there was a huge discrepancy between the way Black people viewed themselves and their actual importance to society—a discrepancy he termed "mental illness." In his first publication, The Long Road from Slavery to Mental Illness, he analyzed the specific reasons for the collective mental illness that is pervasive in the Black world. In his essay, "The Authentic American Culture," he writes about the strong and beautiful culture that belongs to Black America and in essence is an intricate part of the American culture. He urges young Blacks to be proud of that culture and to protect it from many of the negative forces trying to destroy it.

238 ALEXIS WILLIAMS

is our youngest contributor to the anthology. At seventeen years old, she had the courage to write about a tragic period in her life. Her essay, "I Have Overcome," is a strong message to other young girls that, despite the tragedies they may experience, there is always hope for success in their future if they do not lose faith in who they are and their worth to the Black race and culture.

Alexis is a beautiful young Black girl with a gift as a writer and an excellent career in her future.

CARRIE WILLIAMS

(no relation to Alexis) is a graduate student at George Washington University in Washington, D.C. She received her Bachelors Degree from Virginian Union University in Richmond, Virginia in 2013. She has a book of poems that she wrote as far back as the seventh grade. Carrie, in a collaborative effort with her father, Frederick Williams, wrote the essay on the four little girls murdered in the Birmingham, Alabama Sixteenth Street Baptist Church bombing in September 1963. She has also included the two young men who were subsequently killed later on that same day.

FREDERICK WILLIAMS

received a Masters Degree and worked on his Doctorate Degree in Political Science at Indiana University prior to receiving a political appointment to serve as a Legislative Aide on the staff of Senator Birch Bayh, a Democrat from Indiana. While a member of Senator Bayh's staff, he helped manage the first Senate bill to make Dr. Martin Luther King Jr.'s birthday a national holiday. He also served on the staff of Congressman Parren Mitchell, Democrat from Baltimore, Maryland. Frederick helped establish the African-American Studies Minor at the University of Texas at San Antonio. He designed and taught a number of courses, including African-American Political Thought, African-American Politics, African-American Literature from Phyllis Wheatley to the Black Arts Movement, Politics of the Civil Rights Movement, and a course on the Novels of the Harlem Renaissance. He is the author of four novels, his most recent being *Fires of Greenwood: The Tulsa Riot of 1921*. He has ghost written three autobiographies and has edited numerous works. In 2011, *San Antonio Magazine* named him one of the five "Men of the Year". Frederick also received the "Friends of the San Antonio Public Library Arts and Letters Award for Contributions to the Community of

239

San Antonio Through His Writings and as an Educator." He has written an essay for the anthology on the work he did to help pass the King Holiday Legislation and co-authored with his daughter Carrie, the final essay, "The Love that Forgives." He also wrote both the Prologue and Epilogue to the anthology.

Secrecy, Sophistry and Gay Sex In The Catholic Church

The Systematic Destruction Of An Oblate Priest

First Edition

Published by The Nazca Plains Corporation
Las Vegas, Nevada
2011

ISBN: 978-1-61098-212-2
E-book: 978-1-61098-213-9

Published by

The Nazca Plains Corporation ®
4640 Paradise Rd, Suite 141
Las Vegas NV 89109-8000

Cover Photo
Ben Mobley

Author Photo
Les Sterling

Art Director
Blake Stephens

Dedicated to Steven E. Webb

Secrecy, Sophistry and Gay Sex In The Catholic Church

The Systematic Destruction Of An Oblate Priest

First Edition

Rev. Richard Wagner Ph.D., ACS

CONTENTS

FOREWORD

There was a murder, you know.

I have a story to tell. It's a true story that provides an intimate and sometimes disturbing look into the unseemly inner-workings of the Catholic Church. It is primarily a story about how this institution deals with dissent in its midst, but it also shows to what lengths the Church will go to silence a whistle-blower. What I am about to recount happened between 1981 and 1994. It involves the highest levels of the Vatican bureaucracy—The Sacred Congregation for Doctrine and Faith and The Sacred Congregation for Institutes of Consecrated Life, secret documents, corporate incompetence, canonical corruption, and institutionalized homophobia on an epic scale. This is my story; a retelling of my 13-year battle I had with my religious community, The Missionary Oblates of Mary Immaculate, following the publication of my doctoral thesis, *Gay Catholic Priests; A Study of Cognitive and Affective Dissonance*. (NOTE: The complete dissertation is included below as Part 2.)

My name is Richard Wagner. I am a Catholic priest, albeit without formal faculties to act as a public minister. I was ordained in Oakland California in 1975. And I am the only Catholic priest in the world with a doctorate in Clinical Sexology. My research into the sexual attitudes and behaviors of gay Catholic priests in the active ministry is unprecedented and is as fresh and timely today as it was the day it was completed. Following the publication of my dissertation there was a firestorm of international publicity. The press dubbed me "The Gay Priest," but my research and what it implies made patently clear that I wasn't the only gay priest. In fact, there is a sizable segment of the clergy population that is gay and these men are forced to live duplicitous lives of repression in secret. This often creates an atmosphere of extreme isolation and loneliness that can and does drive these men to desperate measures to find emotional and moral support they should be receiving from their Church. These men love their Church, but hate what is it doing to them. And as bad as the situation was back in the early 80's, it's even worse today.

My groundbreaking research broke the code of silence surrounding this delicate topic. The Church's single-minded effort to quash the emerging story and silence me showed that I needed to be "dealt with" in the most severe fashion; an example had to be made of me. If other priests started coming out of the closet and demanding to be treated with dignity and respect it would certainly undercut the entirety of Catholic sexual moral theology—there is no place for non-reproductive sexuality within that paradigm. Needless to say, this notoriety (some say infamy) effectively ended my public ministry.

The irony is that at the same time my story was unfolding an unimaginable scandal, involving hundreds of Catholic priests across the globe, was also brewing. Cardinals, bishops and provincials worldwide were, and still are, furtively shuffling pedophile priest from one crime scene to another. They were, and still are, involved in a massive corporate cover up of their own crimes and those of their brother clergy.

While I was singled out for 13 years of Church vitriol, public character assassination, spiritual depravation and communal shunning, my superiors claimed that they were simply trying to protect the Church from scandal. These same Church leaders and others like them were lying, prevaricating and sabotaging any effort to uncover the burgeoning clergy sexual abuse scandal that would soon rock the front pages of newspapers all over the world. And here again they claimed they were only trying to protect the good name of the Church. But in shielding the identities of the perpetrators, covering up their crimes, blaming the victims and ignoring the severity of the problem, they were actually perpetuating the abuse.

The public panic among Church officials toward me—a single up-front gay priest in their midst—is in stark contrast to their apathetic and anemic response to the systemic clergy sexual abuse that now engulfs them. And there's a reason for that. The Church, then as well as now, uses the specter of gay priests as a scapegoat for their ecclesiastical malfeasance. The faithful are being manipulated by cynical Church leaders, including the Pope, who whip up bogus scandals involving homosexuality, both inside the Church and in society at large. They make it a practice to conflate the notion of a happy, healthy, integrated same-sex attraction with pedophilia, which is an outrageous lie. But the deception continues and it poisons the minds of pious people of faith. It also provides the necessary smokescreen for the thousands upon thousands of childhoods they've actually destroyed while bankrupting their dioceses and rupturing the trust of millions of believers.

I am confident in making the comparison between my struggle and the clergy sex abuse scandal, because I have first-hand knowledge of this criminality. I was sexually molested as a 14-year-old boy in an Oblate seminary in southern Illinois. And not one of the religious superiors I told about these incidents, while I was in formation, did anything about it. Any wonder why I would then seem to have an "attitude" problem especially when it involved my religious superiors?

My story is the story of a Church that will go to any length, even violating its core principles—Gospel values that form the fundamental tenets of faith—to protect its public image. In other words, this is a story of a Church out of control.

I've scrupulously included numerous internal documents below, some of them very sensitive in nature, that pertain to my story exclusively. But despite the very specific nature of these documents, they illuminate how Church leaders respond to a crisis. As in the clergy abuse scandal, no one in the Oblate chain of command can or will accept responsibility for any wrongdoing. And since the cast of characters is constantly changing, everyone can avoid accountability. Each individual hides behind the corporate persona; this in effect provides an effective means of deniability.

The Church, which is generally a stickler for precision and accuracy, can and does claim collective amnesia when the historical record points directly back to it. There is a pattern of evasion and sidestepping, of innuendo and disinformation, lying and public shaming, all in an effort to shift blame and avoid accountability.

As any clergy abuse survivor advocate will tell you, establishing an accurate historical record is essential for making his case; it's also a painstakingly arduous task. However, Church internal documents are often "sub rosa"—put under the seal of ecclesiastical secrecy. The penalty for divulging these documents, or even alluding to them, is excommunication, the same penalty for breaking the seal of confession.

Nor can anyone in a leadership position in the Church truly apologize for injuries inflected, either personally or collectively. When there is a statement of regret it is always halfhearted and presented in the most passive and innocuous way. Such statements may actually concede that an injury happened, but it is never because of anything Church leaders have done or failed to do. And their preferred remedy for this inconvenience is that we all should pray for healing. However, when these same Church leaders are pressed to address the issue of restitution for their egregious deeds, they stonewall. When amends are finally wrestled from them, they claim it is due to their charity and good will, never from their moral obligation. In other words, their deep "regret" is for hardships *endured*, but never remorse for hardships *inflicted*.

When I pressed the Oblate leadership for accountability in my case, as so many advocates for rights of those effected by the clergy abuse scandal have done in their dealing with the Church, the leadership reflexively inverts the blame; they villainize the victim. We victims of ecclesiastical crimes as well as our advocates are immediately recast as malicious persecutors of the Church. Our quest for justice is generally reduced to a grubbing after money. Money, they say, that belongs to God's people. They accuse us of bullying them, the defenseless long-suffering Church leadership. They claim our true objective is to destroy or demean God's Church and to undermine the integrity of Church teaching.

My story begins at its end. On July 28, 1993 I received a formal obedience from my legitimate Provincial superior, Fr. Paul Nourie, OMI. Under my vow of obedience I am obligated to do his bidding. However, both he and I knew that this was a sham obedience, one I actually helped him concoct. This final kabuki-like dance we were doing was purely for show. It was to overcome the only remaining canonical impediment to sealing my fate as an Oblate of Mary Immaculate.

When I refused the obedience, as I had to, my 25-year membership in the community would soon come to an end. While this was a very sad time in my life, the truth of the matter is that everything that could be lost in terms of my religious affiliation and my priesthood had already been taken from me. I had already been in an ecclesiastical limbo for 13 years. Every possible punishment had already been meted out.

To be clear; Fr. Nourie's contrived obedience was a face-saving effort for the Oblate leadership. Once I'm out of the way no one would ever know what really happened. No one, least of all my brother Oblates, would know that my sacred vows were subverted by our community's leadership to cleanse themselves of any responsibility for the destruction of my priesthood and ministry and the massive breakdown in canonical due process.

It was indeed a sad time for me, but it also set a dangerous precedent, which has the gravest implications for every Oblate, and indeed every Catholic religious, as a bearer of rights. What follows is my last gift to the Church. It is a letter I sent to every member of the Provincial Council, the men who were soon to decide my fate. It is as thorough a presentation of the facts as possible of all the events that lead up to this imminent ecclesiastical fratricide.

CHAPTER 1

Introduction

February 23, 1994

My fellow Oblates,

Fr. Nourie's obedience of six months ago, ordering me to dissolve all my personal, professional, and financial affairs in San Francisco within 15 days and to move to an Oblate house in Seattle, is not a morally binding or even a coherent requirement. By the leadership's own fault I have not been an Oblate except in name for many years, and until this obedience I have had no official dealings with Fr. Nourie during his entire tenure as Provincial Superior. This obedience is an attempt by the General leadership, under whose direct instructions Fr. Nourie is acting, to bring about my *de jure* dismissal from the Congregation without having to face inquiry into my *de facto* dismissal.

As an Oblate I was killed off long ago; and now the leadership is attempting to exhume my Oblate corpse and administer to it the appearance of a legal hanging—hoping all the while that no one notices. You owe it to one another if not to me to stop this grotesque deception and to insist conclusively upon the right of every Oblate to just and equitable treatment. If any of you has the least regard for the kind of society you live in, and hence for the kind of men you are, you will at long last *hear* me.

Before I lay out the extraordinary details of this case, I shall devote the rest of this section to a brief survey.

In 1981, following my public self-identification as a gay priest, the Superior General stirred the provincial leadership to initiate dismissal proceedings against me. The latter pressed these proceedings even though I tendered apologies for any scandal I may have caused, provided explanations of my actions and beliefs, and offered a full retraction of any statements that my superiors deemed contrary to Church teachings. Even before the local leadership forwarded the acts of dismissal to Rome, they dissolved all financial and spiritual bonds uniting me with the Congregation and set me adrift. But once the acts were in Rome the formal process stalled, and the general leadership adopted an indecisive and irregular course of action whose overall effect was my dismissal in practice. This aberrant state of affairs, with one illusory interruption in 1988, has gone on for nearly 13 years. During all this time, with no semblance of due process having been applied, I have had no canonical standing in the Congregation, enjoyed no part in the spiritual life of the community, and received no contributions to my livelihood.

The first part of my ordeal consisted of a protracted and diffuse process that no one party to it could define. My requests that the leadership arrange an impartial hearing to examine the history of the case and to clarify my status went unheeded, and the process degenerated into an intermittent, open-ended interrogation into my beliefs and dispositions that the leadership allowed to drag on for seven years. No matter how often or how thoroughly I answered their questions, the representatives and leaders with whom I had to deal—and they were many—resorted to further insinuations of misconduct as the only way to explain a state of affairs that they did not know how to resolve without acknowledging their own egregious errors. The more I protested the lack of due process and observed that my uncanonical separation was becoming more final with every month, the more the leadership judged me to be negative, uncooperative, and unfit to be an Oblate.

Those years involved great personal suffering for me, not only because of the process itself, which was a torment, but also because of the practical termination of my religious and priestly vocations and the consequent need to reshape my life entirely as a layman. The effect of those years was that all viable membership in the Congregation, and indeed its very worth in my eyes, expired. Realizing as well that the leadership was determined that I should leave, my sole concern then was to save my priesthood.

Therefore in 1987 I reached an understanding with representatives of the General Leadership to leave the Congregation voluntarily by finding a bishop who would incardinate me into his diocese. I agreed to this solution, with three conditions: 1) That the leadership publicly affirm me an Oblate in good standing; 2) That they acknowledge at a minimum the doubtfulness of the process to which they had subjected me; 3) That they assure me of a good faith effort to help me in my transition to secular priesthood. The Superior General, Fr. Marcello Zago, OMI, appeared to have met the first two conditions in his letter to me of June 1988, in which he expressed his regrets for the hardships I had sustained since 1981 and embraced me as a brother Oblate. The worth of his gesture, however, depended crucially upon whether the leadership was prepared to follow through with positive efforts to facilitate my transition.

Considering the ruin that the leadership had visited upon my vocation, the personal injuries that I had needlessly and uncanonically sustained, and my willingness to forgive these and leave the Congregation so long as I received help in saving my priesthood, the leadership had the deepest obligation to accord me gracious and unstinting help. Their verbal solicitude and mutual character-witnessing over the years notwithstanding, that obligation was never met, nor was even the semblance of normal standing in the Congregation achieved. Quite the contrary. The local leadership, guided by the General Administration, constantly played interference with my efforts to incardinate in the Archdiocese of San Francisco, while simultaneously refusing to normalize my status by assigning me to the ministry that I had developed after Fr. Zago's apparent exoneration of me in 1988. Two years of hard work toward establishing myself in the Archdiocese of San Francisco—which had every promise of succeeding with a minimum of patience and creative effort by the leadership— were consequently made to fail. That was when my hope of surviving as a priest failed as well.

In 1990 I wrote to Fr. Zago to request information about the appeal process and to lay before him a summary of my grievance, citing the General Administration itself as the party ultimately responsible for all that had happened to me. I wanted the leadership to acknowledge that whatever may have been their individual motives regarding me; their *collective* behavior was unacceptable and wrong. Following the pattern of his predecessor never to allude to the specifics of what I might say in defense of myself, the most Fr. Zago had to say in reply was that my grievance was "most negative". He patronizingly waved it away and instructed me to begin a dialogue with yet a third provincial about other options.

Since I had already lost a quarter of my life in futile effort along those lines, not to mention all the years I had spent preparing for my vocation, I resolved to lose no more. Therefore I have refused to let the case revert again to the provincial level and I have clung to Fr. Zago as the person finally responsible to provide remedy. The history of this case proves beyond question that the leadership has accumulated an enormous moral and material debt to me, and I maintain that a due sense of equity toward a fellow Oblate calls for voluntary and full restitution. This call is the immediate cause of Fr. Zago's instruction to Fr. Nourie to place me under obedience. It is precisely to evade accountability for my degraded condition as an Oblate and as a priest and to elide the Congregation's outstanding debt toward me that now leads the General Administration to contrive this *second* dismissal process.

Key to the leadership's success in this endeavor is simplicity to the point of deception. This simplicity is manifested in Fr. Zago's mock-bewildered summation of my case in his last note to me of June 25, 1993: "I cannot see how you can pretend to have a financial claim towards the Congregation from whom you received your formation without giving back the promised missionary commitment." And again it is shown in Fr. Nourie's laconic remark in August 1993 when he states that my moving into an Oblate residence was necessary "... if being an Oblate is to have any significance whatsoever."

The leadership hopes that such vague insinuations of misconduct— couched always in protestations of their unflagging good will—will justify this obedience and my eventual dismissal. In a letter written to me after I declined his obedience, Fr. Nourie wrote: "...your absence from the community is considered illegitimate. As you know, such absence, if protracted, can constitute cause for your dismissal from the Congregation." But three years before this, at the time of my appeal to the General Administration, Fr. Zago remarked: "When I wrote to you in June of 1988, I did not sanction in any way the continuation of your absence from community."

The innuendo centered on the word 'absence' is crucial to the leadership's effort to obtain my *de jure* dismissal, and I shall examine it closely toward the end of this history. For now I shall simply note that the term entered the process in the summer of 1987, when certain Oblate representatives surreptitiously defined my situation as "tolerated absence." Afterward, the leadership deliberately planted this harmless-sounding label in virtually all their official documentation of my case. The meaning of the term and the reason for its concerted repetition are unmistakable in hindsight: it is propaganda designed to create the false impression that my peripheral standing in the Congregation is the result of my unlawfully absenting myself at some indeterminate point in the past rather than the result of the leadership unlawfully banishing me.

In short, it is an attempt to sweep the history of this 13-year legal aberration under the rug of Canon 665 §2, simply by *declaring* me guilty of unlawful absence. This attempt to transfer culpability through the repetition of a word, however, cannot survive an impartial reading of the dossier. Thus the leadership hopes that the present obedience and the ensuing six-month "absence" will be sufficient to procure my dismissal without having to look any deeper into the history that explains the emergence and persistence of the much longer "absence."

My defense—as always—is to bring that history to the fore.

CHAPTER 2

1980 - 1983

On November 21, 1980, I published an article in *The National Catholic Reporter* entitled *Being Gay and Celibate—Another View*, written in response to an anonymous article published earlier in the same paper. The anonymous author began his article by stating, "Right now, I do not have the courage to sign this with my name. I stand alone in faith. Perhaps I shall write again and take that risk." He went on to explain: "I am writing to share my reflections with the many gay priests and religious who are suffering while coming to grips with their identity— those who are alienated, isolated, confused, afraid and hurting."

The author was concerned with the repressive, even phobic atmosphere that surrounds this subject in the Church and with the consequent hiddenness that typifies the lives of homosexual priests and religious. He wanted to spread the good news of his experience that one can be gay and celibate and acceptable to God. I fully sympathized with the unknown author's sense of isolation and with his wish to be open about his sexual identity without fear of reprisals, and I agreed with his opinion that sexual orientation does not condemn a person in the eyes of God or disqualify him or her for a celibate vocation.

On the other hand, I was struck by his simplistic and judgmental attitude toward gay priests or religious who, for whatever reason, engage in sexual activity. His running toward epithets such as 'cheaters,' 'hypocrites,' and 'exploiters' to characterize such priests seemed to me an evasion of the human depth and seriousness of the problem. Such condemnation, I wrote, "can only serve to reinforce the feeling of isolation and anguish which so many gay priests and religious experience in today's church."

At the time I wrote this reply, I was also completing my doctoral dissertation, *Gay Catholic Priests: A Study of Cognitive and Affective Dissonance*, based on three years of extensive study of gay Catholic priests, in the active ministry, across the United States. This research had made me sensitive to the thoughts and emotions with which homosexual priests were grappling with their dual identities and practices, and I had little patience for dismissive platitudes, especially coming from one who was himself a gay priest.

My article did contain some provocative-sounding statements, such as the one quoted by the *New York Times*: "One should not underestimate the severe psychological conflict and self-preoccupation, which total sexual self-denial, can engender in some people." But my object was not to condone, much less to encourage, sexual activity by anyone. My sole aim was to bring a critical perspective to bear on a subject that was all too easily locked away with the key labeled "bad priest." Being gay myself and "out" to my superiors, I had long felt that homosexuality in the Church eventually had to be brought into the open and discussed with candor and maturity. That is why I requested permission from my superiors to develop an up-front gay ministry in the first place and why they had sent me to graduate school to obtain credentials qualifying me for such work.

During my personal development I gradually came to believe that the first step toward bringing this subject into the open was for gay priests and religious to make ourselves known—in much the same way as gay people were coming out in society at large—and that was the prime motive for adopting gay Catholic priests as the subject of my dissertation and for submitting my article. Together they were my own coming out, and my encouragement of others to do the same. I took the risk, in other words, that the anonymous author had the prudent good sense not to take. I ended my article with the following remark (eliminated by the editor of *The National Catholic Reporter*, along with much else unfortunately, from the published version):

> The anonymous author concludes with a call to courage, the courage to believe that we are acceptable to God regardless of our sexual identity. I agree wholeheartedly that we must have that courage. But we must have the courage for more than that. We must have the courage also to break out of our anonymity and isolation, and the courage to ask openly, honestly, and deeply the questions, which press upon us so urgently.

I would repeat this coming out in a disastrous television interview taped on February 6, 1981, on which I shall have much more to say below.

These acts of public self-identification are the "crimes" that ultimately would bring ruin to my religious and priestly vocations and have brought us, 13 years later, to our present deliberation.

Superior General Fernand Jetté, OMI, after reading my article in Rome, wrote to Provincial Superior Paul Waldie, OMI, on February 8, 1981, with the following instructions:

> [Fr. Wagner's] declaration: "I, too, am a gay priest..." and the principles he expresses in that article are incompatible with the teachings of the Church and with the vows he has pronounced.
>
> If there isn't in [Fr. Wagner] a sincere disposition to change his way of life and to fully accept the requisites of the commitments he has taken, the simplest solution would be that he personally ask to leave the priesthood and religious life. Otherwise—even though the solution would be a still more sorrowful one—he will be dismissed from the Congregation.
>
> ...By doing nothing, we are not helping this confrere who has installed himself in a false life, nor are we helping the People of God who are scandalized by such attitudes, nor are we helping the Religious Institute which loses all credibility.

Attached to Fr. Jetté's letter was an even more explicit document entitled *How to Proceed?* written by the Procurator General of the Institute, Fr. Michael O'Reilly, OMI. It began:

> Father Wagner should be made to face up to the incompatibility of is life-style with the commitment he made by Religious Profession and the reception of Sacred Orders.
>
> If he is not prepared to make an honest effort to abstain from homosexual activity, he should be helped to come to a decision to seek release from his obligations as a priest and religious.

From my public self-identification as a gay priest, Frs. Jetté and O'Reilly concluded that I had adopted patterns of belief and conduct amounting to an active abandonment of my religious commitments. This was a completely false assumption on their part. But neither official so much as suggested the need for further inquiry to ascertain the facts. Guilt was presumed from the beginning, and despite my vigorous protests in the months to come of this mode of administering justice, the process Frs. Jetté and O'Reilly set in motion moved inexorably forward.

Fr. Waldie received Fr. Jetté's letter on February 20 and called me to the Provincial House the following day to read it. I was stunned. Since its publication in late November, the *National Catholic Reporter* article had generated no fallout at all, of which I was aware. No letters to the editor were published condemning the piece; I received no negative mail or phone calls; the response of friends and acquaintances was mostly bland; and Fr. Waldie, who read the article when it was published, responded mildly, certainly not with alarm.

My coming out in the press was a non-event on the local scene and virtually forgotten by early February. Of greater concern at that time were the alarming events associated with an interview taped for the local television program, *Bay Scene 7*. From the perspective predating Fr. Jetté's letter this interview was the first sign that I was on the wrong track.

On February 6, 1981, the date the TV interview was taped, I was an Oblate in good standing, not accused of misconduct, under no ban, and certainly not figured as a renegade priest intent upon scandalizing the Christian community. I was an Oblate scholar whose research was regarded as an illuminating contribution to the understanding of a long-hidden aspect of Church life and was being received with a sobriety appropriate to the theme. I was also an out and proud gay priest. I was out to my provincial and most of the men I lived with before I was ordained and I was now out publicly thanks to the *National Catholic Reporter* article.

Looking back, one easily sees the danger lurking in my success. It was all but inevitable that identifying myself as a gay priest while discussing a large sample of gay priests who were at once sexually active and critical of the vow of mandatory celibacy would lead many viewers to infer that I myself must be one of the sample.

I should point out that when I designed my research project, with the help of my advisor, Wardell Pomeroy, Alfred Kinsey's associate, I proposed to find a sample of 50 self-identifying gay priests, not 50 sexually active gay priests. Although I expected that there would be some sexual activity in my sample, I could not have anticipated that 48 of them would be currently involved in partnered sex, a surprising and remarkable result. In hindsight it is difficult to see how I could have expected that my own public coming out, a risky endeavor all by itself, could possibly be combined with a public discussion of the results of my research without disaster resulting. "Pride goeth before a fall," as scripture says. But in this case the pride was not rebellion but simply the satisfaction of knowing that I had done my job well and the conviction with which I publicly "stood up" for gay priests and religious.

In neither the NCR article or the taped television interview was I condoning the behaviors of my sample, much less intending a public exhibition to my private life. At that time I had no sense of danger, much less that I had placed my vocation in mortal peril. In short, I believed—deluded as I no doubt was—that as a self-identified gay priest I could give an interview on my research, that I was qualified to do it, and that the result, though inevitably controversial, would be overall constructive. I could not have anticipated the ghastly impression that the media's craving for sensation on the one hand and the Church's dread of scandal on the other would together generate.

How did the *Bay Scene* fiasco come about? In mid-January the program's director approached the president of my graduate institute (The Institute for the Advanced Study of Human Sexuality) about the possibility of doing a segment on the Institute. The president told the director of my dissertation and suggested that I would be a good representative of the Institute. Within days I was introduced to the director. I assure you that before doing the interview I asked for guarantees about the type of questions that they would ask, and I pointedly stressed the seriousness of the matter, the importance of keeping attention focused on the dissertation, and the need to avoid any hint of sensationalism. Moreover, I inquired with others about how much I could rely upon the director and the host of the program to keep their focus on my research, and I was told I could trust them.

The interview was taped during a two-hour session. Several times I interrupted the interviewer to insist that certain questions not be asked. I objected in particular to his repeated attempt to turn the conversation to my private life. I have also recorded my conviction that I did not answer what I take to be the most provocative question from the point of view of Fr. Waldie's subsequent allegations, but that that question was provided with an answer from a different part of the interview after taping. I was completely inexperienced at this sort of thing and had no idea of the editorial liberties that television programmers take with taped interviews. On the whole, however, despite some misgivings, I felt that the taping had gone well, and I signed the release before leaving the studio. As it turned out, the station reduced and rearranged two hours of tape to a bare 15 minutes of airtime, and the result was as far removed as it could possibility be from what I had expected.

From my point of view, it is what happened to the tapes after I signed the release that constitutes the real scandal of the *Bay Scene* interview. While I am not saying that two wrongs make a right, a second wrong can make the first look very much worse than it actually was. In this case the first wrong—I have never denied this and virtually begged to be forgiven for it—was that I gave myself to such an enterprise to begin with. The second wrong was that the program was hijacked and turned into an opportunity to discredit my work and me. The story of how the tapes on February 6 passed into other people's hands and became theirs to tamper with at will is fantastic; and were it not that it all happened to me and the proof for it all exists, I would myself not believe that members of the local church could stoop to such tactics. Here, however, I shall keep the details to a minimum.

Fr. Robert Sunderland, SJ, a Jesuit working on the editorial board at KGO-TV heard that a program involving a homosexual Catholic priest had been taped and was scheduled for airing on February 14. The Jesuit apparently found the very idea preposterous and concluded that Richard Wagner must surely be a priest impostor. He contacted the Archdiocese with this information, and the Archdiocese then contacted Fr. Waldie. Fr. Waldie informed the Archdiocese that, yes, Fr. Wagner is a Catholic priest and an Oblate in good standing. Having learned that Fr. Wagner was not only a legitimate priest but enjoyed the good opinion of his superior, Archdiocesan representatives contacted the management of KGO-TV, arranged a private viewing of the tapes, and persuaded the management to cancel the original program date.

These representatives made no further attempt to contact Fr. Waldie to determine what was at issue or to arrange a happier solution. Nor did they contact me to see if I would not agree to changes that they would find more acceptable or even to cancel the program altogether, an alternative I certainly would have preferred under the circumstances. Instead the solution, from their point of view, was to re-edit the tape and end it with a five-minute "rebuttal" by Fr. Gerald Coleman, SS, an instructor of moral theology at St. Patrick's Seminary in Menlo Park, California. Fr. Coleman's remarks decisively shaped the subsequent perception of my character and views and more than anything else explains the uncritical acquiescence and haste with which Fr. Waldie set about to expedite Fr. Jetté's instructions. Fr. Coleman's remarks were a frame-up, a conscious and deliberate attempt to defame me. And in the tumultuous and panicked aftermath of the program, Fr. Waldie, despite having no reservations about me, or my work up until this point, discards everything he knows about me after years of living together and accepts Fr. Coleman's every word as the truth.

Fr. Coleman's contributions were nothing more than a string of *ad hominem* statements. This is so clear that it is difficult to understand how intelligent people, especially those responsible for assuring that I was treated fairly, were unable to see through them.

Fr. Coleman attempted to do three things: to discredit my research, which to him meant denying that homosexuals exist in the priesthood; to attribute to me the preposterous view that the dictionary definition of celibacy somehow exempts homosexual priests from the requirement to live a sexually abstinent life; and to insinuate, to the extent of directly asserting, that everyone must assume that I personally am sexually active.

It was Fr. Coleman's remarks, not mine, that finally condemned me. His reasoning was essentially the same as Fr. Jetté's and it provides an excellent illustration of what gay priests and religious mean when they talk about their sense of repression, fear, and isolation in the Church. Here is a sampling of the logic with which any gay priest who dares to speak his sexual identity in public can expect to be confronted.

Fr. Coleman begins his part of the interview with an admission that he has "never read or seen" my dissertation, and then he sets out to show that its conclusions cannot possibly be true. One might wonder how he could challenge the study's conclusions without having read the study, and the answer is, with a syllogism. He observes that a study published by sociologists Alan Bell and Martin Weinberg entitled *Homosexualities* had been "critiqued" because "homosexuals studied homosexuals". He then generalizes: "Whenever that happens you will automatically get a bit of prejudice and bias [in favor of homosexuals]. Inevitably that is so in this situation as well." Since Richard Wagner has admitted being homosexual, Fr. Coleman reasons, there is no need to review his research to know that its conclusions—whatever they might be—are "automatically" and "inevitably" unreliable. (NOTE: Coleman is wrong; both Alan Bell and Martin Weinberg are heterosexual men.)

After disposing of my research, Fr. Coleman then turns to the idea that my work and remarks were an attempt to rationalize or justify homosexual activity on the part of homosexual priests. "I think," he says "it is very important to redefine what Fr. Wagner was indicating; that [to the contrary] celibacy is really a very positive commitment on the part of priests to serve the church in a chaste sort of way, which rules out any kind of genital activity. And thus…I do not see how anyone can justify the two positions simultaneously."

The interviewer's next line of questioning has to do with the dictionary definition of celibacy, and it is here that Fr. Coleman insinuates that I was attempting to justify homosexual activity by citing the dictionary definition. Fr. Coleman reminds the audience that the concept of celibacy "is taken over into an ecclesial, theological context" and thus is made to include homosexual activity. On the whole, the viewer is left with the impression that Fr. Wagner prefers the "secular" definition over the "ecclesial" definition, that he does not think of celibacy as a positive commitment, and that he personally is trying to have it both ways.

Fr. Coleman is simply repeating in a vague, pedantic way an idea that I had stated more precisely: "The church presumes that there is no [licit] sexual activity outside heterosexual marriage, and thus she feels that a renunciation of heterosexual marriage is enough to satisfy a commitment to sexual abstinence." Again, the overwhelming impression Fr. Coleman leaves with the viewer is that not only is Fr. Wagner automatically and inevitably biased in his research and personally trying to have it both ways but he is theologically stupid as well.

Fr. Coleman's closing remark—the remark that also ends the program and informs the passive viewer as to the meaning of what he or she has just seen— is the noose around Fr. Wagner's neck: "...when one says that term 'homosexual priest,' the assumption is that they are acting out their homosexuality; as we wouldn't normally use the term 'heterosexual priest' because if we say that we are acting it out." Since Fr. Wagner applied "that term" to himself, he must be assumed to be acting out his sexuality. So declares Fr. Coleman. (NOTE: Coleman is wrong again, because no heterosexual priest would hesitate to identify himself as straight. And no one would think less of him if he did.)

Now if Fr. Coleman had not been on a mission to destroy my reputation, he might have said that while many uninformed or careless people resort to this *ad hominem* argument, it is wrong for them to do so considering Church teaching, which has distinguished between the morally neutral homosexual condition and overt homosexual conduct since 1976. He might also have pointed out that the distinction between orientation and behavior has been a virtual cliché in the scientific, legal, and moral literature on homosexuality for more than a century.

Interestingly, shortly after the *Bay Scene* controversy died down, Fr. Coleman himself, in a series of articles on homosexuality in the archdiocesan newspaper, stressed the importance of the distinction between the homosexual condition and homosexual behavior. In his commission to rebut Fr. Wagner, however, Fr. Coleman did not mention the distinction and elevated the *ad hominem* fallacy of inferring overt conduct from psycho-sexual identity to a rule of thumb that everyone ought to apply in the case of self-identified gay priests and religious.

Of course it is simply false to say, as Fr. Coleman does in the quotation above, that if a heterosexual priest were to discuss his sexuality "we" would assume that he is involved in sexual activity. From St. Augustine right down to our own day there is a vast body of literature by celibate men discussing the difficulties of the celibate life given the power of the sexual urge and the attractions of the female sex. A strikingly pertinent example of this was provided when the public furor over the Bay Scene program was in full swing. Fr. Miles O'Brien Riley, a spokesman for the San Francisco Archdiocese and a Bay Area television and radio personality, when asked by the *New York Times* (February 27, 1981) to respond to the controversy, remarked: "I'm heterosexual and it's damned hard to be celibate and heterosexual with the pressures we face and to go home to an empty room at night. I'm lonely for a woman—he [Richard Wager] is lonely for a man."

None of my public remarks about my same-sex orientation come close to this type of graphic language, and that Fr. Riley or any other self-identifying heterosexual priest can talk about his sexual desires in the context of his celibate commitment with impunity is a remarkable illustration of the double standard that applies to homosexual persons. You can be sure that if Fr. Coleman were to suggest in public that Fr. Miles, given his statement, must be acting out his sexuality, it would not be Fr. Miles who would find himself in trouble.

Of course Fr. Coleman was right when he said that heterosexual priests do not normally refer to themselves as heterosexuals. But the explanation of that is the same as the explanation of why Fr. Miles was not silenced for confessing his longings for a woman. The prevailing assumption has always been that *all* priests are "good" heterosexual men. Moreover, there are those who feel duty bound to deny and conceal that the church has in her service a significant population of men and women who happen to be homosexual. Again, the very reason I spent three long years compiling the data for my dissertation.

After the take-over of the *Bay Scene* program, the producer, who had been taken off the assignment, kept me informed of developments. Because he had persuaded me to do the program in the first place, he was effusively apologetic, explaining that the events then taking place were "the craziest thing I have ever seen." On February 19, he brought VCR equipment and a copy of the final version of the program to my apartment. I felt sick when I saw what a shambles it had become and what a devastating impression it was bound to make.

Two days later, on February 21, Fr. Waldie showed me Fr. Jetté's letter. The following evening of February 22, with no prior announcement, the *Bay Scene* program aired—and from that point forward my voice was drowned out.

During our meeting the previous day, with the TV interview still pending, Fr. Waldie asked me to write a letter explaining my two-month-old article in the light of Fr. Jetté's reaction. The following day the program was broadcast. Within two days "scandal" was breaking all over the Bay Area, and shortly thereafter it was picked up by the wire services. The coincidence of the arrival of Fr. Jetté's letter just as the *Bay Scene* scandal was breaking made my situation extremely precarious. The only plan of action I could come up with was to go ahead with the letter Fr. Waldie had asked me to write. If I could provide a satisfactory explanation and apology for my November article, hopefully the television imbroglio could be dealt with on its own later.

At the same time, I realized that the Superior General's assertions were essentially of the same *ad hominem* variety as Fr. Coleman's and that to answer the one was largely to answer the other, and I wrote my letter with that in mind. Nevertheless, it was imperative to keep the two events distinct; for if they were allowed to merge into a single blurred impression of misconduct, then truly all hope for justice would be lost.

In the first five days of pandemonium following the TV interview, I composed the letter Fr. Waldie requested, completed it on February 26, and hand-delivered it to the Provincial House the same day. In the letter I clarified the distinction between being gay and being sexually active; reaffirmed my commitment to religious life by denying the presumption that I had "installed" myself in any other life; offered to repudiate any views my superiors deemed offensive or unorthodox; and forswore further public discussion of homosexuality in the press or media. Above all, I expressed my apologies, because despite my deep commitment to the issue of gay identity in religious life, membership in my religious community and survival as a priest were my paramount values. From the day I delivered this letter to its final acceptance by the Oblate leadership seven years later, I consistently argued that it provided the only authentic basis for reconciliation. Given its extremely important role in the controversy, I shall here present the full text.

Dear Father Waldie:

Please forgive this letter's formality, but as Emily Dickenson once wrote, "With death a formal feeling comes." Truly I feel threatened with a kind of death, for priesthood within the Catholic Communion has been my life's blood.

Father, this has been the most agonizing time in my life. When I first entered into this ministry to gay people I knew I would have to face hardships and that these would include suspicion, rumor, and open hostility. But what have I said or done to deserve *this*?

It is one thing for a man to be *accused* of wrong doing, for then he knows he can defend his honor; but it is another to have it *asserted* against him that he is a wrongdoer, for then there can be no question of inquiry and justice. That persons in authority should wish to make serious inquiry into statements I have made or am alleged to have made or into positions I have taken or am alleged to have taken is clearly within their right. But no sound system of jurisprudence begins with a conviction of guilt.

I deny, unequivocally and in good conscience, what has been asserted against me. It has never been my practice to make public profession of my sins; that is a matter strictly between me and my confessor; and no one has the right to demand to know or to presume to know that sacred confidentiality.

As for what I have said in the public forum, my statements must be taken on their own merits and within their proper context. *I have never in any public forum intentionally or knowingly affirmed or denied sexual activity on my part subsequent to my vows of celibacy and chastity.* If in the judgment of my superiors I have made statements, which can be so construed, I am more than willing to deny that in my writing of those statements I intended that they should be so construed.

Father, have I not from the beginning of this pursuit sought your advice and kept you informed? Have I ever practiced deceit or withheld information? Have I not always proceeded in complete openness and good faith?

Prior to you receiving a letter from the Superior General, I had no indication that the path I was pursuing might result in such a calamity. Time and again did you not approve and commend my efforts in this direction? Indeed, just one day before you received that letter was I not greeted with open arms by you and other members of our community for having fulfilled so thoroughly and so well the obligation, which I contracted with you three years before? I now look back on that evening with great sorrow, that our embracing and joy should have become over night such mockery.

From the beginning, as you know, I have made no secret of my being gay. From the first I have tirelessly repeated the difference between being gay and being genitally active. And by no means is this distinction peculiar to me; psychologists and sexologists universally acknowledge the truth and usefulness of this distinction. So that there may be no mistake, I will quote in full my dissertation on this subject:

"Also something should be said about the use of the term 'gay.' The choice of this term over the more pervasively used 'homosexual' or 'homophile' is more than a personal preference. It is used to indicate a higher degree of homoerotic self-awareness. Though an individual might experience homoerotic feelings, and even give them physical expression, the term 'gay' would not be used to describe him unless his homoeroticism was part of his self-identification. In other words, the term 'gay' is used to denote a person's conscious effort to integrate his homosexual orientation with the rest of his personality. This conscious effort presupposes a conceptual framework in terms of which the person tries to understand himself and interact with others. It is important to point out that this definition does not necessarily denote a sexually active lifestyle. It is possible for an individual to self-identify as gay without having a single overt same-sex experience."

Father, when I reached the stage in my course of study of choosing a dissertation topic, I discussed with you on many occasions what the nature of this study would be. Again you approved and supported my efforts. You know and can confirm that I obeyed you and your council's recommendations and prescriptions to the letter, that I did not shirk your advice or resist your instructions and that in every respect I acted honorably and in good faith.

You were among the first people to read my dissertation. Again you commended and encouraged my work. Again you offered no caution or warning, either with respect to its contents or the proper vehicles for making it public. You also read my article in NCR, to which Father Jetté has taken such exception. And it is clear that you thought the article was within the limits of legitimate inquiry, that the issues raised were important ones deserving a rational Christian response and that I neither implicated myself nor in any way degraded or put at risk the clerical dignity.

I mention these things to encourage you to come forward, should it be necessary, to defend my good name.

Father, as you know, special circumstances surrounded my article's publication in NCR, and it is *imperative* that Father Jetté be made aware of these. Let me say without further ado, however, that *it was never my intention to advocate or defend sexual activity on the part of priests and religious, or in any*

way to challenge the teaching authority of the church in such
matters.

As you know, the article, which appeared in NCR
was a serious abridgment of the original manuscript, which I
submitted. I had never published before and had no idea of
the liberties an editor might take with a manuscript, especially
one, which treated subjects as complex and controversial as
these. As you know, I was shocked to discover how my original
manuscript had been edited and immediately wrote the man
responsible, expressing my astonishment and disappointment.
I have a copy of my letter as well as this man's reply in defense
of his actions; and he himself, if he is an honorable man, will
confirm these facts.

Then what were my intentions in writing this article?
As you know, it was written in response to an article by another
gay priest. And let me point out from the start, with respect to
both his article and my own, that the difference between being
gay and genitally active, is unambiguously clear.

My article was a response to what I perceived to be
three troublesome aspects of his.

First, that the author felt constrained to remain
anonymous, that he was *fearful* to disclose his identity, despite
his being faithful to his vows. I wanted to assure this person
that he need not fear disclosing his identity, and to encourage
him to enter into fraternal relationship and dialogue with others
who share his plight of hiddenness, isolation and anguish.

Second, I was responding to what I perceived to be
the illogic of *his* arguments and the semantic confusion of
his distinctions, which (in my opinion) tempted him to judge
carelessly and harshly those who, for diverse and complex
reasons, might engage in sexual activity. In no sense did I state
or imply that this person represented persons in authority or
that his arguments represented authoritative church teachings
on these matters. The arguments presented in my article
were addressed solely to him and what I perceived to be his
confusion. The arguments in my article are arguments which
persons—"those who would still ask"—might and actually do
bring against arguments such as *his* —*not* those adduced by the
church in support of her doctrines and rules.

In no sense did I intend the teachings of the church as the frame of reference for my article. And let there be no mistake, even if this man's positions happen to be consistent with those of the church, the church's positions are ill-served by the unsound reasons he adduces in their defense. I am persuaded that the church has greatly more cogent and compelling reasons for requiring and enforcing mandatory celibacy for priests and religious than the faulty arguments he adduces. I am convinced that responsible theologians would agree that his arguments are not *the* arguments for a proper and thorough defense of mandatory celibacy. The issue, in other words, was not whether this man was correct in his positions, but whether he was correct in his *defense* of those positions. As for the teachings of the church, they are not for me to judge; they are the province of the duly appointed teachers of the church.

Third, I was responding to what I perceived to be a tendency by this author to assume a facile and dangerous attitude of judgment contrary to Jesus' teaching that we judge not. I wanted to remind this author that as Christians we are under a constant obligation to make every effort to understand, love, and forgive those who fall short in their moral lives. Part of any such effort to understand would be a clear delineation of the questions and reasons such people might pose to explain or justify their behavior. In no sense did I wish to imply that it is not within the clear *right* and *competence* of church teachers to answer such questions and reasons.

In the writing of my article, I made a strenuous effort to put a distance between "those who would still ask" and Richard Wagner, and to avoid assuming a position of advocacy that might be construed as contrary to church teaching. I sincerely thought that I had put the whole complex of issues in a sufficiently clear framework of *inquiry*. For example, crucial arguments are concluded with questions, not declarative sentences; in the presentation of arguments I avoid the first person singular; and in those places where the first person singular is used, I employ locutions such as "I *suggest* that *perhaps*" before the statement that follows. Perhaps I do not know the proper formulas for avoiding advocacy, but I sincerely thought these were adequate. In any case, in the original manuscript I explicitly denied that I was advocating sexual adventuring.

The last paragraph of my original manuscript was a call to Christian courage, understanding and love. This emphasis is at the heart of my ministry to gay people, in or out of religion. The persistent attitude that sums up and dismisses out of hand a whole people as simply degraded and leprous and not worth the time of day is patently contrary to the attitude of the Gospels. In a very real sense, the moral shortcomings of gay people are as a mote compared to the swollen logjam of fear, prejudice, hatred, oppression and complacency in men and women who otherwise strive for righteousness.

Father, anyone who does not understand, or refuses to see, the extraordinary hardships under which these people labor will never appreciate my ministry or the spirit of my article. As you know I personally have had to face the most fanatic intemperance because of being gay and trying to serve gay people. There are those who have condemned my dissertation while openly admitting that they have never read it, those who have shunned my letters apprising them of my work and inviting them to enter into dialogue, and those who have sought to discredit me and my work without ever seeking council with me to determine my true motives and positions. I am convinced that their reactions against me are in fact not against *me* at all, but against some enormity of their own imaginations. The very identification "gay" provokes an almost panic fear in persons who know nothing about my work, and, apparently, do not want to know.

Father, it is pointless for me to further defend my article or my motives for writing it, for, as I have already said, the bottom line is this: *If in the best judgment of my superiors they consider the article or any part of it to be advocating principles contrary to the teachings of the church, then I will freely renounce that article or any part of it that has given offense.*

I would like to say something about my consistent policy with regard to divulging the intimate aspects of my personal moral life. My remarks can be confirmed by numerous individuals both in and out of the church.

From the years of our acquaintance, you yourself can witness to my consistently taking pains to make clear the difference between being gay and being sexually active, and my consistent refusal to discuss the details of my personal moral struggle. Father John Mulligan, SM, of the Institute of Spirituality and Worship in Berkeley, who on several occasions has invited me to speak to groups of priests and religious on sexual topics, will also witness to my carefulness in this regard.

I shall cite only one more salient example. At the Institute for the Advanced Study of Human Sexuality, where I studied for my doctorate and am now an [unsalaried] assistant professor, I have consistently refused inquiries into my personal moral life. In this respect I have been quite unique, for explicit discussion of personal sexual attitudes and behaviors is the rule at this institute, where squeamishness about such topics does not exist. Throughout my three years there I have practiced the utmost guardedness and discretion with respect to my personal moral life, and this in deference and honor to my primary vocation. This can be corroborated by scores of individuals at the Institute, both teachers and students. I might also mention in this context that three of the highest respected professors at the Institute were given copies of the NCR article and asked to comment. They each individually remarked that they could not tell from the article whether I personally was sexually active. To each of them I replied, "That was what I intended, and that is as it should be."

At the beginning of my course of study, my systematic reticence was considered an eccentricity, but by the end, and at present, all understand my position and respect my independence. Throughout my course of study I said nothing, I did nothing, to dishonor my vows. Never has my sojourn at this Institute been an occasion to take my profession lightly or to tolerate tactlessness or insensitivity with regard to my higher calling.

I am persuaded that my life in this highly visible ministry will bear scrutiny. I am not claiming to be free of error but I am convinced that any reasonable person who looks at the evidence and considers the extraordinarily difficult position I occupy will find in me a more than usual disposition and effort to keep within the limits of propriety.

Father, one thing cannot be stressed enough in the process to come, if it must come: *the work into which I entered with the full knowledge and approval of my community is without precedent.* Naturally mistakes were bound to be made. I am the first to admit this. You know that in the past I have sought consultation with authorities in the church to help me formulate legitimate and concrete means of pursuing this ministry. You know that I have been refused such consultations. You know my present willingness and eagerness to enter into dialogue.

As for the trials and errors of these last weeks, I openly confess my share of the responsibility. As you know, prior to you receiving the Superior General's letter, I voluntarily assured you that I would never again use the popular press or media to pursue my ministry. Not even the Holy Father in Rome can remark on sexual topics without his remarks being distorted beyond recognition. How did I imagine that I might be able to do so? In light of this, I am sorry for any injury I may have done the local Church, my community, or my own ministry.

Father, you know that I have never denied the teaching authority of the church. You know that no teaching authority worthy of the name discourages or inhibits free inquiry. The questions and arguments with which I am routinely and inevitably confronted in my work—to which my piece in NCR witnesses—require calm, deliberate, and reasoned answers. For they are not posed in a spirit of defiance; they are an invitation for open, honest, direct dialogue. Our church is preeminently the church of reason; she never shirks dealing with the most complex issues in a dispassionate, detailed, and reasoned way. If I reproduce arguments, which are presented to me, I do so to make clear that those who argue in this vein are more that errant fools to be dismissed or foul sinners to be cursed with epithets. They are human beings endowed with *minds*, who, if they are wrong in their reasoning, must be brought to the truth, not with silence or condemnation (they know these only too well), but with patient reason inspired by love.

Father, you of all people embody and represent this patient reasoning love for me, and I have faith that Father Jetté, too, is a man of patience, reason, and love. In the difficult time to come, if it must come, I pray that we turn a deaf ear to those who slander others; who traffic in hearsay and innuendo; who arrogate to themselves the judgment of God; who make hateful caricatures of those they should strive to understand and love; who systematically seek to discredit rather than reason with those with whom they disagree; who deny that any need exists rather than meet the need with courage, charity, and love.

Finally, I must express my gratefulness for your assurance that during the process to come, if it must come, everything will be done according to law. Never in my life have I had so vivid an insight into the value of the rule of law as against the rule of men. I invite you to begin the process which—I have faith—will justify me in the eyes of the law. As for the eyes of men, let us ceaselessly pray that they may be opened, so that we may at last see face to face and be reconciled in Christ.

Father Waldie, you are always in my prayers.

———————

This letter was as clean an act of abjuration as my superiors could have asked for, and I fully expected Fr. Waldie to forward it to Rome and help me allay Fr. Jetté's misapprehensions. Fr. Waldie, besides being my superior, was a close personal friend, and our relationship was confiding and even confessional in nature. We trusted each other completely, and while hearing his confessions I shared with him more about my personal life and struggles than most religious would share with their peers, much less their major superior. Open-minded, sensitive, prayerful, deeply committed to his religious calling, Fr. Waldie was a role model for me, not least because of the humanity and lack of prejudice with which he befriended me as a brother.

As my major superior, he more than anyone else, encouraged and supported my efforts to develop an up-front gay ministry. When I offered discussion groups on homosexuality to priests and religious at the Graduate Theological Union in Berkeley, he defended me against detractors in the Congregation. He assured me that the community would stand beside me when the going got tough, as we both knew it inevitably would. He sanctioned and arranged community financing for my graduate studies in San Francisco, and I met and talked with him regularly throughout my years of study. I told him of my dissertation topic and arranged with him for payment of my travel expenses when my research required travel to other cities. He read my article in the *National Catholic Reporter* when it was published and he found nothing objectionable in it. I called to tell him about the television interview the day after I taped it. He advised caution and recommended I write an advisory to the bishops of San Francisco and Oakland, which I did. He was among the first to read my dissertation when it was finished in early February and he congratulated me on a job well done. Only two days before the Superior

General's letter arrived from Rome, I was greeted with embraces and pats on the back at Mount Mary Immaculate. On the day we met to discuss the General's letter, Fr. Waldie agreed with me that the General was overreacting, and he urged me to write an explanation with that in mind.

But when the TV interview aired and the heat was on, everything changed between Fr. Waldie and me. In a startling turnabout that I shall never forget as long as I live, he abruptly pushed me away from him and immediately began to pursue the alternatives Fr. Jetté had posed to him: to urge my voluntary departure from the Congregation, or failing that, to begin dismissal proceedings.

On March 2, 1981, Fr. Waldie published an issue of the provincial newsletter devoted entirely to putting as much distance as possible between the Oblates of Mary Immaculate and the impressions created by my television appearance. It was of course imperative under the circumstances for Fr. Waldie to apprise the community of the situation and to try to introduce calm so that the community could make a more dispassionate inquiry. But his letter went far beyond that. In his anxiety to protect himself and the community from any hint of blame, Fr. Waldie uncritically, and probably unconsciously, adopted *in toto* Fr. Coleman's caricature of my views and proceeded to paint a picture of me as a just-discovered anomaly in the Congregation's midst. This letter is fascinating for a number of other reasons, and I would like to examine its two most important paragraphs:

> Without prejudice to the history of our efforts to understand, support, and encourage Father WAGNER in his professed desire to live within the framework of the Roman Catholic Priesthood and the guidelines of religious life upon the disclosure of his "homosexual orientation" to us after his ordination, it can be stated without qualification that the views of Father WAGNER presently expressed via the media on the subject of homosexuality and particularly as they bear on the question of priestly celibacy and chastity are singularly and uniquely his own personal views and they in no way represent or should be implied to represent the thinking, the attitude, the viewpoint or the understanding let alone the practice of the Missionary Oblates of Mary Immaculate. At this point it is clear that Richard WAGNER has given a different definition to priestly celibacy than is commonly understood within the Catholic ecclesiastical and theological community and as understood by us as Missionary Oblates.

...At the present moment, Father Richard WAGNER has been asked to answer in writing his explanation [sic] of his public statements. The official process has begun. We are following the procedure of due process in order to protect both Father WAGNER's rights as well as the rights of the Congregation. Again, our community has attempted to support and stand by Richard WAGNER during these last few years after he had identified himself to us as having a homosexual orientation. This was not improper behavior on our part given the fact that he wanted to remain a priest and religious and we had the duty and our religious commitment to each other to help him do that. Homosexual orientation of itself does not preclude the possibility of faithfully living out priestly celibacy any more than a heterosexual orientation does. Our conduct during this period has been responsible and accountable and so have Richard WAGNER's up to the present moment. His statements via the media have changed this. Therefore, although we do not disassociate ourselves from Richard WAGNER as a person or as a religious brother, we categorically stand apart from him in his views of homosexuality and priestly celibacy.

In the course of his repudiation of my supposed views Fr. Waldie begins to introduce the very conflation of events that I had relied upon him to help prevent. Note in particular his curious pretense that he had not already received and read my letter of February 26 and his equally curious description of his request for an explanation of my newspaper article as though it were a request for an explanation of the TV flap (which I would not be given a chance to explain until mid-May). I had hand-delivered my letter to the Provincial House the same day I completed it, on February 26, and Fr. Waldie read it the next day upon his return from a weeklong retreat (see Fr. Waldie's *For the record*, May 14, 1981, item #5).

Fr. Waldie's avoidance of any mention either of my newspaper article or of Fr. Jetté's reaction to it was remarkable and was probably the result of his uneasiness at having not objected to a writing whose author *his* superior was prepared to do nothing less than kick out of the Congregation. In his newsletter, Fr. Waldie went so far as to say that my conduct as a self-identified homosexual within the Congregation "has been responsible and accountable up to the present moment" of my media (i.e., television) statements. This was the beginning of his attempt to shift the blame for my trouble from my newspaper article to my

TV appearance. One might also note that Fr. Waldie clearly understood the distinction between orientation and behavior, a matter on which I personally had tutored him. However, he did not use the distinction to any effect. He might have introduced it at the beginning of his newsletter by way of cautioning the Province not to jump to conclusions about my personal life or even my opinions, despite the compromising impressions left by the television program. Instead he deliberately left the question of my conduct vague and used the distinction between orientation and behavior only to explain why such a person as Richard Wagner, once known to be a homosexual, was permitted to remain in religious life at all. I also had to take issue with his statement: "...upon the disclosure of his "homosexual orientation" to us after his ordination,". The truth of the matter was that I had "come-out" to him and his predecessor as Provincial, Fr. Carignan, before I was ordained.

When I first saw Fr. Waldie's newsletter, the ominous code words, "The official process has begun" leapt out at me, and I asked myself—as I would go on asking for the next seven years—What is this process exactly? The supposedly reassuring phrase, "We are following the procedure of due process..." was nonsensical coming at the conclusion of a newsletter that had just pronounced me "in clear and evident opposition to the Church's official teaching."

The first meeting between Fr. Waldie and me after the television interview was on March 11, and it marked the almost total breakdown of communication and comprehension between us. Fr. Waldie expressed his understanding of the meeting the following day in his official reply to the Superior General, and again two months later in a letter and attached document entitled *For the record*. The March 12 letter to Fr. Jetté represents Fr. Waldie at his best and at his worst.

Without a doubt he was the most sensitive and articulate of all the Oblate officials with whom I have had to deal during this controversy, and I am certain that he experienced his part in having to arrange my dismissal with genuine anguish and heartache. Despite his numerous mistakes in judgment and even perception, he ardently wanted a quick and painless solution and he tried sincerely to be above board and honest in all his dealings with me. Moreover, the sureness of his personal commitment to the celibate ideal and the correctness with which he strove to embody it in his life and to encourage his fellow religious to do the same, was matched by a compassion that enabled him sincerely to comprehended and sympathized with people whose struggles were markedly different from his own, both in kind and in degree.

It has often occurred to me that if I had been gifted with any of Fr. Waldie's delicacy of feeling and expression the worst aspects of my own public expressions, especially their bluntness, might have been averted. But these positive aspects of Fr. Waldie's character were not what I noticed about his letter to Fr. Jetté. Before I discuss the negatives, however, let me present the letter itself.

It is with great personal sadness and yet with the firm assurance that the right course of action has been chosen that I write to you concerning the Reverend Richard Wagner, OMI.

After a period of two weeks for personal reflection on the questions you raised within your letter to me regarding his "sincere disposition to change his way of life and to fully accept the requisites of the commitments has taken", Richard has decided that he cannot honestly do that and be true to himself and true to us. Yesterday, we had a long but rather intense talk together. It is my firm conviction that Richard cannot at this moment at least affirm his vowed life as we within the Church and within the Congregation understand and affirm it. We came to the conclusion [that] to get involved in a process of denial and subtle distinctions about what he may or may not have said or written would not be honest. Therefore, although he does not choose personally to resign, he understands that the next procedure for us would be to go the route of canonical dismissal from the Congregation.

As provincial and as I have come to know Richard Wagner even more clearly during the past few weeks, I concur with his decision and judgment. To act otherwise would be patently dishonest and not authentic for him. Our course of action given the facts facing us is clear. Although Richard does not disavow the value and validity of priestly celibacy and chastity as understood within the catholic tradition, he presently holds views contrary to this teaching and cannot bring himself to change his thinking.

This whole experience has been a learning one for me both as a priest, religious, and provincial. It is clear to me that we need to look carefully at this question of human sexuality in both a frank and honest manner within our formation process. In dealing with other provincials I know that Richard Wagner is not unique but most remain in the closet as the expression goes. We need a climate and atmosphere within our ranks that this question of sexuality can be raised and looked at honestly. To make a statement to formators of what ought not to be and then proceed to think that all buy into it will not do. I am grieved and deeply saddened by what appears to be an unspoken problem among us. Although formation is a life long process, we need to face the issue of sexuality as this is integrated into our life as vowed celibates.

How do we help and support our members to deepen the value and meaning of their vow of chastity? It appears that just the negative aspects of not marrying and not having the right to have genital expression of their sexuality is what most are aware of when a discussion ever occurs on this issue. Unless we really grow in our appreciation on the personal level of the meaning and value of this commitment, it should not surprise us that some members will find rationalizations to live contrary to the vow. If celibacy and chastity does not produce within us dispositions and qualities of sensitivity, availability, gentleness, kindness, in a word—that we truly become loving persons, then there will be strong temptations to look for other ways to become loving persons. I strongly believe in our vow of chastity and our oath of celibacy. I think that it can produce these qualities and dispositions. I affirm it even though I too struggle with it within my life.

There will be a formation meeting in April 1981 at Kingshouse in Belleville, Illinois. Formation personnel and provincials will be in attendance. One of the main issues is human sexuality and how we are facing it within our formation houses. I pray that it will be a fruitful discussion and sharing among us. Charles Breault will be in attendance, too. I ask your prayers for this meeting. The present case in point might give a clearer focus and concern to the topic we will discuss. We can learn from this and good can come from it. I believe that.

I am sorry that you have to contend with this, Father Jetté. You have so many concerns and problems to face and deal with each day. I don't know what the exact procedure is and therefore would wait to hear from you. You can be assured that due process has been followed. My concern is that both the rights of the Congregation and Richard Wagner be honored. I feel that so far this has been the case.

Thank you for your attention to this matter.

I detected in these remarks an obsequious unwillingness to contradict Fr. Jetté's "false lifestyle" assertions about me. Fr. Waldie did not even mention my letter of February 26, except to claim that we had agreed in our meeting that it would be dishonest of me "to get involved in a process of denial and subtle distinctions".

The principle "subtle distinction," of course, was the distinction between orientation and behavior, the very ignorance or disregard of which resulted in Fr. Jetté's false inference about my personal life and his instructions to Fr. Waldie that I be persuaded to leave the priesthood voluntarily or face dismissal. In his apparent anxiety to ingratiate himself to Fr. Jetté—reflected also in his anxiety to reassure Fr. Jetté of his own commitment to the celibate ideal—Fr. Waldie was reluctant to suggest any possibility that the Superior General might have acted hastily or inappropriately. Instead he immediately busied himself with trying to confirm Fr. Jetté's presumption of guilt.

Fr. Waldie expressed this two months later in his document *For the record*, which was supposed to be a review of "due process" up to that moment. "Although the General did not make his judgment on solid facts," the document reads, "his assumptions were correct and on target. The problem was method and procedure not truth or honesty." Without alluding to the newspaper article or TV interview, Fr. Waldie based his defense of Fr. Jetté's "truth and honesty" regarding me entirely on his, Fr. Waldie's, personal knowledge and convictions about me.

This was a very dangerous path for him to stray on to. His claim that he had learned things about me in the weeks since the TV interview that he had not know in the previous ten years of our acquaintance was simply false. Fr. Waldie and I, as I have mentioned, had a relationship that was confessional, in the formal sense of that word, for two years up to the time I am discussing. It was our custom during these sacramental occasions to speak without inhibition about our personal moral struggles, our understandings of our vowed lives, and a wide range of related issues of Church doctrine and practice. Our "intense" meeting of March 11 was necessarily an extension of our habit of mutual candor, and neither of us could pretend not to know what he knew of the other. The difference, of course, was that now Fr. Waldie had assumed the role of a prosecutor. In this role he began to toy with information divulged under the most protected circumstances as though it were public evidence to confirm Fr. Jetté's otherwise unfounded judgment of guilt and to justify recommending my dismissal. In other words, he was making no attempt to keep clear in his own mind information that he might know about me as a confidant and confessor and objective information that he might use to support Fr. Jetté's conviction of me.

His entire approach was repeatedly to exhort me to be "honest," that is, to admit that my personal weaknesses and doubts, as well as my convictions, were of such a nature and such a degree as to disqualify me as an Oblate and priest. In short, to forgo defending myself and to give up trying to save my religious vocation.

Fr. Waldie was taking the "If" clause of Fr. Jetté's instruction to him literally: "If there isn't in [Fr. Wagner] a sincere disposition to change his way of life ...." He imagined that in his pursuit of Fr. Jetté's "simplest solution" he was oblige to penetrate behind my written explanation of February 26—which he himself would later describe as "very fine"—to the hidden wellsprings of my thoughts and feelings. My every attempt to bring Fr. Waldie back to objective events and to my written statements addressing Fr. Jetté's concerns elicited only further hectoring to the effect that I wasn't being honest with myself. Because *he* knew that I really didn't believe in celibacy as the Church understands it and that I really didn't want to conform my life according to that understanding. But I threw such exhortations right back at him. What about you? What about your innermost thoughts and emotions, or those of any other Oblate for that matter? The Church does not purge priests and religious for their private genital functions or for their private pondering on Church doctrine and practice or even for their conversations with fellow priests or religious on these issues.

The only suitable objects of inquiry—when inquiry is called for—are publicly expressed opinions and/or publicly known behaviors; and these become dismissible offenses only when repeated, habitual, or pertinacious violations are proven and when the miscreant, even after such proof, cannot be persuaded to renounce his false opinions or sincerely strive to amend his behavior.

Nothing in my public statements and behaviors approaches such a profile of offense and obduracy. Just the opposite is true. In my written reply of February 26 I had offered to abjure any opinions that my superiors deemed contrary to Church teachings, I reaffirmed my commitment to religious life by denying the presumption of being otherwise committed despite my shortcomings, and I agreed to keep out of the public eye. That formal statement was all that Fr. Waldie or anyone else had any right to demand of me by way of answer to the specific "charges" put forth by him and Fr. Jetté.

For Fr. Waldie to claim that he had knowledge about my private life and opinions that rendered my formal defense unacceptable and that justified his setting it aside was not only canonically wrong but morally suspect as well.

But Fr. Waldie had another reason for disregarding my defense. Somehow he persuaded himself that "about the same time" as I was writing my defense I was also going on television in a blatant act of bad faith that rendered my defense "dishonest." He expressed this chronological error most clearly in his letter to me of May 14:

> In his letter [of February 8] the General evidently judged that you were de facto living a life style not in alignment with your vowed commitment and asked me to bring you to acceptability. …I did not send your explanation of the NCR article to the Superior General because in the meantime you appeared on public television and expressed ideas and values seemingly in contradiction to what you wrote in your explanation of the NCR article. I, as your provincial, had made the judgment that your written response would place you in a bad light, in a dishonest position, because of what you subsequently had said on television that seemingly countermanded your written explanation. Therefore I did not send your letter on to the General.

Fr. Waldie's confusion was no doubt partly due to his having seen the television program for the first time on videotape after his return from retreat on February 27 and after he had read my letter. That, combined with the public furor caused by the program, gave him neither the time nor the calm to reconstruct the actual relationship between events. But it remains a mystery to me how he could have completely forgotten that I had informed him of the program immediately after its taping on February 6th.

It was at that time that he had instructed me to write an advisory to the bishops. He had spoken with the Archdiocese to confirm my standing as a priest and Oblate, and that my letter of February 26 itself alludes to the interview. Fr. Waldie carried his imagined picture of the relationship between my written defense and my TV appearance right into our meeting of March 11 and held to it even in the face of my vigorous head-shaking and protests, "No, Paul, that's *not* how it happened! Why do you keep saying that?" Try as I might to bring him back to objective events and to my written defense of February 26, he would not let go of what he considered to be his main proof of my dishonesty. And he would persist with this picture until June 5, when I finally put before him a written account of the TV interview, its relationship to earlier events, and his disastrous and probably irreparable misrepresentations of me to the Congregation and to our superiors in Rome.

Apart from wishful thinking or self-deception, what could account for Fr. Waldie's remark, in his March 12 letter to Fr. Jetté, which convinced him that during our meeting of March 11 I had somehow agreed to give up my written defense? The stressed wording of Fr. Waldie's letter—"Although Richard does not disavow the value and validity of priestly celibacy and chastity ... he presently holds views contrary to this teaching..."—indicates that something is not as it was being represented.

Let me back up to give an idea of where I stood with the Oblates before the roof fell in. I had been assigned to postgraduate study to obtain credentials that would qualify me for an up-front gay ministry and I completed that assignment in early February.

Under normal circumstances the natural next step would be for Fr. Waldie and me to discuss the specific shape of the new ministry for which my education had prepared me. Obviously Fr. Jetté's reaction to the newspaper article and the uproar produced by the TV interview put a serious crimp in my dealings with my community. From my point of view, however, the situation was by no means hopeless. My sincere desire to make amends as reflected in my apology of February 26, combined with a little patience to let the storm pass—and public outrage, however intense, does move swiftly—should have brought my superiors and me to a calmer moment. We could then discuss my future ministry and the ground rules for preventing a recurrence of unwanted events. But this would never be allowed to happen.

During my fateful meeting with Fr. Waldie on March 11, when it became clear that he was not going to accept my written statement and that he wanted me to leave the congregation voluntarily, I told him emphatically that I would not do so. There simply was no reason for me to leave. I then asked, "What would it take to bring about reconciliation?" Fr. Waldie replied that I would have to accept official church teaching concerning homosexuality and celibacy and to affirm that I was willing to live my life accordingly. Since I had already given those assurances in my letter of February 26, I said, "I have no problem with that. What comes next?"

This was the decisive moment of our meeting, the parting of the ways, which would never again converge—and it is precisely this moment that goes unmentioned in Fr. Waldie's official recollections of what took place between us.

In effect Fr. Waldie answered *Punishment*. Of course he did not use the word 'punishment' but that was exactly what he meant. If I insisted on staying, he told me, I would be required to end all contacts and associations with the gay community, the object of my ministry; be required to undergo a psychiatric evaluation; be forbidden to identify myself as a gay person; and be barred from ever again writing, speaking, or teaching on the subject of sexuality. He may as well have proposed to put me in a straightjacket and lock me away. My response at that point was, "No, I won't accept that!" Such a punishment would be professionally and personally disastrous to me, not to mention absurdly out of proportion to the "crime" of public self-identification as gay.

When I consider why Fr. Waldie thought such a harsh expedient necessary, I could only see it as a wish to make amends with his superiors by impressing them with his toughness. He too, after all, was in the hot seat and was working to tidy his own name at roughly the same speed he was sullying mine.

So naturally I "agreed" not to pursue my defense further. The writing was on the wall. My defense was discarded, Fr. Jetté's conviction of me was allowed to stand unaddressed, and the only hope of my remaining in the Congregation was to accept whatever punishment my superiors might capriciously wish to mete out. Furthermore, it was suddenly clear to me that by not accepting the proposed punishment I was going to be dismissed—not for my supposed false lifestyle and/ or heterodox principles, but simply and solely on the grounds of disobedience.

Fr. Waldie ended his March 12 letter to Fr. Jetté with a request for information on the dismissal process. He could not have known when he confronted me with the outline of his punitive obedience that he had also inadvertently stumbled onto the dismissal process itself, namely, to *engineer* a truly dismissible offense by means of my vow of obedience. For in fact no one had any intention of following up on Fr. Jetté's assertions about false lifestyle and contrary principles, Fr. Waldie's assiduous digging in those directions notwithstanding. No evidence other than Fr. Waldie's belated convictions concerning my dishonesty and unworthiness to be a priest was ever produced to prove my supposed false lifestyle, and in all the hoopla no one bothered to cite a single statement by me that needed retraction.

In early April Fr. Waldie attended the formation conference in Illinois. Also attending was Vicar General Francis George, OMI, (NOTE: He, Francis George, is now Cardinal Archbishop of Chicago) who brought with him from Rome the guidelines about the dismissal process that Fr. Waldie had requested. The document's typographical quirks, which I reproduce to some extent here, indicate that it was hastily thrown together. Considering that my very priesthood was at stake, the document's slapdash appearance and its use of a monogram to refer to me were profoundly disturbing. I actually wept to see how completely I had already been "dismissed" in the minds of those who had an obligation to see that I was treated fairly.

(NOTE: The only reason I have a copy of the following documents is Fr. Waldie gave them to me. During our March 11th meeting he promised me that the dismissal process would be totally above board, that there would be complete transparency. He gave me these documents in the spirit of that commitment. This proved to be a huge mistake. These were sub rosa documents sent him from Rome for his eyes only. It's clear that Fr. Waldie was duly chastised for this blunder, because he would never share another internal document with me. His commitment to transparency was as fickle as his original commitment to stand by me when things got rough when he launched me on my up-front gay ministry.)

DISMISSAL

BEFORE THE DISMISSAL PROCESS IS BEGUN

1) There must be a serious external fault, imputable to the individual. This fault can be either against the common law or against the particular constitutions of the Institute.

2) To establish this, an ENQUIRY should be made and all the relevant EVIDENCE collected.

   The existence of the crime should be established with MORAL CERTAINTY. This can be done [if]:

   (a) the crime and its imputability are NOTORIOUS;

   (b) the accused has CONFESSED to the CRIME, either during the ENQUIRY or OUTSIDE THE ENQUIRY.

   (c) the existence of the Crime is proven v.g. i) documentary proof, ii) evidence of witnesses, iii) expert evidence.

3) In the case of R.W.... great care is needed to proceed in such a way so that we are fair to him and to the Congregation and Church. Justice must not only be done but be seen to be done.

4) [sic] In this case, probably the best, if not the only way, would be for the PROVINCIAL to give R.W. A FORMAL OBEDIENCE UNDER VOW & in writing:

   i) to return to live in a determined Oblate House or Residence on or before a given date ... everything very precise;

   ii) (possibly) to abstain altogether from his present ministry regarding homosexuals and to refrain altogether from any public pronouncements (press, radio, television) in the matter.

SHOULD R.W. fail to do that which has been formally demanded of him, then the FORMAL PROCESS OF DISMISSAL could be begun by the Provincial.

[Here the document outlines the first canonical steps.]

It is essential that all the documentation be kept. Also, any defense, which the accused makes must be faithfully forwarded for presentation in the final stages of the case to the Holy See. AT EACH STAGE ... before each warning ... the accused should be afforded an opportunity to defend himself.

[Further information on canonical steps.]

[In all of this] perhaps it is better to heed the adage: festina lente!

[Concluding canonical steps culminating in confirmation by the Holy See.]

The document's author virtually admits—even without benefit of having read my defense—that Fr. Jetté's assertions concerning my lifestyle and beliefs were not a credible basis on which to press for my dismissal. Instead "the best, if not the only way" to achieve that end would be simply to set aside Fr. Jetté's (and Fr. Waldie's) convictions of me and start all over by manufacturing an altogether new "crime" more likely to pass the scrutiny of the review authorities in the Holy See.

Let there be no mistake: the document addressed the method for achieving my *dismissal*; it contained no suggestion that the obedience, whatever its content, might facilitate reconciliation. The leadership was to manipulate my vow of obedience into a coercive device to bring about an end that they were unable to achieve in any other way. Fr. Waldie, as I have stated, had already given me a pretty good idea of the punitive content of any future obedience. He never withdrew those depressing prospects or tried to reassure me that after a period of healing I might be able to take up, with appropriate guidelines and precautions naturally, the ministry that I had worked so hard to develop. My work up to that time—and the Congregation's considerable investment—was simply to be discarded, and there would be no two ways about it. Likewise the leadership would not accept my original defense and thus they would not move to retract the judgments handed down concerning me, nor would they inform the Congregation of my efforts to explain myself and to apologize to them.

If I stayed in the Congregation it would be as someone branded guilty of crimes that no one had any intention of proving, or clearly defining for that matter, and I would apparently spend the rest of my life marking amends for those assumed misdeeds.

Overall the cynicism of the document *Dismissal* is simply incredible. Considering its depersonalized way of referring to me and its startling recommendation that Fr. Jetté's precipitate judgments be allowed to drift into the background unanswered while a new and provable "crime" is hewn out of my vow of obedience, the document's professed concern for my just treatment and its almost cheery "Festina lente!" were to my ears little more than mockery.

Following the advice from Rome to proceed cautiously, Fr. Waldie told me in a meeting on May 3 that he saw this as a possible opening to reconciliation. He made no positive suggestions, however, about how we could achieve such an outcome and he continued to press for Fr. Jetté's "simplest solution" (my resignation from the priesthood) as the only "honest" option open to me. Moreover, he clung even more doggedly to the three parts of his own "indictment" of me, as reflected in his May 14 cover letter and attached document *For the record.*

The first part was his claim that I had rendered unacceptable my "very fine" defense February 26 because my "subsequent" act of going on television was blatantly dishonest and self-refuting. The second part was that during the interview I had (now quoting Fr. Waldie) "...attempted to give a definition to the promise of celibacy that suggested that one who had taken this promise could still legitimately involve himself in homosexual activity". And the third part was his insinuation, always expressed hypothetically, that my private life was inconsistent with my vowed life. "*If* you are in fact living in a life and life style that is incompatible with our Oblate life style and commitment ... then you should make a definite decision to choose which life and life style you will live in and by. You cannot have it both ways." (My emphasis.)

The assertions about promoting a redefinition of celibacy to accommodate homosexual behavior and trying personally to have it both ways obviously came straight from Fr. Coleman's remarks at the end of the television interview. As for Fr. Waldie's original contribution—based supposedly on his quite recent insights into my private life and thinking—that I had adopted a lifestyle in contradiction to my religious commitments and thus had placed myself in a dilemma that I could resolve only by leaving the Congregation and the priesthood, I rejected that repeatedly. Whatever my personal shortcomings, I told Fr. Waldie, I did not see myself as being in any such dilemma. I resented his badgering presumption that he knew me better than I knew myself and his insistence that if only I would see myself as he now saw me—and ultimately that was what he meant by my being honest—then naturally I would fold my tent and migrate elsewhere.

Fr. Waldie summarized our meeting of May 2, and his understanding of the events and conversations preceding it, in his communications to me of May 14. At the end of his cover letter, he announced the immanent end of all financial support of me (and he did terminate it that month, without so much as a second thought as to how I was going to survive). Then, in the next paragraph, he expressed his and his council's concern that due process had been followed and he made the following request: "...I have specifically asked you whether you judged that I had been following due process to your satisfaction. I would appreciate in writing from you your estimation or acceptance of this fact or not."

This was the first time he had asked me to give a written account of his perceptions and activities during the two months since he rejected my defense of February 26. While I was drafting my response, Fr. Waldie arranged still another meeting for June 7, 1981, to review again the matters we had discussed on March 11 and May 2. However, in attendance this time would be Jesuit canonist Fr. Richard Hill, SJ, to serve as witness to the discussion. Since I was unable to finish my response until June 5, I decided to take it with me to the meeting. When the three of us took our seats, I produced copies and asked that we read them together, since it presented my position in a methodical way that would probably get lost in a free-for-all conversation.

The letter rejected outright any suggestion that the community followed due process in my case. I carefully reviewed Fr. Waldie's attempt to use his confused chronology to dismiss my defense of February 26, thus allowing Fr. Jetté's original assertions about my newspaper article to be set aside in favor of pushing an identical set of assertions based on the television interview. I went on to show that Fr. Waldie based his claim that I attempted to redefine celibacy on Fr. Coleman's remarks, not on mine, and that my supposed admission of sexual misconduct was the result of creative editing after the taping of the program. In any case, my letter of February 26 was an honest and thorough offer to make amends, and I announced clearly that I had always stood by and continued to stand by that letter. I concluded by turning directly and pointedly to Fr. Waldie's repeated insinuations based on his personal knowledge of me and related this to his wanting me to confirm in writing that due process had been followed in my case. Here I quote the relevant paragraphs from my letter:

> Paul, for some time now you seem to have taken
> the position that any defense I might offer would necessarily

be a subterfuge. You have used your own unsubstantiated convictions about me as if they were decisive, when in fact, apart from evidence, they have no weight at all. Need I remind you that judges are as subject to law as anyone else, that that is why there are laws and due process, that that is the only thing that distinguishes the rule of law from the rule of men? Judges are obliged to judge on specific and precise charges, holding strictly to the evidence pertaining to the case, according to predefined criteria of what constitutes proper evidence, and following step-by-step procedures established by law and tradition. Now if a judge were to convict someone in lieu of evidence simply because he really *believes* the accused to be guilty, he would, in any system of justice worthy of the name, be subject to impeachment.

Now you consistently indicate in your remarks that no evidence is relevant because you personally are not convinced of my innocence, that is, you imply that the General's presumption of guilt has somehow assumed the status of something other than a presumption simply because you have come to share it. You further state in your *For the Record*: "Although the General did not make his judgment on solid facts, his assumptions were correct and on target. The problem was method and procedure not truth or honesty." What a piece of legal sophistry that is. Surely you know that in a legal proceeding truth and honesty are not separate from method and procedure; that they are inextricably bound together.

You say that though the General had no solid evidence for his allegation, he is nonetheless right. And why? Because you, you say, know the truth. But how do you know the truth in these matters? In other words, (1) do you have independent solid evidence to substantiate this presumption of guilt; and (2) if you do, is this evidence of such a kind as would be appropriate, given the principles of our church, to present in this case? Specifically, in what one respect has my alleged notorious lifestyle changed from more than one and a half years prior to the NCR article to this present day? What fragment of information do you have now that you did not have then? And what is it about this information now that makes you suddenly unable or unwilling to do your level best to ensure that I am protected according to law in these fantastically convoluted proceedings? More specifically, do you have pictures of me in compromising embraces? Do you have depositions from those who may have collaborated in my presumed lifestyle? Have you gained the confidence of my confessor and acquired information from him, which he is vowed never to divulge? Or are you, as my superior and friend, in possession of certain confidences, which I may have shared with you? And are these hypothetical confidences different in kind or degree from the confidences you possess of other Oblates but under no circumstances would think appropriate to make public? To put it bluntly, were you to be in possession of such hypothetical confidences would you be prepared to set a precedent as ugly and repressive as all this implies?

You have asked me to declare directly whether due process has been followed. I have told you before, and I repeat now, I haven't the vaguest idea what due process might be in a case such as this.

I have not been afforded competent and reliable counsel, and my only recourse has been to seek your advice— only to have my conversations with you misreported and thrown back in my face as if they were a signed confession of guilt. When you ask me if due process has been followed, I can only reply not according to the common understanding of due process in a humane system of justice.

According to such a system of justice, or any approximation to it, the proceedings of these last months have been nothing less than a farce, though the consequences have been anything but funny. I refer not only to the realities discussed above, but also to the following. You continue to talk as if, were I to remain a priest, certain exactions would be demanded of me. But you know full well that practically all the punishment that can be meted out already has been, and this, I should add, out all proportion to any reasonable charge, which might be brought against me.

I have been effectively silenced (I'm still holding to my promise), I have been ostracized from my community, I have been stripped of my faculties, and I have been denied all financial support, and have had my medical insurance revoked (these last two things prior to any ruling by the council). Since practically all the punishments that can be inflicted already have been, all that remains is the one, last act of humiliation, namely, to strip me of my *de jure* title, the *de facto* priesthood having long ago been scrapped.

I can only conclude that you have a most unusual understanding of due process. To you it seems to mean two things only: (1) moving at a snail's pace, perhaps on the outside chance that the accused may incriminate himself further; and (2) presenting a chronology of the given sequence of events and asking the accused to confirm its correctness. (Whatever else it might mean vis-a-vis your obligations to your superiors is hardly a question for me to judge.)

Now neither of these understandings of due process is correct. Due process, in this country at least, has always denoted a *speedy* trial, and this for the purpose of removing the onus of guilt from the innocent as quickly as possible. More than this, due process means, to resort to the dictionary, "a course of legal proceedings carried out regularly and in accordance with established rules and principles." I think that I have shown sufficiently that the proceedings of these last months have been at best irregular and *ad hoc*, the very opposite of what is meant my due process. In fact, they have been so irregular that punishments have been inflicted out of all proportion to any reasonable allegation, which might be brought against me on the prior assumption that I am guilty, period.

Being *a priori* guilty, I was given three recourses: (1) to admit my guilt by leaving the priesthood voluntarily; (2) to seek reconciliation, which in this situation clearly means to accept any exaction which might be imposed on me given the presumption of guilt; or (3) to stand my ground and be dismissed. Can any question remain why I have consistently chosen the last alternative?

Now given your limited understanding of due process, I have shown that you have not followed it on the second point, namely in your chronology of events. How you can present these errors in typescript and ask me to confirm them as if they were the simple truths in this matter is incredible to me. I cannot believe my eyes. These are not subtleties; they are errors so gross that they sting like a slap to the face. If you wish to have me dismissed on the tonality of what I am alleged to have said, or on what I am recorded to have said despite all the mitigating circumstances, or on your own unsubstantiated, quite late-to-develop convictions about my personal moral struggle, go ahead. Do what you must do. Do it, and accept the consequences. But in the name of God, please, Paul, at least get the facts right and in proper order. I prize my priesthood too dearly; it has been so much my identity and lifestyle, to see it thrown away so cavalierly. I cried to see how unworthy it had become of peoples' most careful attention.

When the reading ended, Fr. Waldie was the first to break the silence. His exact words were, "Oh my God, I think I've made a terrible mistake." After a pause, Fr. Hill spoke. It is noteworthy that he did not ask, "In what way?" He said simply, "Let us assume you did make a mistake. Where does that leave us?"

I do not exaggerate when I say that from that moment the objective grounds for having me removed from the Congregation had completely evaporated; in any event the leadership had so mishandled the process up to then that it was an embarrassment to consider it further.

What, then, were we to do? Setting aside my letter without further discussion, Fr. Hill turned the conversation in an entirely different direction. For whatever reasons, Fr. Hill argued, the situation between the Oblates and me had developed to the point where, justly or unjustly, I had been thoroughly discredited as an Oblate and priest. Matters had evolved to the point where the community regarded the situation as beyond mending, the truth or falseness of the original conviction being by now wholly beside the point. Given the Oblate leadership's strong preference for my departure, it was impossible to see what future I might have as an Oblate. However, since I interpreted a voluntary departure as tantamount to an admission of guilt for crimes that no one was prepared to support with a shred of evidence, the only remaining option to resolve the impasse was dismissal. But dismissal is a difficult thing to procure, and the Holy See does not endorse such moves for light and transient reasons. Therefore, the community must provide objective grounds for dismissal, and one need look no further for those than the vow of obedience.

Fr. Waldie agreed entirely with Fr. Hill's recommendation, which of course was the route Oblate officials in Rome had already proposed to him. Thus my awareness as early as March 11, 1981 that the leadership would shift my supposed guilt for unorthodox views and/or false lifestyle *in toto* to my vow of obedience came true.

My position at that point was surrender. If the Congregation was resolved to sever its relations with me no matter what I might have to say in defense of myself, and if the only remaining question was the means to achieve that end, then a contrived obedience it would have to be.

So on June 7—strange as it may sound—I entered into a "gentlemen's agreement" with Fr. Waldie. While the whole scenario, like the document it was predicated on, struck me as unbelievably cynical, I agreed to give the leadership the objective grounds it needed to have my *de facto* dismissal formalized. Fr. Waldie and I agreed, with Fr. Hill as our guide and witness, that: (a) I would be given a peremptory order under vow to take up residence at St. Mary's parish in Oakland (an indifferent choice); (b) that I would refuse in writing to obey that order; (c) that Fr. Waldie would send to me the two required canonical warnings; (d) that I would not respond to these warnings; (e) that Fr. Waldie would forward the relevant documents to Rome with the recommendation that I be dismissed from the Congregation on the proven grounds of disobedience.

Fr. Waldie issued his obedience on June 22, 1981. I replied as rehearsed on June 27. Since this act was to mark the death of my religious vocation, however, I felt compelled to register my outrage at the deliberate abuse of my vow of obedience as a device to dispose of me when all other reasons for such action had disappeared. While I was willing to give my superiors the disobedience they needed to remove me, I wanted them to know that what they were doing was wrong. I wrote

> This absolute, unilateral obedience, is an affront to what I have always appreciated the vow of obedience to mean, namely, the collegial responsibility binding you and me to seek together the will of God in our lives. I know that as my duly appointed superior you have the authority to do what you will, but I believe such a demand does not reflect the fundamental theology of this evangelical council to which I pledged myself in perpetual commitment. Therefore I reject any assumption that this obedience is or could ever be a true test of my fidelity.
>
> ...I believe that any true community must acknowledge and respect the uniqueness and integrity of its individual members. And this not only for the wellbeing of its members, but for its own wellbeing, the two in the final analysis being one. Certainly never should an individual member be sacrificed to maintain an appearance, an illusion, that the community enjoys unanimity; or to free itself of the continual need for self-examination; or to exempt itself from the obligation to seek out and purify the meaning and spirit of fidelity. Without a constant

wariness of itself *any* community can become faceless, rigid, and without compassion. It can crush individual creativity within its ranks and thus undermine its very own resources for maintaining itself and building its future.

Community cannot designate conformity for conformity's sake, discipline for discipline's sake, obedience for obedience's sake, nor any narrow and arbitrary "tests" for the purpose of proving a member's loyalty. Community is the result of individual persons freely joining in diverse ways toward a common good—in trust—each bringing the fruits of his individual work to the common work of all. But whenever the solemn intonations of power and command are invoked against a loyal member in order to save face, community has already cracked at its foundation. It has ever been the case, in all times and places, for the sake of community, that responsible men have *had* to say "No".

Despite the Oblate leadership's talk about observing due process and respecting my rights as an individual, by June 1981 the provincial leadership had severed all financial support of me and every vital tie with the community. Two months later they forwarded the acts of dismissal to Rome for review by the General Administration and eventually the Holy See. From that moment on I was suspended in a non-canonical state; and even though, as it happened, the General Administration never forwarded the acts to the Holy See for confirmation, I have remained in that state to the present day. The only right I retained, as I shall presently narrate, was the "right" to diffuse and redundant interrogations whose putative aim was reconciliation but whose net result was to reinforce the estrangement between me and the community and to further erode my priestly vocation. Though in principle I was a fully entitled Oblate, for all practical purposes the leadership had dismissed me from the Congregation, and I immediately had to arrange my life accordingly.

On November 10, 1981, Fr. Waldie and Fr. Leo Dummer, OMI, came to my apartment in San Francisco to take back my Oblate car, the last remaining material link I had with the Congregation. During his visit Fr. Waldie told me that the Procurator General, Fr. Michael O'Reilly, had recently asked him for more information about my case. I had a right to defend myself, he told Fr. Waldie, and he encouraged me to write the Superior General directly and, in Fr. Waldie's words, "...let him ask you precise questions so that he can come to understand what you are saying." I assumed that the acts of dismissal forwarded to Rome in August included my correspondence to Fr. Waldie, and I could see nothing I might add to what I had already said there. Besides I was anxious and depressed much of the time, shifting back and forth between anger at what I experienced as betrayal and grief at the sudden and permanent loss of religious fellowship. Also, except for odd jobs, I was unemployed and looking for work and had no leisure for difficult correspondence. Consequently I did not view the general leadership's solicitation of a defense as a hopeful sign. To me it indicated nothing more than a wish to put the last procedural touches on my dismissal.

I do not know if canon law prescribes a time limit beyond which deliberation on a proposed dismissal becomes unreasonable and injurious to the person concerned, but by March 29, 1982, more than a year after Fr. Jetté convicted me on grave matters and eight months after the acts of my case were forward to Rome, I was astonished to read in a letter from Fr. Waldie: "The Superior General wrote to me recently indicating that the General Administration does not want to proceed too rapidly on this important matter." Suddenly there was talk of dialogue, even though, as I have mentioned, anything that might signify practical and spiritual membership in the Congregation had already vanished.

My only contacts with the Oblates since August 1981 were a few brief telephone exchanges with Fr. Waldie. He acknowledged the deterioration of my standing in the community in the first paragraph of his letter: "I surely grant you that you have been in limbo as far as our response to you as individuals and as a province goes. ...Given the relationships that did exist before, this remains difficult and painful for you and those of us who were in relationship with you." With everything in the past tense, the natural question I had was: Dialogue about *what*?

In his correspondence to me of March 29, 1982, Fr. Waldie quotes Superior General Jetté, who, interestingly, now rephrases the two items of his original conviction of me as questions that he wants Fr. Waldie to put to me:

...in dialogue with Father Wagner, I think it is necessary to always come back to two essential points:

1) concerning doctrine, does he integrally accept the Church's and the Congregation's position regarding the nature and the obligations of the vow of chastity?

2) in practice, does he sincerely want to conform his life to it and help other priests and religious to do likewise? It is

a question of honesty with himself and with the religious institute to which he has committed himself.

In a meeting with Fr. Waldie on April 30, I answered "Yes" to both questions. As I had already satisfactorily replied to these points in my letter of February 26, 1981, I saw no reason to repeat myself. Yes, I accepted the Church's and the Congregation's understanding of the nature and obligations of the vow of chastity. Yes, I sincerely strove to live accordingly—and I rejected any insinuation that I influenced priests and religious to do otherwise. As for the *sincerity* or *honesty* of my replies—the *deep* questions that got Fr. Waldie into such a muddle—what could possibly satisfy them besides my direct answers? Yes meant Yes! Those answers, combined with my previous discussions of my opinions and practices, ought to have been enough. In a letter to me the day after our meeting, Fr. Waldie announced: "I will write to the General and tell him that you would answer 'yes' to both questions and I would invite him to write you directly to begin a direct dialogue with you." But as events would prove, Fr. Jetté, like Fr. Waldie before him, was very reluctant to take 'yes' for an answer. In fact, he was unavailable for any answer at all.

CHAPTER 3

1984 - 1986

Two years later, Fr. Charles Breault, OMI, General Councillor for the United States, invited me to meet with him at the Provincial House to discuss my case. The meeting was held on March 26, 1984. There Fr. Breault presented me with a letter from Fr. Jetté dated February 8, 1984, and he requested that I read and respond to it in his company, with Fr. Seamus Finn, OMI, my good friend and classmate, attending as a witness.

Before I discuss this letter, I must emphasize that in all the intervening time between my last meeting with Fr. Waldie in April 1982 and my meeting with Fr. Breault in March 1984, the sum of my contacts with the Oblates was a few bewildered telephone conversations with Fr. Waldie. Fr. Waldie's explanation for the extraordinary hiatus—though he too thought it excessive—was that Fr. Jetté had many pressing responsibilities and that I should not presume that my case had any special priority with him.

It had been three years—very long years I might add—since Fr. Jetté had declared me guilty of grave offenses and steered Fr. Waldie toward arranging my removal from the Congregation. At the time of Fr. Breault's contact, I was in every respect living the life of an independent agent. I had begun to get on my own feet financially with a small house-cleaning business, and in my off hours I nursed along a private practice of psychotherapy. Though I was far from emotionally reconciled to losing my religious vocation and all my former friends and associates, I entertained no hope—given the abruptness and completeness with which the leadership had thrust me from community—that the formal severance would not eventually be forthcoming. I interpreted the faint murmuring of "dialogue" and "reconciliation" as an indication that the dismissal based on a trumped up obedience had no merit. And what was left was little more than bureaucratic prudence and a needless prolonging of the pain of separation.

Consequently I was surprised to read Fr. Jetté's first paragraph to me: "For the past three years, this situation has been quite uncertain...." What was uncertain? I had refused a direct obedience from my major superior; that was established beyond a doubt. Was Fr. Jetté acknowledging that the reasons for my refusal might have merit? Was he perhaps prepared to accept my Yes answers to the two questions he posed to Fr. Waldie two years earlier? Needless to say, it was a crucial letter and deserved the closest scrutiny.

Fr. Jetté acknowledged that he had finally read my defense of February 26, 1981, and quoted a passage from it that denied that I advocated sexual activity by priests and religious or challenged Church teachings. But then Fr. Jetté simply dropped the letter and the passage without further comment and turned immediately to a series of new accusations, the most important being that I disobeyed my Provincial two and a half years earlier when he ordered me to take up residence in an Oblate house.

In another unexpected turn, Fr. Jetté then held out the possibility of reconciliation, but he quickly followed this with a clear signal that my dismissal—despite his personal reluctance to follow through on it—was still very much a live option. Of course, this made no sense at all. Because in all of this he made no allusion to the reasons I had previously tendered for refusing Fr. Waldie's obedience: namely, that the obedience and the resultant dismissal process originated when Fr. Jetté pronounced me guilty without inquiry; that Fr. Waldie dismissed out of hand my letter of defense; and that Fr. Waldie, following the General Administration's guidelines, engineered the obedience precisely to side-step these uncomfortable facts.

By ignoring entirely the direct relationship between his own unjust assertions, Fr. Waldie's refusal to tender my response to them, the resort to a punitive obedience as the only way to procure my dismissal, and my obliging refusal of that obedience, Fr. Jetté was free to awaken a new suspicion. Abstracting my specific act of disobedience from its defining context, he now proposed to treat it as indicative of a more general indisposition to obey.

In short, despite the solicitous word 'reconciliation,' Fr. Jetté's letter represented no movement at all. On the contrary, matters had become considerably more obscure if only because of the three-year gulf that had opened up between my *de facto* removal from the Congregation and this belated, diffuse inquiry into my disposition to obey. What did the leadership, really, want of me that I had not provided several times already?

Three years into my banishment, the leadership could have taken obvious procedural steps that could have broken down the ever-building wall of suspicion behind which they were isolating me. Those steps were: accept my letter of February 26, 1981 on its merits. Retract the false judgments that lead to the unacceptable obedience and bring explicit closure to the two-and-a-half-year dismissal process. Cleanse the atmosphere of the rhetoric of guilt and punishment and pave the way for a good faith dialogue concerning appropriate reassurances to the community and an honorable assignment for me. We would then *see* if I acquit myself according to my professed vows.

This direct procedural approach was exactly what the leadership failed to adopt because to do so would require that it acknowledge gross procedural errors on its part up to that point. Instead the leadership opted for what amounted to an *ad hoc* psychological inquiry while doing nothing to remedy the non-canonical state to which they themselves had consigned me since 1981. The putative aim of this inquiry was reconciliation but its context was the unresolved dismissal process. It disregarded my written defenses of myself in the face of baseless assertions of guilt. The *illegitimate* obedience that grew out of that disregard now eclipsed my defenses with an open-ended suspicion of my disposition to obey the *legitimate* requests of my superiors *under normal circumstances*.

Aside from sketching his understanding of the situation, the specific purpose of Fr. Jetté letter was to introduce Fr. Breault, who, on Fr. Jetté's behalf, would ask me to respond to five questions. Here is how Fr. Jetté itemized the questions:

(1) Do you accept the teachings of the Church concerning consecrated chastity and ecclesiastical celibacy? What, in your opinion, is the content of this teaching?

(2) Do you agree to maintain an external behavior which is in conformity with this teaching and which does not contradict it either in word, in writing or in act?

(3) Do you agree to live in an Oblate community and to accept, from your Provincial, an apostolate which would not be that of ministry to homosexuals?

(4) Do you agree not to give any talk, nor to publish anything, on the question of sexuality, without the explicit permission from your Provincial?

(5) Do you agree not to present yourself publicly as "gay"?

The meeting was held at the Provincial House on March 26, 1984. I repeat—and I cannot stress this enough—no one gave me a copy of this letter until the beginning of the interrogation by Fr. Breault on that day. Obviously it was impossible for me on the spur of the moment to clearly apprehend its contents, although I was able to divine during my "witnessed" reading that all was not right with it.

The worst for me was not the contents of the letter, which I was far from clearly assimilating, but the manner in which Fr. Breault confronted me with it. To spring such a difficult document on me out of the blue—even though it had been available to others for almost two months—and to expect me to respond to it without preparation and before witnesses was unconscionable.

I shall not review here Fr. Breault's notes on the "jeremiad" I delivered during that grueling three-hour session. I remember little of it myself. The heat of anger, the sweat running down my back, an earthquake occurring almost on cue—those I recall. And my pathetic appeals: "Is there anyone who can help me with my rights? Can anyone help me?" "My friends! It's tremendously hurtful to me."

Fr. Breault invited me to write directly to the Superior General.

On June 11, 1984, I sent Fr. Jetté a 17-page, single-spaced account of my case up to the time the local leadership forwarded the acts of dismissal to him. I included answers to his five questions, and I outlined the procedural route by which the general leadership might resolve the situation. Needless to say, I was disgusted with the process and quite pessimistic about its outcome. I had so few expectations for it that I wound up mailing Fr. Jetté the next-to-last draft, replete with typos and misspellings. Producing the final typescript seemed like the labors of Sisyphus—and how I longed to be out from under that accursed stone. This was 1984, the strangely apropos Orwellian allusions aside, and before I caught my second wind.

I do not wish to quote from this letter extensively, but if my readers are willing to pick their way through the poor typescript, they will see that it did successfully restore the historical context and proposed the general terms of the solution that the general leadership would adopt more than four years later.

There are three things to notice in the following excerpts: (1) my insistence on hewing to the history of the case, (2) my insistence that the leadership openly acknowledge its procedural errors and set them right, (3) and my objection to the renewed effort to make obedience the issue upon which everything would turn:

> While I appreciate the conciliatory spirit of your letter, I am amazed to find no reference to the historical context, which has brought us to this day. Excuse me if I speak with candor, but from my point of view any attempt at reconciliation without such a context is doomed to the fate of every previous attempt. I contend that a careful analysis of the facts and sequence of events show that I have been the victim of a grave injustice.
>
> [My review of the history of the case.]
>
> ...This is the context of the 'situation' without which we cannot possibly discern what would constitute an authentic reconciliation, if such is really wanted. While no one has ever asked me to air my view of what actions would have to be taken to resolve this impasse, perhaps it is high time I volunteered to give it. Let me stress, however, that this is not a demand on my part, nor even a request. After all the frustration, disappointment, and anguish I have been through these past years, I would be foolish to allow myself the hope of a happy ending.
>
> Bearing all the foregoing in mind, I tell you with the utmost sincerity and without the least hesitation or doubt that the only way to rectify the situation is to restore forthwith the *status quo ante* Fr. Waldie's misguided rejection of my defense of February 26, 1981. His decision, based as it was on his quite erroneous reading of the situation, set this case fatefully on a course of confrontation, which found its issue in the manufactured disobedience of June 27, 1981. My letter of February 26, 1981 provided the grounds for a speedy and, above all, *clean* resolution of the problem. In it I abjectly begged forgiveness for my blunder; I answered the Superior General's misunderstanding with regard to my lifestyle vis-à-vis my self-identification as gay; I provided abundant reassurances with regard to repudiating statements my superiors objected to; I forswore resorting to the press or media in the future; I reaffirmed my vow of celibacy and chastity by rejecting any insinuation that I was living in any other way. I think that any reasonable person who took it upon himself to understand the actual sequence of events and the extraordinary circumstances

surrounding them would find in my letter of February 26 more than enough to allay the need for more radical measures.

Restoring the *status quo ante* of February 26, 1981 would require two courageous moves.

First, the obedience of June 22, 1981—or *any latter-day, disguised version of it* —would have to be revoked without qualification. One would have to forthrightly acknowledge that the orchestrated attempt to use my vow of obedience as the best, indeed the only way of fixing the outcome of my dismissal was itself a violation of the spirit of that solemn vow. At this point, there is no way I can accept any peremptory command, no matter how innocuously phrased, to return to community, because given the context, such an order can only be interpreted as a repeat of Fr. Waldie's obedience of June 22, 1981. I have made it abundantly clear why I can never go back on my refusal of that obedience. I remind you that these unhappy events have left me with nothing except my honor, and I would have to be a very perverted character indeed to throw that away. Apart from living in community, I have to live with myself. While to ignore the history of that obedience and my reasons for rejecting it might in fact restore me to community, I would return a worthless person deserving of no one's respect, least of all my own.

The second move would have to be an acceptance of my apology and reassurances of February 26, 1981. Moreover, the last three years of being an outcast, of receiving no support, of being without faculties, and of being kept in ignorance of my fate (although certain of eventual dismissal) would have to be acknowledged as *punishment enough.* That being acknowledged, and my apology and assurances accepted, I would then be restored as an Oblate who has made good on his past mistakes and who is worthy of being embraced again by the Congregation. After a reasonable period of time, when all are adjusted to my restored membership, I would then be able to enter into fraternal dialogue in an atmosphere of mutual trust to determine how I might best serve the church—either within the Congregation or in another community or diocese.

At the end of my letter, I proceeded to answer the five questions put to me by Fr. Breault the previous March 26.

Father, at last we are brought up even with the questions you put to me in your letter of February 8, 1984. I shall now answer them in serial order.

1) The teaching of the church concerning chastity and celibacy is that all persons who take these vows shall not engage in genital activity. I have never maintained that these vows meant anything other than this, nor have I ever disavowed their positive content. In the case of homosexuals, however, I have pointed out the *INARTICULATENESS* of what it means to be a vowed celibate. For one thing, I believe that the homosexual's vow is binding indirectly in this specific sense: "Since the church recognizes no licit sex outside the institution of marriage she feels that a renunciation of heterosexual marriage is enough to satisfy a commitment to sexual abstinence and that nothing more needs to be said." For another thing, I have observed that the homosexual's vow of celibacy has a highly ironic quality. Unlike a heterosexual man, when the homosexual man takes this vow he is pledging to forgo sexual relations, which he is morally required to forego even if he does not take it.

Obviously pointing out the indirectness and irony of the homosexual's vow of celibacy can never be construed as somehow condoning sexual activity on his part. Similarly, it would be nonsensical to suggest that the dictionary definition of celibacy might be used as some kind of loophole, which would justify sexual activity on the part of a homosexual priest.

Why even mention the indirectness and irony of the homosexual's vow? Simply to emphasize that homosexual priests and religious come to take their vows from a quite different social and psychological direction than their heterosexual counterparts. Not only does the church require them to live celibately even when they do not vow to do so, but the special quality of their situation is never dealt with directly and explicitly. On the contrary, the secrecy that surrounds the subject is so great that a homosexual usually feels compelled to conceal the fact of his orientation for fear of reprisals.

It is the fear and anxiety engendered by the hiddenness that is the real issue in all of this. With respect to homosexuals, the formation process is a complete failure, because there is no attempt to deal frankly and forthrightly with their unique situation. So we should hardly be surprised to discover that persons who live in extreme isolation and loneliness might seek other avenues of human contact. And while it is true that sexual activity is incompatible with celibacy, surely there is nothing gained by calling such persons hypocrites.

Everyone acknowledges the difficulty of living a life of sexual abstinence. What surprises me is how little compassion and understanding there is when we discover that not all are equally close to fulfilling the ideal. Certainly it is my firm conviction that the crisis in today's church regarding the issues of homosexuality and celibacy is not going to be resolved by redoubling the repression and hiddenness in the hope that homosexual men and women in religion will remain "our little secret." Homosexual men and women are not morally culpable for being such and it is wrong and wrong and wrong to treat them as if they were.

2) Yes.

3) This is the obedience of June 22, 1981 restated. I can honestly say that I do not reject the idea of living in community; in fact I look forward to the opportunity when I can once again enter into dialogue with my superiors to discern the Spirit of how I may best serve the church. However, if reconciliation is possible only if I blindly agree to this demand without my superiors first attending the task of clearing my good name, as outlined in my case above, then you have no choice but to issue the decree of dismissal.

4) Yes.

5) Even though I find this last request most disquieting and believe it only adds to the atmosphere of repression and